WALKING ON
Ocean Floors

WALKING ON
Ocean Floors

Mike "SPIKE" Mcgettigan

To order additional copies of this book, contact:
Xlibris
1-800-455-039
www.Xlibris.com.au
Orders@Xlibris.com.au
791887

CONTENTS

Acknowledgments

I would like to thank Xlibris for their support.
Thank you, Cherry Noel, for your organisation of someone who doesn't know anything about being a writer or writing a book.

Thank you, Sarah Perkins at Author Solutions, for turning pages of misspelt words and bad grammar into a readable book.

I don't think I would have gotten as far as I did without the support from my lovely wife, Christina.

I joke that she is my handbrake—she slows me down. But without her, I would have smashed into a wall at high speed or drowned riding one wave too many.

But jokes aside, she has been my rock, someone to come home to, waiting patiently, and sometimes not so patiently, with two children for months on end for me to walk through the door. It has not always been very easy. Thank you.

My two children, Ryan and Jay, for growing into good adults even though I missed so much of their childhood and some very important times as they grew up.

My mum and dad back in Napier for the countless times they have had to cover for me—money here, money there—when I had been in a bind and for helping out our small family when needed and, most importantly, for giving advice that I never listen to, like, 'When are you going to give up that dangerous job? Aren't you getting too old for that?' Ha ha, parents never stop worrying about their children.

A special thanks to Loretta and Drew, Krissy and Gordon, Paula and Nat, and Rev and Sharon, our Perth family whom I could count on to help Christina with the kids for those long two-to-four-month trips I used to do when our family was young.

Thanks also to part of the Wellservicer crew to whom I handed out the first four chapters to see if my story was, in fact, worth reading. The feedback I got from them and Amber, my niece, and Nick was the encouragement I needed to continue the story.

Thank you.

Introduction

Would you like to go where I normally go after we have gone where we are going?

I am sitting on the edge of a stainless steel seat. I'm dressed, ready to dive, and so are my bell partners, Cliff and Richard. We are hanging in the hooks over the top of the moon pool waiting. It's hot in this medium-sized bell of about two metres round and two and a half metres tall. They have had the hot water running for a while, and we are sitting waiting and sweating. We have to wait because they told us to hurry up because they are ready to dive. When the *Deep Discoverer* is in its final position, the DP systems are checked, and the bridge confirms it is safe to dive. The supervisor will get a green light on his panel, and we will be lowered to the seabed.

Cliff is the bellman today, and he will lock Richard and then myself out of the bell to work on a closing spool to bring one of Shell's main trunk pipelines back online. We are not that deep, only living at seventy-nine metres, but I'm not sure what the seabed depth is because I wasn't really listening to the dive brief by the supervisor back in the chamber. My mind was elsewhere, probably surfing in an exotic location or something like that. But it will be about ninety metres. The seabed is a light firm sand, and the visibility is not bad, so diving here is relatively easy. I'm on the edge of the seat because before I can drop to the seabed, I have to put on an SLS. It's a lot heavier than a standard bailout, and it's obvious that the guy that designed it has never worn one. But apparently, it could save my life. My wife would say, 'I bet a man designed that.' It's lucky we rushed up to the bell because we are still waiting.

How did I end up here in the North Sea in the summer of 2019? Well, I'm not really known for being a storyteller, but I'll try and explain.

I have always loved the water. Going to the beaches or local swimming pools and rivers of my home town are memories throughout my childhood.

I wonder if being born an Aquarius star sign has much to do with it, or was it just a roll on from our family upbringing? As a large family, we often had gatherings at the beaches and rivers of Hawke's Bay, on the east coast of New Zealand. What a playground. We were all schooled in swimming, but the funniest visions of me are not from my memories but old Super 8 film footage taken at the Onekawa Olympic pool in Napier. My mum and dad had to watch me like hawks once I could walk. I would run straight to the pool; not just any pool—the bloody ten-foot-deep diving pool. Ha ha, bloody maniac from grasshopper age. I was a nightmare for them, so swimming lessons were the only way they thought they could relax, I guess. I was even a nightmare in the bath. I used to stay underwater holding my breath and pretending I had drowned until Mum would come flying in freaking out, yelling and screaming.

So through the school years, summers were swimming and winters were soccer. My dad immigrated to New Zealand from Glasgow, Scotland. Chasing him around the front yard with a ball was the other mainstay of my part in the early home movies. I was a mad footballer in my school days, playing for my school teams but also representing Napier and Hawke's Bay in the county tournaments.

Like a lot of kids, I had a pair of flippers and a mask and snorkel. There was a programme on one of the two TV channels we had back then that was a scuba diving series that I'm pretty sure was called *Primus,* and the famous Jacques Cousteau was our David Attenborough of the time. After those programmes, I'd go and swim around my bedroom out the back of the garage with my diving gear on, pretending I was in some deep interesting place.

When I was at intermediate school (Marist, eleven and twelve years old), I had a paper run in town on the Napier Hill. On Saturday mornings, we had to go around the houses on our run and pick up the weekly money. It was called the rounds, and it was our payday when we arrived back to the paper house. Often, the tips we received from the households were as much as our pay, sometimes more. The paper wasn't printed until 3:30 p.m., so I would have three hours in town getting up to mischief as you do.

One weekend in summer, I spotted a couple of guys I knew from school down the wharf. They were snorkelling around looking for fish and paua. I hung out with them that day, and the next weekend, I took my diving gear and met them. The water was cold but clear. We actually found three or four paua that day, and a couple of Asian crew members off a coastal freighter docked on our pier spotted them. Next thing, we were the centre of attention and in the money. They were going spazzo. Well, they were probably just talking normal but excited, but it sounded spazzo to us kids. They gave us about two weeks' pay and took off jabbering and laughing. We met up a few more times over that summer. The next year, I went to high school, and it was all forgotten about.

The summer of my last school year, I was introduced to surfing. It didn't take long to get the bug. Then I was hooked. I could safely say I have been a mad surfer ever since. I am probably in my best place when I'm sitting on a board waiting for the next wave. It clears my head, resets my attitude, and on those really good days, puts me on a high that nothing else can come close to. In our younger days, my mates and I would work to save up enough money to do a surf trip up or down the coast, dragging our girls along sometimes. We had lots of fun, and maybe that was the ingredient that got me up and out of our little country town to see what was up the road, around the next corner, over the next hill.

I wasn't that good at planning things and just seem to roll with the moment. When I decide to go on a holiday or return home to visit family, I don't think next year or in six months' time. I leave the next day or the next week. A product from my working life maybe where a phone call can mean grabbing the bag from the garage and being at the airport the next day. I do some really cool stuff after I left my family and friends in 1984. I also do some crazy stuff, some really dumb stuff, and some very scary stuff. I travel through some amazing countries and meet amazing people. Sometimes I'm alone, and sometimes I wish I was alone. I'm happy with my life and the people I've spent it with.

I often wonder, if you could think a thought faster than the speed of thought, would you think a thought before you thought of it?

If you're not up to much, join me for a stroll around the ocean floors of the world. The stories are as I saw them and remember them. I have told them true to my memory, and if you are in some of the following stories, I hope your memory is similar to mine. But mostly, I hope you get a laugh at the picture from the past.

Chapter 1

BEFORE THE FIRST FAREWELL

D o you believe in fate or fateful decisions? I guess I do. Why? Because I made a decision once that put me unknowingly on a path that ended up on the seabed of the oceans all over the world. Let me explain.

In mid-1978, electronics were in their infancy, and I was an infant in the workforce, seventeen years old, and working for a little electronics company in Napier, New Zealand, called IEA, Industrial Electronics and Automation. I was hired with six others to put about two hundred cigarette vending machines together, test them, and send them off to whatever hotel hallway or lobby they would end up dropping out their wares to the smoking masses of the day.

On completion of that project, I was asked if I wanted to stay on and work on the production line of the 10 hp electric motor speed controller. This consisted of five of us on a big table with a soldering iron each and basically screwing all the parts onto the mainframe and soldering all the looms in place, testing them, and sending them off to do their role in the automation of the world. Exciting stuff.

Now this is where I meet Mary. Why is that important, you may think? Well, back in the late 1970s, we had fuel rationing, and you had to nominate two days a week that you didn't drive your car. Now I was still living at my parents' house, and Mary used to drive past me because she and her husband Roger lived in a caravan park five minutes up the road, and this is where I meet Roger. Why is that important, you might think? Well, meeting Roger was another door opening onto a different road.

Both Roger and Mary were lovely people. When it was my turn to drive Mary to and from work, I would drop in and have a beer with Roger. He was working on the Tomoana Showgrounds freezing works construction site as a fitter welder for a company that was from Auckland, which is why there were a lot of them at the caravan park. And they were on good money working six days a week. They all had nice cars and flash caravans, which is pretty impressive when you're a kid on your first real job out of school.

So here's the big missed opportunity, the fate-making decisions that my silly childish mind made that quite possibly governed the rest of my working life. And this is how it worked out.

During the beer drinking conversations with Roger and his workmates, I asked if he could get me a job. I wanted to work hard for a while, save up some cash, and travel the world. 'No probs,' he said and organised a meeting with Bill, his boss, who was also at the camping ground. This worked out OK, and if I wanted to, I'd be a trades assistant, or glorified labourer, you might say.

The same week this was going on, I get called into the boss's office at IEA; he's a nice bloke, but I can't remember his name. He tells me they are looking at taking on an apprentice starting as an electrician and expanding to electronics technician. What an opportunity. But dumb me, already thinking of the money I will make with Roger and being able to get out of little old boring New Zealand in about eight months instead of being stuck there for another four years. I honestly thought on it for a while. But I didn't consult anyone.

I made a decision the next day and turned my back on electronics. What a mug, but it was obviously the path I was meant to go on. I handed my notice in, and two weeks later, I was a TA with Roger. I worked on the site until the completion of the project. I didn't have enough money saved to leave the country, so I bought a new surfboard and went on a surf trip instead.

About a year and a half later, I was employed as an apprentice fitter/welder/turner for Whakatu freezing works. I had met a lovely lady, and you could say that maybe that was meant to happen. I did my time, and by the end of that, I was twenty-two years old, owned a block of land close to Mahanga Beach on the Mahia Peninsula, and had a bit of money saved up and was ready to move on and do something with my life.

On 26 January 1984, I watched Robert Plant play in Auckland, and the next day, I flew off on a one-way ticket to Singapore via Bali for as long as my money would hold out.

So was that a bad decision? Who knows what would have happened if I ended up an electronics engineer. *Que sera sera*, whatever will be will be. Remember that song? Doris Day, bless her. What I do know is in the four years it took me to leave my hometown, I had amassed a small group of friends that was very hard to say goodbye to; five of whom I consider my best friends, and one of them I'm still happily married to.

Chapter 2

A One Way Ticket from Home

After two nights in a YMCA hostel in Sydney, I arrived in Bali's Kuta Beach in the early evening of 29 January 1984 and scored a room to stay in Melasti Beach bungalows next to the Kuta village markets. It was dark when I arrived, so I had no clue where I was. I was hungry, though, and keen to check out this totally different planet I had landed on. I walked out of my room onto a porch and spotted four Aussie blokes that looked like they were heading out, so I asked if I could tag along, and off I went. It was my birthday. I was twenty-three. I ended up having magic mushrooms for dessert and got lost, and when I finally found my hotel at whatever time in the morning, I couldn't remember much of what I'd done, ha ha.

So Bali was a pretty quiet and really neat place back then. There were only six or seven clubs or big bars. There was like a pub circuit thing where different bars had their party nights, so everyone got their share of the tourists' money. It was fun going off surfing every day on a motorbike. The food was great as long as you didn't get the wrong meal. It was cheap, and everyone was in party mode even when they were relaxing. The Balinese are very mellow and friendly people, mostly Hindu. There is always a ceremony happening somewhere, with lines of locals walking with drums and dressed in traditional clothes, very colourful.

The tourist strip of Kuta, back in the 1980s, stretched down Jalan Legian from Kuta village to Double Six Road on the border of Legian and Seminyak. From Double Six Road, the rice paddies stretched in terraces all the way up to Mount Agung. On a sunny day, it is an absolutely beautiful scene, often with a sphere of cloud capping the peak like a hat. There are temples large and small everywhere, with the Mother Temple over halfway up Mount Agung, giving you a majestic view of the famous terraced rice paddies looking south all the way back to the coast on both sides of the island. The irrigation system the Balinese use is unique and recently was named as a world heritage site.

Back in the Kuta Legian stretch, you can buy a pair of board shorts and a Bali singlet or shirt for a dollar each. Everywhere you go, they are trying to sell you something. They love bartering and pretend they are making no money in the end. The clothes are very colourful but after a few washes start to fall apart.

Over the next four years, I would spend all my time off from work chasing waves around the Bali coast. There was an English couple on holiday from Cornwall, with their two kids staying at Melasti in the losmen next to mine, who often talked about the surf that day and stuff. While out for dinner one night with them and a Canadian lady, Cathy, who was in the rag trade buying stuff for her shops in Canada. Anyway, they asked us if we wanted to join them on a trip up to the northern beaches on the other side of the island, a place called Lovina Beach, not far from a town called Singaraja.

So it was organised, and a few days later, we climbed into a bemo, and off we went on a really cool, if not sometimes radically dangerous, drive up through a place called Ubud, which back then was known just for art and jewellery. We stopped at the Monkey

Forest and got some of our shit stolen by monkeys. I think the locals train them to steal anything they can. Then you have to buy a bag of peanuts off the local, and he has to trick the monkey into giving your shit back. So it cost me a bag of peanuts, but I got my shit back. From there, we carried on up towards the Mother Temple, stopping at a bat cave and only having about three serious head-on crashes.

We broke out of the dense bush and onto the rice paddies around evening and pulled into a small hotel with lovely views back over the south end of the island. The next day, we wandered through the Mother Temple, which, I must say, on a nice day is worth the trip by itself. We circled the top of Mount Agung down the other side, stopped at a pretty neat waterfall called Gitgit, and made our way into a picturesque beach and pulled up at a hotel with losmen right on the beach. The food was amazing, and everything was super cheap.

But after three days out of the surf, I was keen to head back, and Cathy had some meetings with a clothes maker. So the following day, we left the family, who wanted a few more days of peace and quiet, and we headed back for another series of Russian roulette with other drivers passing trucks and buses on blind corners. Man, I tell ya, it sure scares the shit out of you. You need a bloody drink when you finally reach your destination.

I think it was Cathy that told me about a new bar opening up a short time later, and I'm sure it was the opening night of the Sari Club Bar in mid-February that I met another Kiwi surfer that would open another door of opportunity. His name was Des. We got along OK and ended up surfing together for a few days before he left to go back to Singapore, where he worked. He had given me his contacts and invited me to stay at his joint while I looked for a job if I wanted. 'Oh, choice, mate, cheers. See you there.'

A couple of weeks later, my Bali allocated funds were getting low, so time to leave that lovely little island with its friendly locals and move on to the next phase—look for a job in Singapore.

I left Bali with mixed emotions, not only sad to leave such a lovely spot, not sure when I would surf again, saying goodbye to people I had met and shared good times, but also a bit hyped up to be moving into another unknown, another step out of the comfort zone. And that is how I landed in Singapore.

I didn't want to just lob in on Des and his friends, so I made my way to Bencoolen Street to find a cheap hotel to base from to locate Des in the hope that he was still in town. Wow, what a location warp. The contrast from little beach island lifestyle to full-on megacity took my breath away and made me spin. I thought Bali was hot; Singapore is hot but in a different way. I called it concrete hot; not enough trees and grass around to suck up the heat, so the heat just bounces all over the place, attacking you from everywhere, not just the sun. In fact, there are lots of trees and parks around the city centre, and they are beautiful. You just have to look for them.

The next day, I jumped on a bus and went looking for Des's place. They had no ph there, so I just lobbed up and knocked on the door. I was so hot; it was the middle of the day, and I must have looked like a vertical puddle. Anyway, the door opens, and there's Des. 'Son, how you doing? You made it,' in his powerful, happy voice. He's standing there in a sarong, the standard clothing for home life in Singapore, as I would get to know. I was introduced to his flatmate and work buddy, Ron, from the States and later to Lingy, Ron's girlfriend. Des and Ron worked for a down whole wireline company called Core Lab.

That night, they invited me to join them in Bugis Street for dinner with the rest of their Singapore friends, so, of course, that's what I did. Bugis Street back then was an infamous tourist centre with a lot of colourful history. Everyone that ever went to the old original Bugis Street has a story to tell. And some like me have many. With the cheap drinks, amazing food, and colourful locals, it was the after-dark tourist mecca full of expats and backpackers, and as I would find out, the billy boys' local hangout. So I said the old original Bugis Street because it no longer exists, as best described by the following excerpt from *Wikipedia*.

> Bugis, in Singapore, was renowned internationally from the 1950s to the1980s for its nightly gathering of transvestites and transsexuals, a phenomenon which made it one of Singapore's top tourist destinations during that period.
>
> In the mid-1980s, Bugis Street underwent major urban redevelopment into a retail complex of modern shopping malls, restaurants and night spots mixed with regulated back-alley roadside vendors. Underground digging to construct the Bugis MRT station prior to that also caused the upheaval and termination of the nightly transgender sex bazaar culture, marking the end of a colourful and unique era in Singapore's history.

So on my first night in Bugis Street, we have a table. There are about ten of us, all Des and Ron's mates with their girlfriends. There's shit going on all over the place; chicks everywhere. I look up, and there is this absolutely stunning six-foot goddess walking along towards our table. It was pretty obvious my jaw was on the ground because everyone at our table started pissing themselves.

I said, 'Far out, did you see that hot piece of arse walking past?' still blown away. They stopped laughing enough to let my dumb arse know I had just seen my first *billy boy*. Ha ha, how disappointing was that. I couldn't believe men could look that pretty, and I wasn't even drunk. Oh my god.

So over my first couple of times living in Singapore, we used to go there a lot, sometimes to drink until the wee hours of the morning. You always met funny people that were passing through or worked there. Then we would go down to the Indian restaurants along Bencoolen Street and have roti pratas for breakfast. They are a fluffy flaky Indian pancake with your choice of spicy curry. I never thought I'd ever like curry for breakfast, but far out, they are nice and bloody cheap to boot.

I was invited to stay with Des in a spare room while I set myself up to start knocking on doors, and over the week, that's all I did. Singapore was in a go slow as far as oil and gas were concerned, so it wasn't looking that good. Luckily, Des was in town for a week or so and showed me the oilfield expats' hangouts where you just hangout, hoping to hear of a company hiring. It was in one of those bars, Jack's Place, under the city bank in Orchard Road, that I bumped into another Kiwi guy from Christchurch. He was heading home after a trip offshore as a rigger with a company called Brown & Root, an American pipeline and oilfield construction company.

He said, 'Mate, if you're a mechanical fitter, you should go out to this company called Taylor Diving. They work on the Brown & Root barges, doing all the diving work. They like hiring mechanical fitters as tenders to help keep their gear running while their divers are in the water.'

'Cheers, mate.' I bought him a beer and never saw him again.

The next day, I took my resume out and filled in a job application. The day after that, I was called and asked if I was interested in going out as a tender on a job for Taylor Diving, and I said yes. I was given instructions and flight details, and that was that. I've got my first job. *Wow.* Trouble was the job mobilized on the Monday; my two-week visa expired on the Sunday. So on Saturday, I went over the bridge to Johor Bahru on what would be my first but not my last visa run. On Monday, I went to the airport.

Chapter 3

I Have a Job in a New World

I was met at the Changi Airport and given tickets and instructions to fly to the island of Labuan, above Borneo and below the Philippines. It wasn't until arriving there and boarding a bus for a short trip to a jetty to board a small tugboat that I really started to meet the guys I was going to work with. We sailed down a beautiful waterway that led out to a large open harbour area with all types of vessels anchored with boats going to and from, some with big cranes, some with large drilling derricks.

Although I was talking to a couple of Kiwis, an American and a Canadian, nothing was really sinking in. A few of them knew each other, and they were mainly talking about where they had been and whom they had been working with. I just stood there looking around, most likely with a dumb look on my face, ha ha.

We arrived at another jetty, which was on the actual island of Labuan, where we went into a hotel restaurant and handed over our passports. Our names were ticked off a list, and we were given lunch. An hour later, we were back on the tug and chugged out to this big rusty barge with a big crane. Once on board, we were ticked off another list, given cabin numbers, and told what shift we would be on.

So here I was on board the Brown & Root derrick lay barge called the 264. Lay means it lays pipe off the back, this one on starboard side, and derrick means it has a big fuck-off crane on it on the stern with a small crane that drives up and down the deck as well. It was bloody hot on the deck, and it was bloody noisy. It's an American company, so there were Americans all over the place going, 'Goddamn, motherfucker.' If I wasn't so blown away by the whole situation, I would have laughed. There is no doubt I would have looked laughable to them. *Goddamn greenhorn motherfucker that one*, they would have thought.

I was put on the night shift, which is 0000 hrs (midnight) to 1200 hrs (lunchtime); while day shift is 1200 hrs to 0000 hrs. They use the twenty-four-hour clock in the offshore world, I was told. I was told to put my gear in my cabin. I was taken to the store room, where a guy gave me a set of PPE (overalls, boots, hard hat, and safety glasses). I was shown around the accommodation area, where to have meals in the galley, the TV and recreation room, etc. Then I went back to my cabin shared with a few others and lay in the dark, listening to the noises until I fell asleep.

At 11:30 p.m., I joined my shift gathered in an area on the starboard stern, in front of the big crane; that is where the dive station is. We were all introduced to each other and to our shift supervisor, an Aussie guy called Tony. The two Kiwis, Stuart and Glyn, plus the Canadian, Gerry, and I think the American was on my shift. His name may have been Paul or Phil or Steve; I know it wasn't Peter or Richard. Anyway, there were a couple of others, but their names escape me. We had a Malay, a Singaporean, and an English ex-taxi driver. So we had a United Nations meeting covered if we needed to solve any problems. Tony put us into pairs and gave us jobs to start on.

At the end of that first shift, I was absolutely exhausted. I had a shower and a meal, and I was lying on my bunk in a dark cabin under the deck of this huge steel tank. I know my head was spinning trying to take it all in. What I was doing? There was a mix of excitement of the unknown and trepidation about whether I was going to do OK. I know when I finally fell asleep, I was dead to it.

So the next day, I was out on deck working on a saturation diving system. And the job the barge had to do was a hyperbaric welding repair of a twenty-inch pipeline on the seabed at forty feet in the Sabah Gas field. We had two welds to do.

There is a lot to explain, so let me try and paint a picture to help get your head around it. I didn't even know what a diver was until the day before, so I've been thrown right in the deep end, but that's OK. I'll explain.

Commercial divers dive down from the surface breathing air but are limited to the time they can stay at whatever depths they are at because the nitrogen in the air can cause the bends. So each time they dive down, they have to decompress back so they can walk around and help the next guy do his dive. This is called air diving.

When divers have to weld pipelines together under the ocean, they need to stay down for long times. This means air diving is not an option, so they use gas divers. To use gas divers, you have to have a gas diving system. This is called a saturation system. They are called saturation systems because the divers live inside these large round chambers about two metres in diameter and about six metres long. They are filled with a mix of helium and oxygen. And they are blown down to the pressure equal to the depth they will work at.

So at the start, six divers climb into a chamber and shut the door. A life support technician opens up valves and blows the chamber down monitoring the oxygen levels and temperature. Once at the required depth, they stop. The divers make their beds and prepare to go diving in teams of two or three, depending on the requirement. When they need to go diving, they climb into another chamber called the dive bell. Once in there, they shut the door, and the gas between both chambers is taken away, similar to astronauts in movies. The bell is trolleyed along until it is over the side of the vessel and then lowered into the water and down to the working depth. Once there, the pressure on the outside becomes equal to the pressure on the inside, and they can lift the door, put their dive gear on, and go out and do the work.

When they have done their shift, it's all reversed; they come up, lock back on to the system, and swap out with the next team of divers. They then have a shower, have something to eat, and then sleep until they are woken up the next day to do it all again. It doesn't matter how long it takes to do the job; they do no decompression until the job is finished. Anything from three to thirty days is normal. Then they just do one decompression. That is called saturation diving.

And I learnt all that in my first day, but don't worry, I didn't understand it either. Funny enough, as I write this, I have three hours left of a decompression from 128 metres, four days, and nineteen hours. I'm in a chamber with five other guys. We blew into saturation twenty-five days and nineteen hours ago. My team did eleven bell runs, and I spent a total time of thirty-six hours working on the seabed up to my knees in mud off the coast of Venezuela. It's October 2017. These are the sorts of figures that are the norm for this style of diving. Your body is saturated in the gas, so there is no nitrogen in your system. That is why it's called saturation diving. And, yes, because it is helium, we talk funny like ducks in a cartoon. You will notice I move from feet to metres throughout the book. This is because different companies have different policies; some use metric, others imperial.

So the reason I remember Stuart, Glyn, and Gerry is they took me under their wing and told me what things were and explained shit and set me up for shit so they could laugh and take the piss out of me. They were funny guys, and we got along well. They were divers and had been around for a while already.

Over the next few days, we got the sat system ready. The American hyperbaric welder divers arrived, and the barge was towed out to the work location, and tugboats chugged around, setting up all the anchors to hold it in place over the pipeline. The welder diver gods came out and climbed in to the chambers, and the life support technician blew them down, and we started the job. Now, to do a hyperbaric weld, you need a habitat. A habitat is a steel box that goes over the pipe. You seal it and blow all the water out with a similar breathing mix to what you have in the chambers. The divers lock out of the diving bell, swim over to the habitat, climb in, take off the diving gear, put on the welding gear, and set the pipe up and start welding it. That's the simplified version. There is actually a shitload involved, and it is a big operation.

The habitat that Taylor Diving had was huge. It weighs twenty tons and has big hydraulic clamps to pick up the pipeline and help line it all up. It is called the SPAR unit, submersible pipe aligning rig. It was twenty feet high, so in the water, the top of it was only twenty feet from the surface, and the visibility was pretty good, so we could sit on the side of the barge and watch what was going on. Sometimes we would jump in and swim down with a mask and snorkel and check it out—something you wouldn't be able to do now.

As the days went by, I got more comfortable with my surroundings. Tony was a really good supervisor and had a bit of a sense of humour, and we all got along well. The days were hot, and we used to look forward to the sunset. The cooler nights were entertaining because with the SPAR unit down with lights all over it, we had heaps of things to watch if we weren't running around doing shit. There were lots of fish, but the biggest buzz was watching the dolphins chase flying fish. They swim upside down so they can see the flying fish while they are flying through the air. Until you see it, you wouldn't believe it. Sometimes the fish would fly into the side of the barge and even onto the deck three metres off the waterline.

After a couple of weeks, we had the first weld completed, but the next location was not ready, so the barge was towed back into Labuan, and I would get my first run ashore as an offshore worker. The barge superintendent had taxi boats organised to leave a half hour after shift change and return five hours later for each shift. We were dropped at a jetty with a short walk to a large sports park. Down the far end was a yacht club that Gerry, Stuart, and I aimed for. Glyn saw a basketball court so went off and bought a ball in the small town down the road. We had a few beers there and then headed into the town. Glyn joined us as we walked past. In the bars in town, the beer was cheaper but too warm, so we staggered back to the yacht club. By then, it had filled up with more guys off the barge, including Tony, the supervisor. The drinks went down fast, and time went fast. Next thing, we were staggering back to the tugboat to get our way back to the barge. We had three days doing this and had a lot of fun.

On the night we left, I was on shift. We were all sitting around the dive station in the dark as the barge was being pulled back out to the field. At about two o'clock in the morning, there was this Zodiac with two ROV pilots. One was crashed out in the front; the other, driving, comes flying up alongside, yelling out and waking us up. 'Come down the stern and help me get him up, will ya?' the driver yelled. So down the back we went.

The barge was probably doing about four knots. The guy drove the Zodiac hard into the back of the barge where the ladder was. We managed to get the unconscious guy up without dropping him.

The driver asked for a knife and slashed the Zodiac, so it started sinking. He quickly climbed up the ladder and cut the Zodiac loose. The last we saw before it dropped out of our lights was the engine going around in circles, getting deeper and deeper. You could smell alcohol for miles around. These two, they had missed the crew boat, and we reckon he probably stole the boat even though he reckons he bought it.

I would see a lot of this over the next years. It sort of came with the job, you might say, ha ha. Missing a crew boat or a flight is pretty bad in this industry, and you gain legend status for it amongst the bar stories for ages, if not for ever, if it's a good story. So the next weld went pretty well. We finished and DE mobed all the gear, packed everything away, and then packed our bags and returned to Singapore.

I think I was paid for forty-four days all up and earned twice as much money as what I had saved up over two years in New Zealand. I had met some new friends that lived in Singapore, so all in all, I thought I was the man. I put half the money in an a/c in city bank, went out to Taylor Diving, and picked up a reference from the bosses on the job, picked up my surfboard, and went back to Bali.

Hang on, I got another Bugis Street story for you. So the deal was to meet Glen, Gerry, Stew, and a couple of others in Bugis Street. Back in the 1980s, I didn't have a card to get money out of an ATM, but I took enough cash to last the night. I was staying at Des and Ron's place in upper Serangoon Road. This was probably the wildest night that I had at the infamous party street; it must have been a weekend. Anyway, we ended up with a big crew shit going down all over the place. These oilfields guys go full on, shouting rounds, so there were heaps of chicks hanging around; it was awesome. Some Kiwi army boys were down there making their own mess and matching us for front-page antics. Then they stepped it up. Three or four of them climbed on top of the toilet block building and did something I'll never forget—the dance of the flaming arseholes. A group on the ground, five or six, were doing the haka, and these other guys had ripped their pants down, whacked toilet paper up there arse, and lit it. I have never seen anything so funny in my life. It didn't last long, and I don't know what damage it had done to them, but it lives on in my memories like it was yesterday. All hell broke loose afterwards.

At around 6 a.m., we staggered down Bencoolen Street for some rotis. Stu and Gerry had motorbikes, so off they went. I jumped on the bus just down from the roti stall. I couldn't believe all my money was gone; I had $1.30, but luckily, it was only eighty cents. My shirt was ripped. I was absolutely trashed, and I watched the locals all getting on the bus as we ambled along. They would give me weird looks as they went to their seats. I was woken by the bus driver shaking me. 'You pay, you pay.'

I looked around. Shit, I was up at the Punggol, a fishing village at the end of the line. I pushed him off and pretended to throw up. He walked back down the bus, raving on in whatever form of Asian dialect he spoke. From the looks of the locals getting on the bus as it started of its journey back, I was obviously looking pretty messed up. So I was thinking, *Right, keep your shit together. Don't fall asleep. No money left.* I could have drunk a small swimming pool dry if I had one. Bang! What the hell was that? I jerked awake. Looking around, I see the roti stall go past. *Oh, no, you dumb arse shit.* I hit the buzzer and staggered off the bus one stop further away than I had gotten on two hours earlier. By now, it was heating up. I was in jeans with a ripped shirt; I looked like total chick magnet—not. By the time I walked all the way back to Des's, I was at least sober, although I had my vertical puddle costume back on. I showered and then I died. A fitting end to what I think was possibly my best night at Bugis Street. I'm going to Bali. I need a surf.

Chapter 4

BACK TO BALI

As the plane banked over the ocean to line up with the runway, I had my first glimpse of what looked like a lot of swell, deep lines stretching out as far as I could see in a deep blue ocean that looked peaceful and relaxing. I was at the window looking north towards the Kuta Legian coast, and the deep lines were throwing back rainbow spray as they crashed onto the beaches. Then right under me, Kuta reef peaked up and barrelled off as the plane came in and screeched onto the tarmac. It was only about 1:30 p.m., and I was in hyper mode, wondering how fast I can get through the airport, get organised with accommodation and a bike, and get to the surf.

Arriving in Bali, this time with instructions from Des, I headed straight down to the Legian Seminyak border to Eddies Garden, a private villa property with traditional two-storey bungalows. I introduced myself to Eddie, the owner and caretaker, and asked for a place to stay. He sent me to his brother's place up the road—cheap, clean, with air con. And his brother set me up with a good Suzuki 125 for $2 a day, and the brakes worked, what a bonus.

While I was throwing my gear in the room and sorting out my board, I met four Aussie surfers that were next door. I asked them where they had surfed and told them Kuta was pumping and asked if they wanted to join me. One did, and off we went. We surfed till dark and had a lot of really good waves. Kuta reef in the six-foot range has got to be one of the top five waves in Bali, and that evening, it was perfect. I went out with my new neighbours, and we got along real good. They were a bit younger than me but heaps of fun. We partied and surfed together over the next three weeks and got up to heaps of mischief. Quite often we practice our mono's on the Kuta/Legian Beach on our way back home late at night. They disappeared on certain swell sizes to so-called secret spots and never let me in on it.

I was sad to see them go, but not long after they left, Des turned up, so we were hanging out together. Because he and his friends lived and owned villas in Bali, they knew a whole different set of people, garment traders, jewellers, etc. So that was interesting. And I was introduced to the European side of the Bali tourist scene, which was more prominent at the Jalan Double Six end of Legian. Des and his friends that lived in Eddies Garden had originally lived in Jakarta in housing estates paid for by the companies they worked for. They told me they were moved out back to Singapore because in the late 1970s, the police were going around shooting anyone with a tattoo on suspicion of being gang members. Because a lot of them had tattoos, they just relocated all workers to Singapore, which was a bummer for the surfers because they had the surf worked out based from Jakarta with another friend of theirs, Martin (Martin Daly of Indies Trader fame), who was a diver as well. They pretty much surfed most of the Sumatra coast and islands before anyone else and named most of the breaks. I meet Martin later in the story and end up doing a job in Indonesia for him. So anyway, no waves in Singapore, and hence them buying their own places in Bali.

When I googled the tattoo story before I included it in this book, I found out that they had been 'purging criminals' until as late as 1983. And apparently, canals often had bodies floating in them.

Getting back to Bali. Cruising around on a motorbike down little dirt tracks, through rice paddies and farmland, looking for waves away from the crowds, was part of the fun of the day. Then one day, I came across a spot where I knew my four Aussie mates had been sneaking off to. No wonder they kept this quiet, and so did I. I think it was a whole year before I walked over the hill, and there was someone at my little barrelling left hander (it is called Bingin). I was devastated, but it was inevitable. Riding the bikes along the beach from the Blue Ocean all the way to Chungu was fun. Places to surf were decided on by tide and swell size at sunrise. Usually an afternoon siesta and then evening surf on the beach at Jalan Padma or Rum Jungle, the better two beach breaks, and then a meal—different restaurant most nights—and then off along the bar circuit, depending on the night, but usually ending at a bar called Kiawapi's, which was on Jalan Legian just up from Jalen Padma. They usually had a good band playing until midnight.

The Balos (Balinese) are very good copy artists, from music to art to clothing and jewellery. Hence, the expat traders would bring their good-quality wares that are in fashion, get them copied by local Balinese for a fraction of the cost, and ship it home and sell them for large profits.

After nearly two months, I was starting to get low on the funds I allocated to spend in Bali and had to think about a return to Singapore. Des and I were asked if we wanted to join a couple of other guys in a fishing boat charter to search the neighbouring islands of Lombok and Sumbawa for waves—two weeks for US$500. I only had $200 left and decided not to, and I still kick myself to this day. But the reality was it's lucky I didn't because getting a job back in Singapore didn't turn out as easy as I thought it would be.

When I arrived in Singapore, Ron and Lingy had moved to a nicer place, and I was allowed to borrow a guy's room that was offshore. I set about looking for work doing the same system as last time. After a couple of weeks, things were very quiet. The guy that resided in the room I was using arrived home and basically kicked me out. Poor old Ron; he was pretty embarrassed, but it had to be done. Ron was too nice to kick me out. So I got on the phone to Stew, told him I was in a bind, and asked if I could drop in until I get a game plan. He was in a big kampong (large open shed-style house) out in Sembawang with an American called Chuck and an English guy called Pierre. Chuck OK'd it. Bye, Don; hello, Chuck.

Chuck was also a diver. He was building a thirty-foot Warren catamaran in his kampong. Pierre was a model and was helping Chuck. When I walked in, there were two upside-down hulls in the house, a basketball court out the front, and native bush out the back. This was country Singapore. So Chuck said I was welcome to stay with them but had to help work on the boat for the bed. 'That's a no-brainer,' I said, and we shook hands.

The routine over the next month was from 0900 hrs to 1800 hrs. Most days, we would get stuff done on the hulls. It was fun. We were all waiting for a job to materialize. In the evenings, we would go down to Charlie's Bar, a two-block walk through the residential kampong suburb. There was a food circle up the road with really nice local food at pretty good prices. Then further up near the end of Sembawang Road was a stretch of bars that catered for the New Zealand army barracks stationed there. The Sembawang area was scattered with divers and other oilfield workers and, of course, lots of army or ex-army personnel.

Most of the guys I met around Chuck's had motorbikes, and Stew took me over to a mate of his that had a shop, and I bought an old Yamaha 250 for $300, I think. And that was a good move, saving on taxi and bus transport and time. Every now and then, we would hit the city for some live entertainment—Rainbow Nightclub had some really good Filipino bands that would cover the latest rock—and finish off in Bugis Street and Bencoolen Street for roti pratas, and then head back for a drunk game of basketball. Whatever time we woke up, we would get some more done on the cat.

Stew and Pierre had a friend with a yacht at Changi Yacht Club, and we used to crew his yacht for the weekend cruises. Through that, we managed to score a charter. A guy from the club needed a twenty-six-foot yacht sailed down from Port Kwang in Malaysia. So off we went, Stew, his girlfriend, Manny, Pierre, a Canadian diver called Brian, and myself. We took four days, with Brian and myself sailing the night shift. It was fun, very relaxing cruising down the Malacca Strait around the small islands that surround Singapore and into Changi.

After two months at Chuck's place, things were not looking good on the work front. My girlfriend from home was now in Brisbane, Australia, so I told her if I didn't have a job soon, I would fly there before I ran out of money. After telling Stew my thoughts, he said, 'What we need to do is make up a bullshit resume, say you have worked in Queensland as a diver for three years, and we'll drop it into a company called Oceaneering out in Jurong on the other side of the island. He says the boss is a Kiwi, and if we say you did your course at Pro-Dive, the school in Auckland, he might give you a job because the guy that runs that school is his mate.' So that's what we did. Then we added that I had worked for a couple of years around Queensland doing civvies. I wish I had a copy of that bullshit resume.

So a couple of days later, we were out at the Oceaneering office 'guardhouse'. I didn't get to talk to anyone; it was like Fort Knox. The guard came back from the office and said, 'Leave resume,' and that was it. A taxi finally picked us up, and Stew said, 'Well, can't do much more than that,' and we laughed at the situation.

The next day, I got a phone call from Lynda, Ian Johnson's secretary at Oceaneering. 'Hello, is this Mike McGettigan?' in a Chinese/Mandarin accent.

'Yes,' I said.

'Ian Johnson wants to see you tomorrow. Ten o'clock OK for you?'

'Yes,' I said.

'OK. Don't be late, huh?' And she hung up.

When Stew came home, he said, 'Bullshit,' and we laughed. He said, 'No one gets to see him, you wanker.'

So another taxi out too Jurong because I didn't want to be seen pulling up on a motorbike. I got called from the guardhouse at 9:55. The guard introduced me to Lynda; she is Chinese Malay. She took me into Ian's office. I was nervous as hell, mainly because I can't remember what bullshit Stew wrote in my resume. My hands were sweating like a mountain rock face in the wet season. The interview was a bit of a blur. He did ask me about Australia but not enough to blow my cover because I had only ever spent one night in transit through Sydney on my way to Bali. It was my trade cert he was really interested in because he had a stuffed Airman compressor that had just come back from Indonesia not working, and he wanted it sorted. It was out of my league because I wasn't a diesel mechanic, but I wasn't going to say that. He asked if I was interested in working on that.

'Yeah, sure, I'll get that working for you.' I hoped.

'I can only pay you $40 sing a day.'

I said, 'I'll soak that up if you put me on a diving job to make it up later.'

'We'll see how we go,' he said. 'Oh, I've got a guy called Bill Ensor arriving off a job Monday. You can work together. See you Monday, eight o'clock.'

'OK,' I said. 'Thank you.' We shook hands, and I walked out to Lynda's desk.

Lynda was smiling and said, 'OK?'

'Yes,' I said. 'I'm to come in Monday to work with Bill.'

'Good,' she said. 'See you Monday.'

She called the guard. The guard picked me up and took me back to the guardhouse and called me a taxi. I stepped out on to the roadside and took a deep breath. I've got a job, but what have I gotten myself into? When I got back to Chuck's, they were all pissing; they couldn't believe I was in his office yet alone walked out with a job. I took everyone out to Charlie's.

The road that Chuck's kampong was on was called Jalan Sembawang, and it was a gateway road from the main Upper Sembawang Road to a vast country-style area in the north of the island. There were rice paddies and little farms and lots of kampongs hidden amongst the bush, a stark contrast to the southern city side of the island. Jurong is in the south-west corner of the island and is one of two main hubs for the offshore oil and gas industry, with the Loyang marine base close to Changi being the other, though way smaller.

So Monday morning, I decided to cut through the maze of roads that would bring me out close to the Singapore Zoo. From there, it was all highways and parkways (motorways); from memory, maybe a thirty-minute ride at the most to Kwong Min Road. I met Bill, and Ian gave us an update of what he wanted. He and Bill shot the shit for a bit, and then we started looking into this Airman compressor.

It turned out neither of us were diesel mechanics, so we had a laugh at the fact that we didn't have much chance of fixing it because it was seized. Anyway, it didn't really matter because other jobs kept coming up, and we only played with the Airman when there was nothing else to do.

Bill was pretty out there but a real hard case, and we got along good and ate for next to nothing at the local food circles. Every couple of weeks, I had to do a visa run across to Johor Bahru. After about three weeks, Bill had been sent off to a job, and I was freaking out that I could get sent out on an emergency fill-in, which happened a lot. One Wednesday night, I was talking to Stew about it. The fact I had never even done a scuba dive but claimed to have three years' experience as a commercial diver had me a bit worried. So Stew called a mate of his that has a dive shop and tells him that I have just gotten back from a job offshore, but I have no tickets, and I need a ticket for a job that's coming up.

'Anything you can do to help?'

'Yes, I have open water course this weekend. Come in shop on Friday, pay, and pick up paperwork. We do theory exam Saturday and two open water dives on Sunday to sixty feet.'

'Thanks, mate,' Stew said and hung up. 'All sorted,' he said.

I was thinking, *Perfect, I get to at least do my first dive.*

Friday night was spent with Stew drumming all the necessary physics of diving into my little brain. Saturday, I passed the test. I said, 'Cool. What's the story for tomorrow?'

He said, 'Oh, don't worry about it.'

I said, 'Oh, I've been looking forward to it.'

He said, 'No, you'll make my class look like idiots.' He gave me my ticket, and that was that.

I walked out onto the East Coast Parkway. I didn't know whether to laugh or cry; not only had I skipped the first PADI training ticket, but also I had been given an open water PADI ticket without even diving. The bummer was that's what I needed to do the most. Oh, shit.

So life carried on at Oceaneering's yard with different divers joining me as they came and went on and off jobs around Asia. One Monday morning, I arrived an hour late into the yard after a big party night at the Changi Yacht Club. I took my helmet off, and my name was blasting over the Tannoy speakers in the yard. I was thinking, *Far out, I'm not that late, am I?*

I went up, and there's Lynda with a big smile on her face. She was always nice to me. Anyway, she said, 'Do you want to go to Dubai as a baby diver? We only pay US$80 a day, though' (experienced divers, $90/100).

'Yes,' I said without thinking.

'OK. Go pack bag. You go this afternoon.'

Holy shit. I asked if I could get paid because I needed to pay some debts before I left.

'Come back half hour.'

When I came back, she said I was flying tomorrow afternoon. *Thank God*, I thought. That gave me some breathing space. I thanked Lynda and promised I'd drop in and say hi on my return, which I did. That night, the smart arse jibes from the Jalan Sembawang kampong crew were fast and furious, ha ha. 'Oh, deep-sea baby diver boy.' The next day, I was on a flight to Dubai, UAE.

Chapter 5

SURVIVING DUBAI

On the flight, I was seated next to an Aussie guy called Pat. Once we had established the fact that we were both working for the same company, he started asking questions about whom I had been working for, etc. Once again, I was wishing I could remember what Stew had written on my resume. Luckily, I didn't mention working in Aussie because he was from Brisbane area and would have sniffed out my bullshit. Then he asked me where I did my dive school. Because I can't remember lies, I thought safer to tell the truth. Big bloody mistake that was and would haunt me over the next two to three months and nearly got me bent, not to mention killed.

I didn't want to mention Pro-Dive in Auckland because I thought he would have been there, so I said, 'I haven't been to dive school. I got in the back door. Where did you do yours?'

'I did mine in the States at CCC's, cost $10,000. How much are you on a day?'

'US$80,' I said.

'Me too.' And that was pretty much the end of the conversation.

I just thought he was a quiet bikie-looking dude. What I found out later was he was absolutely pissed that I was on the same money as him. He was a bit of a bikie, though. And although he had a major hand in possibly making the next two to three months the hardest I had ever had, I still see him on jobs around the world, and we are reasonably good friends, I think. He's an OCM (offshore construction manager); I'm still just a low-life diver.

It was the end of September 1984 when we got off the plane at a small Dubai airport at about 2 a.m. We were picked up and taken to a guest house in the yard of a company called Hydrospace International, a subsidiary of Oceaneering, on the side of the Dubai Creek. On top of the workshop, there is a kitchen lounge and four rooms full of bunks and a toilet shower block. In the morning, we went across the yard to the office, did paperwork sign contracts, and got introduced to some of the people I will work with. We were kitted out with safety gear and started working around the yard mobilising equipment onto trucks to go down to the harbour and onto the boats and barges for the job we were to do. The deal here is you have to do three months to pay for your airfares; if you go home early, a percentage of your pay will be deducted for the cost of flights.

There were English, Scottish, Americans, Canadians, Australian and Kiwis, an Egyptian, and a Maltese. It's hot, and it's dry. There were also Indians and Filipinos that were riggers and welders. And, of course, there were locals who stand out wearing their traditional garments. Pat and I got teamed up with some of the Kiwi Aussie guys that have been around for a while, and then I saw Tony, the supervisor, from the Taylor diving job I did. We had a chat. He obviously knew my real background but never mentioned it. He introduced me to Bill, another Kiwi supervisor, who took me and Pat onto his team, which was real handy. Bill and I clicked straight away probably because we're both half-arse jokers always looking for a laugh and some fun.

Bill, Toni, Mat, a superintendent, and Brent, a Kiwi diver, with some other Oceaneering guys from Australia took us down to the Dubai Ski Club when we knocked off work, and we had a few beers and a bit of storytelling, which gets the ice broken, and you meet the real person you're going to work with, and they get to meet the real you. It was just a five-minute dusty taxi drive. The club was air conned with pool tables, a nice bar, swimming pool outside, and, of course, access to ski boats and equipment, plus windsurfers. As Hydrospace employees, we were complimentary members.

Over the three years I worked here, we had some good parties, live bands, and there was a really good local and expat society. Sometimes I would go there by myself and hang out with the local working crew, mostly English but a couple of Kiwis and an Aussie. The manager of the club was part of the royal family, and although he didn't drink, he often sat with us, and sometimes when I was there by myself, he would serve my beers, and we would just chat. Looking back, I guess there is a bit of a distance between the educated and the non-educated, but then it doesn't matter what nation you are in; the same applies. Mohammed, like his large family, I assume, was well educated and quite westernized.

Dubai is split into two towns by the Dubai Creek, with Dubai one side and Deira on the other. Bill took me for our first foray into Dubai the next night, the desert cut up by large tar-sealed roads with huge roundabouts in the middle of nowhere. I remember thinking they must have bought all these roundabouts in bulk to get a discount, but it was obviously good future planning by the sheik because now you hardly notice them. Pulling up and jumping out of the taxi in Dubai was like jumping onto the set of *Lawrence of Arabia*. I would not get to see the gold souks until next time in town.

We got some offshore supplies like books, toothpaste, etc., and then went to the Astoria Hotel and an American bar for a beer, and then went to the Ambassador Hotel to a bar called Baker Street. An English band run the bar, and of course, they played there most nights, and they were pretty good. In fact, the live music scene in Dubai was really good. With four different bars with bands, the only problem was there were no women. I remember being in Baker Street sometimes with up to a hundred men and three women. Every now and then, the nurses, mainly British from the Sharjah hospital, would come over, and the place would nearly look normal. Sharjah is about forty minutes away and was a wet town when I first arrived, but within six months, it had stopped serving alcohol after a deal with Saudi Arabia meant they got a new mosque. I was told that the local Arabs mainly worked in government jobs, and labouring jobs of such were carried out by expat workers from India, Thailand, and Philippines, or other Arabs from outside the sheikdom.

In the 1980s, Dubai was a small city even when you included Deira, but it was spread out with large hotel and apartment complexes seemingly in the middle of nowhere. The Hyatt Galleria was the only high-rise building in the city. With a hotel block and apartment block, it was on the Deira side at the mouth of the creek. The Sheraton was up the creek Dubai side city centre but was not that tall. There was no palm or anything. In fact, we used to go to Jumeirah Beach and ride wind swell waves with mini mells on Fridays with an expat teacher called Lance, also a Kiwi, whom I had met one night at Thatchers, one of the good early evening bars. Lance and I became good mates and still catch up to this day. Friday is their religious day off, and a hotel complex called the Metropolitan used to have jam sessions mid-afternoon onwards in the Red Lion Bar.

So getting back to work, Bill was to take out a small single-shift crew on a supply boat with a small air dive system consisting of a container with a decompression chamber and an air diving panel with umbilicals and all the gear needed. So the names I remember were Bill, Pat, Aubrey, Paul, Dennis, Claude, and an American, Neil. We mobed the boat and sailed out to DPC's (Dubai Petroleum Company) south-west Fateh Field.

I shared a cabin with Bill and a couple of others. I didn't get a lot of sleep. It wasn't purely the fact that I was going to have to dive for the first time but the fact that Bill snored like a bulldozer. Bloody hell, the only time he stopped was when he would roll over and fart like a hurricane; a moment silence and then the bulldozer was back in the house. When it was brought up over breakfast, he said he doesn't hear anything, but he used to wonder why he would wake up surrounded by shoes, boots, and anything else that could be thrown at him, ha ha.

The other shift of the complete crew was coming out a day later on an ETPM barge called 401. ETPM was a French offshore construction company similar to Brown & Root. They were nicknamed Easy Time Plenty of Money. So we were to go around the platforms the barge had to work on and put buoys on the pipelines that lead off so the barge doesn't drop its anchors on them.

MY FIRST DIVE

So the morning started off with organising a scuba replacement system, which consists of two G size air bottles, a little dive panel, and a radio comms box, a three-hundred-foot umbilical with a Kirby Morgan ten-band mask attached to it, and checking the comms worked. We also had twin set scuba tanks for the standby diver. We loaded it all into a large Zodiac. We all jumped in, and off we went over to the first platform. Can't remember who dove first, but after a few dives, the G bottles were getting low.

Bill said to me, 'I'll put you in on scuba with Claude to run the last buoy out as far as you can get.'

We said OK. Inside, I was freaking out a bit; outside, I don't know if it was obvious. So when the time came when Claude put his tanks on, I put mine on; when he put his fins on, I put mine on. Then the knife, then washed and spat in the mask, then tested the reg, gas is on, yep. Claude looked at his stops board. A stops board is a homemade Perspex sandwich with a set of tables typed up on the inside that tells you bottom time and water deco stops time for the depth you get to. I didn't have one.

Dennis asked, 'Where's your stops board?'

'Um, haven't got one.'

'What? You'll need one around here. I'll lend you mine. Don't lose it. I've only just made it.'

'Thanks, mate. I won't.'

Claude rolled over the side, grabbed the last buoy's rope, and left the surface, and I was right behind him. He got to the bottom, looked back, gave me a thumbs up, and pointed up the pipeline, and off we went. He must have checked depth and worked out the time because I can't remember any of that; I just remember not to lose those fins in front of me. He stopped and started digging under the pipe. It was a sort of sandy mud, and I dug on the other side. We got the rope around. He tied a knot and gave me another thumbs up, and we left bottom.

Coming up was a lot slower, so I was able to actually take note of my surroundings. The visibility wasn't too bad, and although I might have calmed down a bit, I was still sucking the air out big time. We were told to do a no deco dive so came straight up to the surface. The boys in the Zodiac came over, and we climbed back in. The only thing, I think, I did wrong was lose Dennis's stops board. I think he just did the old rollover eyes while looking at everyone else. Later in my career, I would do the same tactic to other baby divers. It's the silent speak for, *This guy's bloody useless. I don't think he'll last long*, and we all sort of laugh behind our eyes.

So behind my eyes at that time was a tonne of emotion. I couldn't let any of that out. I was definitely sheepish because I was disappointed I lost his board, but I was also elated that I had just done a dive to 105 feet, first dive ever, and I was pretty relaxed about the whole ordeal. According to my first page in my first logbook, a bottom time of twenty-four minutes. The boat was called the *Catharina*, and it was 6/10/84. We left surface at 1010.

When we arrived back at the *Catharina*, two guys jumped up, and we starting passing gear up. This was where I got the second secret eye talk. I was passing up the comms box when the Zodiac bounced on the end of the bow rope. I went in the drink with the box way above my head, trying to keep it out of the water. Someone managed to grab it out of my hands before total submersion, and Bill managed to get it dry over lunch, and it still worked, thank God.

The damage to me was already done, though, and a division started like a tear in fabric, small but getting bigger, not amongst everyone but most definitely amongst some that will show their colours later in time. I bumbled around trying to keep up with it all, but it was obvious I was green, and to the experienced, probably too green. Bill maintained his jovial character and kept me included in general conversation, and without that, the tear would have been a lot quicker and maybe even non-repairable. I had to work on staying involved, and I think by the end of the first week, some had caught on to Pat's distaste at the fact that they had spent a lot of money to get their dive tickets, and here I was on the same day rate or not much less. I don't blame them really, but at this time, I didn't know it was an issue. It would be two jobs later it would hit me.

So the barge turned up the next day, and we rejoined the rest of the crew and went on to shifts. On 11/10/84, I did my first hat dive. It was my third dive in total and quite a different experience. The hat is actually a Kirby Morgan ten-band mask, a fibreglass faceplate with an oral nasal demand valve. Clamped onto that is a rubber hood. It is tightened around the back of your head with a rubber spider, so your face is sealed against the foam seal by the oral-nasal. You have earphones jammed next to your ears and a microphone in the oral nasal. It is more comfortable than it sounds. The umbilical attaches to the right side of the band mask and loops around the back of your backup air bottle called a bailout and attaches to your harness via a D-ring. It's pretty cool because you can talk to your supervisor, and he can yell at you.

Trouble is now you're dragging this bloody umbilical around; if there is any current, it is actually dragging you around. And although it is your lifeline, it can actually be your killer. Unfortunately, a lot of divers die because of bad umbilical management. In about 2009, I received word a friend of mine from my diving days in Dubai had lost his life in a diving accident in Asia. When I received a report of what happened to Rob, it was disgusting that this sort of thing was still happening in the industry. It is a wake-up call that just because there was such a big emphasis on safety in the modern-day offshore industry, mistakes can still be made. His team had let him down, and he paid the ultimate price. Rob was a real nice English bloke, RIP. As for me, that dive went OK, although I think the only person I impressed was me, ha ha. Yeah, had another little solo celebration again.

My first job offshore as a commercial diver came to an end. We demobed the barge. I had done five commercial dives. The crews got split up, with Bill, Tony, Brent, and Matt joining another crew of Aussies on a seabed core drilling job going out of Fujairah harbour on a vessel called SeaCat. Pat and I were sent on a visa run to Bahrain to return with a residence visa. This had a very important part to play later as it meant I could come and go into Dubai as I pleased.

When we got back, we joined Paul, Aubrey, Dennis, and a couple of Scots; one was the supervisor of that particular short job. All I can remember of this job is when it was my turn to dive, the wind had picked up, it was dark, and the pressure was on to get whatever done before we had to pull off. The current was ripping, and we had trouble getting the previous diver out of the water. The supervisor pointed off the back of the boat to where he wanted me to go and gave me instructions on what I had to do when I got there. I jumped in and straight away got swept under the boat and bounced of the props. I was huffing and puffing, and the supervisor was yelling at me. He has a really strong Scottish accent, and even on deck, I had trouble understanding him, let alone with a hat on underwater. They managed to pull me back to the ladder. My old man is Scottish with a bit of accent, but that was no help with this guy yelling in my ear. I didn't know what he was saying, but I knew he needed me to get to this riser. I was going up and down in the swells, hanging on to this ladder. The umbilical was trying to drag me in the opposite direction. I can't even see the job because it's dark, but I just launched off and went like hell to try getting to the platform. Whoosh, and I was hanging off my waist on my umbilical like a fly on the end of a fishing line in a river. They dragged me back and dragged me up the ladder. First big-time failure. I pulled the hat off. The supervisor was still yelling at me but now in disgust because I had embarrassed him. I still couldn't work out what he was saying, but I knew it wasn't good. I had just been run off my first job on my second job. Oh, dear, not a good start. Don't worry, it gets worse.

So now I really am Nigel No Friends, the guy they laugh at when you're not around. I was sent to the beach by myself, but I'm not sure how I got there. I was stuck here for another two months, so I decided I've got time to turn it around maybe. Because of my trade, John, the yard manager, was happy having me around fixing things and helping around the workshop. The job I had just been run off from came back, and I helped them demob.

Lance, the Kiwi schoolteacher I had met one night at the Dubai Marine Hotel, had invited me to join him at a party. I dragged Pat along. Nothing was mentioned about work. We had a good time and managed to get home safely. We were still unfamiliar with Dubai, and it can be dangerous for a westerner trying to get taxis after drinking in pubs or parties because you're not allowed to be drunk in public. One time, I was waiting for a taxi to come pass, and a police four-wheel drive stopped. I couldn't hide. I was by myself, and even though they offered to give me a ride, I was actually shitting myself until they got on the right road that I recognized. Maybe they were OK, but I wasn't happy until I got out. A few days later, we were mobing another job to go out to DPC on another supply boat. Same guys, but the two Scots had gone home, and the supervisor was an English guy called Brian, I think. So we got the vessel ready to go, and because we weren't sailing until midnight, some of us went into one of the hotel bars on the Deira side because we were tied up on that side of the creek. We had a real laugh, got pretty pissed, and headed back to the boat. I went to the toilet, came out, and walked straight into a major argument—that three to four of my so-called friends a half an hour ago were saying to the supervisor that they didn't want me on the job. It was pretty ugly and made worse by the amount of alcohol that had been drunk.

'I'm not going to dive if he's my standby.'

'He wouldn't be able to save me if I get in trouble.'

'He hasn't been to dive school.'

'This is bullshit.'

All of a sudden, it's back to me and them. I was pretty embarrassed. Paul was sticking up for me. Brian was trying to calm Aubrey and Dennis. Pat was throwing shit in as well, not sure why because he hadn't exactly been a diving legend anyway. But I had no leg to stand on and couldn't say much. Brian said there was nothing he could do at this time of night and we'll sort it out in the morning. That's how we went to bed. The vessel sailed out to the field. How did I feel that night in the dark? With three other divers that had just spilled exactly what they thought of me, no hiding behind doors to laugh anymore, I was pretty freaked out and dreaded the sun coming up. And it was as hard as I thought it would be. Now there was a real wall between me and them. Breakfast was like being at a funeral. Paul gave a bit of reassurance during the morning and told me I'll be all right. I joked that I had more mates on this job than normal. He smiled. 'Don't worry about it.' We went out on deck and got the show on the road.

We were in the Fateh Field, which is deeper with bad visibility, and the job was seabed scrapping. That consists of dropping a basket on the seabed with rope tied on in long lengths on the outside. What you couldn't put in the basket, you put as close to as possible and tie it off. In the mid-afternoon, they had to put me in. We were using a Rat Hat as the main diver's hat, with the standby using the KMB10. I hadn't used a Rat Hat before; it is a fully enclosed hard hat. You put a toilet seat over your head that has a rubber seal that seals around your neck. The steel ring has an O-ring on the outside, and the hat gets clamped onto that. The toilet seat has straps that go around your crutch, and they stop the hat wanting to come off your head. They are a free-flowing hat, and there is a knack to using them properly and efficiently.

I didn't get shown the trick to finding the knack, so I was pretty much set up for disaster. That didn't take long. Brian was OK. I could understand him, he was reassuring, and all I had to do was go down the crane wire to the bottom about 170 feet, take my time, get myself together, and get some work done. They are the magic words to becoming a diver—get some work done. Those words should be in capital because that's all that matters. Surface-oriented air diving is a race against time. Leave the surface, get something done, leave bottom on time. Very important. So here I go; time to redeem myself.

I jumped in and grabbed the crane wire. All good so far. Jesus, this hat's heavy. Bloody hell, I rammed the nose on the nose peg to clear my ears. Now I was upside down flying down this bloody greasy crane wire. My ears were trying to implode. I was scared of slicing my hand open on the wire. I was going so fast, so I was still upside down when the basket at the end of the crane came into view and, bang, I was on the bottom. My ears were trying to blow my eyeballs out. My head was screaming. By jamming my nose on the nose peg and trying to blow, I finally equalised my ears. What a release, like a squeal in my head.

Brian said, 'All OK, Spike?'

'Roger.' I lied.

I went down way too fast. They had just thrown my umbilical over the side and let me go, or hang I should say. I was narced off my tree. Narced is nitrogen narcosis, similar to the spin you get from four shots of good tequila. I was looking around; I can see about ten feet. In my head, it sounded like I can hear every vessel in the field. My vision came and went. My head settled a bit.

Brian said, 'All OK, Spike?'

'Yeah. Roger.' I lied again.

I climbed out of the basket into the mud. I saw what looked like a bit of scrap that looked like I could put in the basket, and I went off to pick it up. It was a small stainless box of some sort and took me a bit to get out of the mud. When I got it out, I stood up and turned to the basket. *Shit, where did that go?* Must be just there, and I started walking in what I thought was the right direction. Now here's where another rule of diving defines the living from the dead. Don't panic. Those words should be in capital as well. So guess what I did. First, I freaked out and thought, *Oh, no, you dickhead, you have to find that basket.*

'How you going down there, Spike?'

'Good, just putting a box in the basket.' I lied again.

See, karma comes back to you when you lie. Still, no basket. Now I started *panicking.* I was running around and totally stuffed up the visibility, and I was now totally lost. I guess Brian had noticed my breathing had doubled.

'You OK?'

'No, I'm lost. Can't find the basket. It was just there. Now I don't know where it is.' There was silence for what seemed like a year.

'OK. Don't panic. We'll drop the standby. He'll come down your umbilical and pull you back to the stage, OK?'

'Yeah. Roger.'

So down came Aubrey. I wasn't happy to see him, though, because I could see the group laughing at me behind his eyes. It was horrible, and although I didn't die, I felt dead. When we got back to the surface, I thanked him for coming down and then just sort of kept a low profile. No eye contact with anyone. I climbed into my music that night and went through my options. I need a surf. I had thrown myself in the deep end; it's not the ten-metre pool from my childhood with the old man close behind. I was in a 170-foot pool, and I was alone, very alone. I told myself I can do this. I just need to get it right.

I got up the next day, and as Nigel No Friends was having breakfast, he told myself it's not over until the green boy drowns. *I'll do better today*, I promised myself. So this time, as they were dressing me in, Paul told me to keep the exhaust shut; it makes the hat light.

'When you get to the bottom, adjust it so it's not trying to blow off your head.'

Why didn't they tell me that yesterday? I thought.

My job this time was easy. Brian was trying to help, as was Paul. I had to take the crane down the down line to the basket, hook it up to the lift rigging, make sure all is secure, and return to the surface. I got to the seabed in better shape, adjusted the exhaust so the hat was just bouncy on my head, and hooked the crane up. I even put some more scrap in the basket, and when my time was up, I left bottom. That wasn't so bad. There we go. I felt like I had broken off some uselessness. I was at thirty feet doing a water stop. They started coming up on the crane. I can see the crane wire, so I was waiting for the basket to go past. Then my world collapsed. There was no basket on the crane hook. With devastated anxiety running through my body, I couldn't believe my eyes. What the hell happened? I hooked the crane up; I did.

Now I told Brian. There was silence and then 'Come back on that.'

'The basket's not on the hook.' Silence.

As I did the time at the stops, I was told to move up to the next stop. Silence. I finally got to the surface, and they took off the hat. Silence. I could feel the laughing behind the eyes. Then Brian went off at me. I was run-off again. That's twice out of three jobs. I was in a pretty big low now. Not even my music helps. I need a surf real bad. I didn't know what went wrong. And no one was explaining anything to me, so I wasn't going to find out. Nigel No Friends was pretty alone now; it looked like a long road out. I got lower the next day when Brian said he has to go home, and I was going back to the beach with him. So now it's official—I was run-off. He explained I wasn't up to it, but in my head, I disagreed.

Back at the guest house, I was the only one there. I helped John in the yard, but he was quiet as well, probably felt sorry for me. While I had been out on that last job, a Western Australian diver that was on the SeaCat crew had a bad CNS bend. He nearly died but recovered and was paralysed from the waist down. He was in the local hospital and every day would be brought out to do therapeutic O2 in our on-site chamber. He was in a bad way but improving slowly. A couple of times, I ran the chamber, and a couple of times, I was in the chamber with him. A week later, he was well enough to be flown home.

A couple of days later, Norb, the boss, walks into the guest house. 'McGettigan!' he yells.

I came into the lounge. 'Hi, Norb.'

'I need someone to go out and help a surveyor on the SeaCat. Can you go?'

'Yeah, of course.'

'I'm only paying you $40 a day.'

'But I'm contracted for $80 a day.'

'You have been run-off the last two jobs. Do this, or you're on a plane out tomorrow.'

'OK,' I said. He stormed off.

Next day, I was on my way out to Fujairah and joined the Kiwi Aussie crew as a surveyor helping an Egyptian run the tide fish and monitor current's direction and speed every hour. When I got on board, I told Bill and Tony what had been happening, told them I had stuffed up no doubt but thought with the right help, I could pull this off. I said I just need someone to give me confidence and guidance instead of setting me up for a fall.

'I'm pretty sure I can turn it around.'

They said, 'Go talk to Matt. He might help you out.'

So I went up and talked to Matt. He said, 'Do your job surveying,' and when he could, he will put me in the water, 'and we'll take it from there.'

'Thanks.' I felt better already.

Over the next few days, the guys got me involved and explained stuff and things to watch out for—all the little things that make a difference, like relax, take your time but hurry, and don't panic. The job was interesting. They had a miniature drill rig sitting on the seabed, with a hydraulics umbilical running a drilling head on about a four-metre drill derrick. The drill cases were core barrels designed to capture a core of the ground you are drilling. Then the rock doctor processes his findings, and that all goes into the design of whatever they want to build on that location. The core strings are one and a half metres long, and sometimes we had to drill thirty-metre cores. So that means drilling down the first core, sending that to the surface, adding another one-and-a-half-metre drill rod to the next core, and repeating the steps. So lots to do, very interesting.

One afternoon, Matt said he'll put me in on the standby gear to observe Brent on the drill rig. Bill and Tony were only divers on this job, so they dressed me in and basically just told me to relax and enjoy the dive. I jumped in, and that's exactly what I did. Brent gave me the thumbs up and then carried on; he was pretty busy. Matt was explaining what Brent was doing. Then I left bottom. What a difference it makes when people have a good attitude. I will remember this forever.

Over the next few days, Matt used me to get some of the easy stuff done, building my confidence. Then he started using me as if I was part of the dive team, and it was fun going underwater but doing a job you associate with being on the surface. It was a very busy time in the water, and time went quick. Around this time, we had a crew change and were alongside in the port of Fujairah. Pat arrived to replace someone that had to go home. I wondered if Pat was going to start getting into everyone's ear like he had with the other crews. It had been pretty good up to then, but I needn't have worried.

While we were alongside, everyone took off to a yacht club five minutes away, but Tony told me I was staying with him to help mix gas for the next part of the project. We had taken a couple of helium quads on board, but the mix of helium/oxygen wasn't right for the depth we were going to dive at. To fix this, we had to dump out some helium and add more oxygen. Once we had the right mix, we were up the road for a few cold beers. I said, 'Gidday,' to Pat, but that was about all. Most of the Australian crew on our job were from the Perth Oceaneering diving company, and they had all been around for a while; they were a pretty hard-case bunch. I just listened and laughed. It was a fun night out.

SURFACE SUPPLIED MIX GAS DIVING

Mixed gas diving involves three types of gas. I'll break it down for you.

Nitrox

When diving was first invented around the 1950s, compressed air was the breathing medium because it was readily available and easy to compress. Unfortunately, air is not the ideal mix because of the high concentration of nitrogen, which is approximately 79 per cent. This causes two complications for divers, the first being nitrogen narcosis (which is a feeling resembling being very drunk) at deeper depths, and decompression sickness (DCS); both of which can be fatal to any diver. To reduce the amount of nitrogen in a diver's breathing mix, they developed nitrox. Basically, it is just air with more oxygen and less nitrogen. Typical percentages common in the industry are 32 and 36 per cent oxygen per volume. As air is 21 per cent oxygen, you wouldn't think 15 per cent would make much difference, but it does. It allowed divers to significantly increase their bottom time while reducing the risk of DCS. While this mix has benefits, it also has associated risks. The major hazard is oxygen toxicity. This comes about when a diver inhales high concentrations of oxygen for an extended period and when a diver exceeds the recreational limits for depth. This could cause epilepsy or seizures and lead to drowning. Sounds like fun, let's go do that. If you're going to do that, you really need to stick to the strict guidelines and special tables.

Helium or gas diving

This is the term used when a diver breathes a mix other than air or nitrox. The main reason for this is to avoid nitrogen narcosis. It also improves decompression and oxygen toxicity. Surface gas diving involves a lot more drama. It is way more complicated and needs a lot more organisation and better equipment and planning. The fact that such dives are performed at deeper depths and for longer times increases the risk of something going wrong. It is very important that the gas mixes are checked because breathing the wrong mix can be fatal. Heliox is the gas mix most common in this line of diving. This mix of 79 per cent helium and 21 per cent oxygen is often used for deep diving with extended bottom times. Unlike nitrogen, helium has no intoxicating effects at any depth. It has a lower density than nitrogen, making it easier to breath, and in cases of long bottom times, improves decompression. Still, heliox has its drawbacks with it being very expensive, has limited availability, and its thermal conductivity is six times greater than nitrogen. This means that a diver breathing heliox will lose body heat six times faster than someone breathing compressed air, making them susceptible to hypothermia. To prevent this, divers can wear a hot water diving suit where hot water is pumped down a hose in their umbilical and which is connected to a valve on the suit that sends the hot water around a perforated small rubber hose that is stitched all around the suit.

Our working depth was only going to be around 165 feet, but due to the depth of the hole we were drilling, we needed the extra time to accomplish an economical dive. We were also using a dive stage instead of just going down the down line. So when it was my turn, I climbed into the stage and left surface, breathing normal air. At thirty feet, I was told that he was changing over to heliox and to start flushing my hat until I hear the gas change and then give him a count. The flushing sound went from a deep low sound to a higher-pitched smoother sound because of the different density, and if you have ever breathed the Christmas balloons, it makes your voice high pitched like Donald Duck. Hence, as I counted, my voice went from normal to duck speak, and Matt knew the gas change was complete and told me to stop flushing.

I carried on down, did the dive, and on returning to surface—the first stop was eighty feet—I was told to flush the hat again. This time, heliox was flushed out for nitrox. When you hear the different gas, you start the count, and when the voice is back to normal, you are asked if you're OK. Then you come up to your next stop. The nitrox helps to flush out the helium from your system. At thirty feet, you flush your hat again, and this puts you back on to standard air mix. Now at the end of that rather long stop, you have five minutes to go from thirty feet to the surface, get your gear off, get down the deck to the chamber, climb in, get a seal, and be blown back down to forty feet. You have to grab an O2 bib as you're trying to equalise your ears as hot air is blasting in on you.

You're in the entry lock, so when you equalise with the main lock, you can open the door, go through, get on an O2 bib, and put your thumbs up to the port hole, and the clock starts. You lie down in a pool of sweat with the mask on, grab your book, and start relaxing. You do twenty minutes on O2, have a five-minute air break where you get to have a drink of water, and then back on the bibs. After the second O2 period, you deco up to thirty feet slowly and then spend another hour or more before you finally deco all the way back to the surface. They pass in a fresh cleaning towel. You clean the chamber bibs, shut the main lock door—they get a seal—and blow it back down for the next diver. After a cup of tea on the go, you check your O2 quads, check the chamber is ready for the next diver, and when he hits the surface and jumps in the entry lock, you're in charge of his deco until he steps out and comes back from his cup of tea on the run. He takes over from you, and you return to the aft deck dive station. And that is the basic operation of a surface gas dive crew. For the first half hour after getting out of the chamber, you feel like someone has blown your chest up.

I had completed four of these dives by the time the job was finished, and Tony collared me and Pat to help him demob the vessel in Fujairah harbour, while the rest of the crew took off in a bus back to Dubai. We rode in the last truck with the gear and arrived at about 2 p.m. in the yard. Everyone was heading out for drinks in town, but I needed a cash advance, which meant I had to go into the office, which meant possibly running into Norb, my boss, something I really wanted to avoid. But I wanted to go out with the boys, so off I went to see Binta, Norb's secretary. I filled out a form and asked Binta if she would go and get Norb to sign it for me. She said, 'Why don't you?' and then looked at my stupid face and laughed because she knew the shit I had been in, and off she went into his office while I hid in hers.

'McGettigan!' Norb bellowed out. 'Where is he?'

I thought, *Oh, no*, and walked in, expecting the firing squad.

He nearly jumped over his desk, grabbed my hand, shaking it, and said, 'Goddamn gas diver eh.' With a big smile on his face, he told me about his first gas dive. I was blown away. 'Heading for some beers with the boys?'

'Yeah, looking forward to that,' I said.

He signed my advance form, and off I went with US$200 and a huge relief. I was told that Matt, Bill, and Brent had all gone in and put a word in for me while we were still coming back. I seemed to be out of trouble for now. I felt pretty good heading out for the night.

We were in Baker Street. The band was good. There were a few girls. Pretty good night nearly ended with us all locked up because when we were acting up waiting for a taxi, Jerry, from Tasmania, ran over the top of the taxi we were getting in and straight into a cop. It took Bill and Brent fifteen minutes to calm the cop down and let us go. Ha ha, we got back to the guest house without any more drama.

The next day, we sweated out the alcohol working in the yard storing the gear from the vessel. Most of the SeaCat crew flew out that arvo, Matt, Tony, Bill, and Brent amongst them. I was now back amongst the English friends of Pat but just kept my head down and worked in the yard with John. We got half rates for working in the yard, so with nothing else to do, why not earn yourself a beer? This was when I started heading to the ski club by myself and hanging out with people that wanted to talk to me.

One day, we had just finished lunch in the guest house, Paul, Dennis, Aubrey, and Pat. Norb walked in and said he had a little job to do in Abu Dhabi, maybe four to five days, and needed a crew and asked Paul if he want to be the supervisor. Paul said he hasn't gotten a supervisor ticket but had filled in for Brian on the job that I was run-off and could take it out if he wanted.

Norb said, 'OK, pick your crew.'

Paul looked at me while he said, 'Well, these guys here will be a start. We just need a couple more.'

'OK,' Norb said. 'I'll organise a vessel.'

We went down to get John to decide what gear we could take, and that was us mobing up another surface air spread. Two days later, we sailed out of the Dubai Creek on the cockroach-infested *Maintainer 2*. Man, it was gross. We would spend a week fighting cockroaches for our food and being woken up with them walking over our face. Oh my god, I will never forget that.

On the job itself, there was still a bit of tension with Pat and his mates, but Paul took me under his wing, gave me a book to read, asked me questions during the day, and set me up with trap questions and call me a wanker and laugh when I fell in the trap.

Thanks, Paul, for making those days bearable and helping me get over that wall.

We arrived back in Dubai and went out for beers as usual, and things were not as hostile as previous nights. Paul never went out very often, choosing to stay at the guest house and drink from our much cheaper bar. We often came back around midnight, and he's crashed out with a whisky on his chest. Too big to move, we would just leave him until morning. I'd wake him for breakfast, and he would scull what was left of the whisky on his chest and get up. Classic.

It would be a couple of weeks before we mobed another job. I spent a bit of time at the ski club and had a bit of a surf day at Jumeirah Beach, twenty minutes out of town, with Lance and a few dangerous beers on the beach. A patrolling police four-wheel drive came past but luckily didn't stop. An American called Norm came back to the guest house one morning and said he'd just made an easy US$200.

'How?' we asked.

'Sold a pint of blood.'

So off we went. The second place we went to, Norm fell over, nearly passing out. He had to give one pint back. Ha ha, what a laugh. We had all made $400 so that night hit the nightclub.

Getting close to Christmas 1984, we mobed a vessel called the *Interprovider* with a surface gas diving spread on it. First, we had to wait for the tide to get to the right height so we could back it up hard against the wharf by the Sheraton Hotel and drive a mobile crane on and then sea fasten it to the deck. We were heading out to DPC field to do seabed scrap survey and debris removal. Divers started arriving, some English and Australian. We had a large crew because we would be doing a lot of gas diving. The survey part of the job was a pain. We would do deep scuba dives to set up lines off the platforms so we knew where we were. Then we would go down with these boards and run around drawing pictures of what we saw. The vis was shit, and I didn't seem to be very good at it.

One day, Aubrey came up to me as I was getting ready to dive. He said, 'Spike, you're shit at this, and I'll tell you why.' I listened. 'What you do is get down there, run along the lines as much as you can, just looking, nothing else. When you're on your stops on the way up, that's when you do your drawing. If you saw a scaffold pipe, you put it down. It doesn't matter where. No one will be going down to check your work. Scaffold pipe here, tire there, piece of piss.'

'Thanks, Aubrey.'

So that's what I did. All of a sudden, I was getting as much done as the others. The fact that Aubrey had actually given me advice to help instead of hinder was what made me realise I had finally started to get accepted with the other divers that I had had trouble with for the last seventy odd days. At this stage, we were only doing surface air dives while we were doing the surveys. Some of the platforms had so much rubbish on the seabed they decided to break the job into two stages.

One evening, just after dinner, Pat came into the TV room. He was worried because his shoulder and elbow were in pain. Aubrey jumped up, and we got Paul up, went down, and blew Pat down for a table 6. I think Dennis went with him as the nurse, who is there in case of any complications. Pat got relief at depth so was treated with the standard table 6. A table 6 is therapeutic table designed to help release trapped gas in the human body. It is basically just a lot of twenty-minute cycles of medical O2. The bent diver and his nurse are blown down until they get relief from whatever pain they have. This is usually forty feet. So Pat and Dennis finally arrived back on the surface, and he was OK. You can't dive for a month after a type 2 bend, so because he had already done his three months, he went home.

I think Ted joined us then. What a cruiser he was. About fifty years old, bloody fossil with a few stories but pretty quiet. He had been in the Royal Navy as a clearance diver and played a large part in the tests they did to make the Royal Navy tables for compressed air diving manuals. By now, Paul, Aubrey, and Dennis had all done their three months and left, and Tony was now the supervisor, with John, a Kiwi from my hometown of Napier but living in Perth, and two other Steves, also from Perth. Arkmed, an American diver, was also on our extended crew. The first stage of this job came to a close on the end of January and was going to start up again in about two months' time. We were on the beach, and I was preparing to go when the Indian travel agent came up to me.

'Hello, Mr Spike.'

'Hello, mate, what's up?'

'You have return ticket to Singapore?'

'Yes, I do. Can you book my flight?'

'You give me ticket, I book and give you return to Dubai instead.'

'OK,' I said.

He hadn't consulted anyone; he just assumed that because they had spent US$3000 on my residence visa that I was coming back. I thought, *That's handy.* I went and saw John in the workshop, checked his latest dates for remobing the *Interprovider,* and flew out to Singapore.

Chapter 6

GOT TO GO SURFING

I dropped in to Oceaneering's office to say hi to Lynda as promised, and Ian was there, so I dropped into his office. He was pretty keen to find out how things went up there. He said I was lucky he was away because he wouldn't have sent me knowing I was full of shit.

I said, 'Lucky you weren't here, then,' and laughed. He called me a wanker, laughed, and kicked me out of his office, and told me to keep in touch. I thanked Lynda and headed back into town to get flights to Bali. I needed a bloody surf.

I was down Scotts Road, close to Orchard Road, and thought, *I'll go into the Jockey pub and see if any friends are around.* It was closed as they were doing a major revamp of that corner. In the next building was a place called the Tropicana. This club had three bars, one big lounge bar for DJs and bands, a small public bar next to it, and another small club above that. It was well known for oilfield workers, hookers, etc. I walked into the public bar for a quick beer. Before I had even gotten a beer, I was getting my arse pinched from two sides by reasonably nice-looking girls on the job. I was thinking, *Far out, what a contrast to the last four months.* I stayed for another beer just to soak it up. I was on a mission; I was heading to Bali, and I had people to see and surfboards to pick up, and I wasn't letting a prostitute get in the way of that. There were plenty of hot chicks to chase in Bali.

On my way out to Sembawang, I dropped in to see Ron. Des was away, but we had a quick catch up, and off I went. Chuck and Alice, his Indian girlfriend, were home at Sembawang, but Pierre and Stew were away. They had finished glossing the hulls and were working on the spreader beams, so things were moving OK, but he said he was getting low on cash and might have to get a diving job. I slung him a couple of hundred and said I'll see him on my way through next time.

Back to the airport. Back to Bali. Back to the waves. Back to having a life. On that flight into Bali with a cold beer and a vodka chaser, the memories of those first two months in Dubai were pushed away by the anticipation of what's going to happen tomorrow when the sun comes up. I was already getting charged.

I pulled up at Eddies Garden and had a catch-up with Eddie and his wife Nyoman. Their kids were so cute running around and very polite, all saying hello and then running away embarrassed as kids do. Eddie's brother's losmen were full, so he took me to a cousin's not far away and closer to the beach. They organised a bike for me, and when it turned up, it was an impressive Binter 125, similar to a Kawasaki trail bike. They were good to ride, handled the muddy rice paddy tracks, and had good height on the handlebars, making it easier to carry your board. It was wet season again; lots of rain and frogs, and most of the waves were Nusa Dua, Greanballs, and Yung Yungs. If a real swell hit Sri Lanka and Turtle Island. I bumped into a couple of surfers from my first time in Bali, but mainly, I was riding solo.

I had organised my old girlfriend that I had left in New Zealand to come over for a couple of weeks, and until she arrived, I was quite happy doing my own thing. I remember it rained a lot those first two weeks, and as it got closer to Christina arriving, the weather started to get better. Towards the end of the third week, I was on my way to the airport to meet Christina. I was a bit nervous and excited. We were good friends and in love when I decided I wanted to leave New Zealand by myself, and we broke up. She left Napier not long after me and had been living in Brisbane. I was looking forward to seeing her again but was worried if things would work. We had three weeks to find out. I remember her walking out into the arrivals hall like it was yesterday.

Sitting in the bemo on the way back, we were both unsure with mixed emotions; two friends back together, smiling and laughing but unsure what to do with each other. I gave her the tour guide stuff as we drove along the beachfront and then down Legian. We had a lovely first night together getting reacquainted, catching up on our lives apart. We walked off down the beachfront for some dinner and finished the evening walking along the beach to Kuta and then all the way along Legian Road, looking at all the shops and talking shit as if we had never been apart. Isn't it funny how when you're with your real friends, things just seem easy—conversation, even silence?

The next day, we carried on as if we had never been apart. She came with me surfing and just hung out on the beach while I was out amongst the waves. It may have been her fourth or fifth night when, for some reason, I just jumped awake, seeing a shadow by the door, and looking down, our bags were gone. A dog was barking, and Agung, our losmen owner, and one of the boys were chasing someone jumping over the border wall. Luckily, they had dropped my pack and had not seen my smaller travel bag with our passports, traveller's cheques, etc., hidden under the bed. They had also dropped a hammer as they jumped the wall, and Agung said it was lucky I didn't wake up earlier; they would have just bashed me with the hammer. It was about two in the morning.

The losmen we were staying at was on Jalan Arjuna towards the beach from Legian Road. But back then, there were lots of paddocks with a cow or two, chickens, and ducks, and two-and-a-half-metre-high walls with spaces big enough to ride a motorbike between them. North from this road were mainly rice paddies through the Seminyak district. We decided to move down closer to the Kuta Legian district and found a place in the laneways not far from the beach. A week or so later, Des turned up and invited us to stay in Paul's private losmen at Eddies Garden. That was a lovely spot and I think to this day is one of the nicer spots that we have stayed in.

I will never forget the Balinese New Year that year and the lead up to it. It's called Nyepi Day, a Hindu New Year celebrating a day of silence. It is in March, but the day is different every year, coinciding with the start of the Saka calendar year. For three to four days leading up to the eve of the Day of Silence, there are processions of papier mâché effigies of naughty gods and spirits they want to expel from their compounds. On the eve itself, they go ballistic crashing pots, banging drums, and setting fire to all the monsters they have built over the last few days. We had gone out that evening walking around Kuta Legian, had some magic mushrooms, and just took in all the crazy entertainment everywhere.

Eventually, we were back on the top veranda sipping a cold Bintang. It's around 4 a.m. It is *silent*, not just normal silent but spooky silent. Normally, you would have chickens clucking as the dawn is breaking, and there is always dogs barking—not this day. It is the weirdest thing to witness. No birds chirping, dogs barking, chickens clucking; no cars, no motorbikes. *No nothing.* Super spooky and extremely enjoyable. The deal is they have scared all the naughty spooks out, and the only way they can get back in is through you doing something naughty and making a noise. It could have been as late as 7 or 8 a.m. before you really hear animals and distant cars. Absolutely amazing, and although you cannot leave your compound until dark, it is well worth experiencing this amazing morning.

So over the last couple of weeks, while Des and I had been chasing waves, Christina had been hunting out quality shops amongst all the cheap Charlie run-of-the-mill Bali stuff. And one afternoon, she had dragged me along to help her find a place she found but couldn't remember where it was so effectively had lost again. We were walking along the Legian Road between Padma and Rum Jungle. I was sitting on the doorstep of a shop she was in. On the other side walking along was a bloke. He looked at me, I looked at him, and we both looked away. I looked at him, he looked at me, and we both looked quickly away again. He carried on walking. I watched him disappear down the road. Christina came out of the shop.

I could just see him down the street, and I said to her, 'See that guy in the hat down there? He so looked like Jonesey.'

She shrugged her shoulders and said, 'That wasn't the shop. It must be up here somewhere.' So we carried on walking.

Five minutes down the street, the guy in the hat came out of a travel shop.

'Hello.'

'Holy shit, Jonesey, how are ya?'

We hadn't seen Niel for years as he had left Napier and was living down in Margaret River in Western Australia. He hadn't recognised me until he saw us both. So we hung out with Niel. He joined us at Eddie and Nyoman's baby christening. That was another beautiful day that the Balinese culture really comes into its own; the costumes, the colours. The Balinese love having the westerners joining in, and they make you so welcome and involved that it is lovely being around. The food is amazing, but watch out you don't have too much arrack. That shit sneaks up and totally kicks your arse.

Eventually, it was time for Christina to head back to Brisbane. A bit of a sombre day, but we had had a good time and promised each other we would do it again.

'Keep in touch. I'll be back here in about four months. Let's see what happens.' And she walked through the departure doors and was gone. I felt pretty hollow and low.

Later that night, Niel suggested heading over to Nusa Lembongan for a couple of nights before I leave. Des had already gone back to Singapore, so off we went the next day. Nusa Lembongan is an island just off the coast of Sanur on the opposite side of the island and has some good surf breaks on it. A good swell hit, and we scored shipwrecks four to six feet for two days. I had to leave to head back to Singapore and Dubai, so that was where I left Niel.

I flew out the next day with a shadow over me. I was sad to be leaving. I had just had a beautiful time. I hadn't been charging around like a lunatic chasing chicks and waves. I was more tuned in to the island life, when to go and not go surfing, and often turned up at the right time. I had had a really relaxing time enjoying and being more immersed in the Bali lifestyle and lived it quite different to my previous two trips. Although I loved having my friends around, I also loved my time alone. So as the plane took off from Bali one more time, I tried to chase the cloud away by telling myself, *It's OK. Three to four months and I'll do it all again.* And that cheered me up. I had decided to bounce straight through Singapore to Dubai and just take my board with me. Lucky I did because it would be nearly a year before I would see Bali again. The problem was I had not been asked to come back; I had just decided that because I had a ticket and a visa. What have I got to lose? So it was with a little apprehension I was on the flight down the back, smoking a cigarette and having a beer. What's going to happen this time, I wondered?

The flight landed in Dubai's small airport at about 2:30 a.m. I jumped in a taxi, headed straight to the guest house, found a bed in one of the rooms, and crashed out. My plan was to wake up around 7:30, grab a coffee, and go and see John, the yard manager, which is what I did.

'Hi, John, how are you?'

'Hi, Spike, when did you get here?'

'Early this morning. What's happening?'

'Not a lot at the moment.'

'When is the DPC second phase of that seabed scrapping job heading out?'

'Oh, that's a couple of weeks away, I think.'

'Oh, that's a bummer,' I said.

'What have you come back for?' he asks.

Because John and I got along pretty well before, I thought I'd just tell him straight up. So I told him about the return ticket and that I just took a gamble. He laughed and said, 'Why not?'

I said, 'Have you got anything you need doing? I might as well give you a hand until I find out what's going on.'

And luckily, he was busy. He gave me a list of gears to test and move around, so I went up, had some brekkie, and put my work gear on. At around one o'clock in the afternoon, I was on the forklift on the other side of the office when I spotted Norb coming down the stairs from the guest house. He often went over for lunch. I thought, *Here we go*, and drove over to face the music, you might say. I pulled up next to him.

'Hello, Norb.'

He looked up. 'McGettigan, what are you doing here?'

'You told me to come back for the DPC work, but John said it's been delayed.'

'Did I?' he said, squinting into the sun, trying to recall the conversation.

I jumped in and said, 'John needed a hand fixing some equipment, so I thought I might as well help him out. When that's done, I'll just hang around until the job goes, if you want?'

He was still squinting into the sun while he was thinking about it. 'Yeah, OK, do that.' Off he walked.

That's it. I'm back in. Wow, cool. I was buzzing thinking, *Thank God I've gotten through that one.*

That afternoon, I went down the ski club. There weren't many people around. I had a little celebration by myself when Mohammed came in. We were having a chat, and I was telling him about my Bali trip. When I mentioned Christina was an old girlfriend from New Zealand, he said, 'I have a girlfriend from New Zealand I met in London while on business last month. She is coming down here soon. I will introduce you.'

I said, 'OK, I'll wait around.'

Mohammed introduced us, and it turned out she is from a place called Havelock north, not far from my hometown—no shit—so we traded schools and local stories, and she said her mother was an acupuncturist in a place called Flaxmere.

I said, 'No way. I had gone to an acupuncturist in Flaxmere to try and kick the smoking.' We laughed because I was sitting having a smoke at the time.

'It obviously didn't work.' She laughed.

And I said, 'Well, actually, it would have if I'd wanted it to, but I just think I wasn't ready to give up.' And it was true, I think. I still wanted that one cigarette a day, but that leads to another and on and on. When I had had the acupuncture, it was ages before I got that craving for a cigarette, and that first one tasted like shit. But as I said, I wasn't ready to give it up.

Over the next few days, I caught up with Lance. Then one morning, Tony was having breakfast in the guest house.

'Hi, Tony, what are you up to?'

'I've just arrived to take out an emergency job to look for a sunken ship in the Strait of Hormuz. What are you doing?'

'Waiting for the DPC job.'

He said, 'OK, you're coming with me.'

That was me back in the yard getting a mixed gas dive spread ready to load onto the trucks. The other guys turned up next day. We mobed the gear on the vessel *Scorpio Del Golfo* and put it all together as we sailed to the straits.

Apparently, while I was in Bali, an American navy cruiser had witnessed a coastal trader sinking, but there were no life boats around. Looking a bit suspicious, they logged the coordinates. Lloyds had been given a claim on a trader that sunk with a dodgy story. So we were sent out to find the vessel and prove it had been scuttled if we could. The straits are very deep in parts, and we were hoping it hadn't landed in the trench because if so, we wouldn't be able to get there. We arrived in the area the next day and set up to drag the sonar fish and try to locate it. About five runs through this area and we had a few possible spots marked with buoys. We anchored and sent in an ROV to look, and on the second location, we came across the wreck. It was in 270 feet and only maybe two hundred metres away from the drop-off into the trench, so we were lucky, but the scuttled trader's captain was not. We spent the rest of that afternoon with the ROV recording and surveying the vessel.

The next morning, we dropped a diver in, but with only thirty minutes on the bottom, he couldn't find a way into a hold to see if the trade goods were there. While he was doing decompression, we had the ROV back in, and they found a hatch in the middle of the vessel open. I dressed in to attempt to get into the hold for a look around and try to locate any goods and get a sample. The vessel was on a slight lean to port, I think, and I was coming down in the stage on the starboard side. The visibility wasn't that good, and we stopped the stage above what we estimated the top of the vessel to be. I had fins on, so I dragged some slack through on my umbilical and launched off into the blackness. I was swimming over but also slowing dropping, and all of a sudden, a big shadow loomed in the dark at the end of my hat light beam. I pumped my fins and tried to get there before I lost the height. My umbilical was just starting to get tight when I threw my hands forward, and my fingers just grabbed the gunner rail. I was huffing and puffing like a billy goat, hanging on the side of this ship, trying to get my breath back. The umbilical was trying to pull me off.

The supervisor was asking me, 'How's it going?'

I was still just sucking hard and holding on until finally I could say, 'Slack the diver.' I got some slack and managed to pull myself up and onto the sloping deck. Now I can start getting in control of my breathing, and after a minute, I was able to tell Tony where I was.

'Good boy, good boy,' he said. 'Now, any idea where you actually are?'

'No, but I'm guessing around midships. I'll go left and see if I find anything.'

It's pretty spooky standing on a big ship on the seabed with maybe twenty feet of visibility, and that is mainly with your hat light beam. There were fish looking at me but no idea what type. They wouldn't have known what type of fish I was either, so we left each other alone. There were ropes floating up, and all of a sudden, another shadow turned into a white superstructure, obviously the accommodation area that we expected.

'Right,' Tony said. 'Turn around. Go back the other way. There is a hold open, must be forward of where you hit the ship. You better get a move on, not a lot of time left.'

It's bloody hard walking in fins, so I went into the swim mode and used my hands to pull me along from one place to the next along the edge of the holds. Then all of a sudden, a big empty space as I came to the hold that the roof was off. Down I went, telling Tony I was in and heading down.

I remember him saying, 'Giving you bubbles,' so he can keep an eye on my depth. As I got down to the bottom of the hold, there was flotsam all over the place. It looked empty. Then all of a sudden, I saw a roll of fabric. Tony told me to cut a piece off for a sample; I did that.

'You have eight minutes left. See if you can find another one.' I do about thirty feet away and cut another sample off that. 'Right, leave bottom.'

'Roger, leaving bottom,' and I made my way through the darkness and out of the hold, back to the dive stage, and started my ascent back to the surface.

It took ages to go through all my water stops, and the water got clearer and clearer as I got shallower and shallower. I just sat on the stage staring out into the clear blue. Occasionally, a school of fish would swim around me to see what was on the other side. Finally, I hit the surface. On deck, I ripped all my dive gear off while heading down to the chamber, climbed in, shut the door, and, bam, compressed air is charging in. My ears were ringing. It was so hot. I was dripping with sweat, holding my nose with one hand, thumb up to the port hole with the other, and finally it stopped. I pushed the door open, cleared my ears for the last time, climbed into the main chamber, put the O2 bib on, and yelled out, 'On O2.' I shut the door. They took the entrance lock away, and I was able to dry myself off with a towel and lie down and relax.

I'm guessing about two hrs later I was back on deck. They had the ROV back in the water, and they were taking photos of an area on the hull, about three to four feet off the seabed. They had found a square hole in the hull. You could see by the edges that it had been cut with a gas torch from the inside because of the round bumpy lip on the outside edge. This is called the slag that an oxyacetylene torch leaves on a mild steel cut.

The next morning, we were going to drop a diver in to locate the hole and take some measurements, but the current was stronger than the day before, and the weather was looking dodgy. We packed up and came back to Dubai. The Lloyds insurance client we had on board was pretty happy with our findings, stating the likely scenario that they had pulled into a port on the African coast not logged and secretly unloaded the goods. Then hoping to scuttle the vessel in an area where no one would find her, they cut the hole, jumped into a life raft, and headed off, claiming it started to take on water very fast at night and they had to abandon ship. Unfortunately for them, the hole they cut wasn't big enough, about two to three inches square. When the sun came up, they were long gone, but the ship wasn't, and the US Navy just happened to be on patrol (because of the Iran/Iraq war) and watched it for three hours without a sign of anyone around before it slipped under the surface to its murky grave. If the ship had landed any other way, we would not have come across the hole, and it would have been harder to prove, but I think that was enough to put the captain and maybe the owner both in jail. A couple of days later, Tony, the ROV pilot, and I gave evidence to a small court hearing, and that was that.

One or two days later and I was sent out to a production vessel in the CPC field off Sharjah called the *Balaka*. This was handy because the DPC job had been delayed. Hydrospace had a maintenance contract with them that meant they had to have a minimum of two divers on board at all times in case of an emergency. When they needed to do maintenance, they called extra divers out to complete whatever was needed. So I and a Dutch guy (name forgotten; sorry, Dutch guy) flew out on a chopper; that could possibly had been my first chopper ride actually. Anyway, we met Ahmet, an Indian from Bombay, the supervisor and a young English guy. This field was in 220 feet, and the water was clear with good visibility on the seabed. We were doing scuba, so you don't have a lot of time down there, but because of the visibility, you actually get to enjoy the dive. It makes such a big difference when you can see all around you. We were diving out of a rib, and we would get six twin sets and all the dive gear set up on the deck of this tanker. The crane would lift us over and drop us in the water, and off we would go. We had to replace four hydraulic lines that went from a control box to a valve station. There was a tonne of fish, big schools of trevally, bonito, and some of the biggest barracuda I had seen. Man, they look mean in the water.

When that job was done, Ahmet asked me if I wanted to stay on for two weeks while his side kick went on leave. Yeah, sure. Our days were spent mucking about just doing general maintenance on equipment but not doing much. Like a little paid holiday, a bit of sunbathing, reading books, and sitting around telling stories. I've been told I'm good at that, so right up my alley, ha ha. He was going on leave soon, so the last week, he made up a bullshit story about having to check the ties on a cable on one of the risers. It was an excuse to take the speargun and get himself some fish to take back home to Bombay. Way to go, Ahmet.

So we headed down the bottom make sure all is in order. On the way up, he hit this three-and-a-half-foot trevally. Bloody hell. He put it on a line without cutting its spine and handed it to me. I had to hang on to the riser—this fish was going psycho—while he went and hit another one. I had never been spearfishing before, so I didn't know what we were doing. We finally got back in the boat, and he told me off for not staying at the right depth for my deco stops and said I could get bent. Bloody hell, Ahmet, you could have at least killed the bloody thing, and we laughed. I enjoyed my little holiday with Ahmet. I caught him up in the guest house once after that while he was on his way to or from work. Nice bloke.

It was the end of April that I came off the *Balaka*. Over the two months I was in and out of Dubai and the DPC fields, I did another short seabed drilling job in Abu Dhabi. Then when we came off that, Tony and I were sent to a job in Qatar. A vessel called the *Ocean Diver 2* was doing a boat landing contract in a field off Halul Island. We had to get visas to work there, so when we arrived, we stayed in a guest house in town, while Greg did the paperwork. He had a Hobie Cat and set it up so I could go for a blast around the harbour on the Sunday afternoon. We were not able to drink there, so the place was very boring. When we finally made it to the vessel, it was full on. The superintendent was an American called Tom. He and Tony didn't get along, and Tony walked off the next day; he may have lasted two.

Anyway, I was on shift with Derrick and Pat again, but there was an English guy called Billy, who was a welder diver, and he was in charge of the welding crew for this job, and he was funny as hell. He was a black belt in karate and sometimes does security for the Miss World contests in the UK. After shift, when we were all jammed into this small cabin, he would be throwing his balls from side to side, telling us all these funny stories about what the miss pretties would get up to once they realised they weren't in the running for a win. We would be pissing ourselves most nights that I can remember. He also had some other good stories of which two are worth a retell.

The first being when he had been working in India one year. He had met this girl before he had gone away and had said on his return he would take her out for dinner. So he got back, they sort out the restaurant, and while there, he had an attack of the dreaded runny bum. They had only ordered a bottle of wine and were chatting. He excused himself and raced into the toilet and exploded all over the place, and when he went to wipe his arse, there wasn't enough toilet paper. Up above the toilet is one of those small narrow windows with a curtain, so he climbed up on top of the cistern, wiped his arse with the curtain, climbed back down, washed his hands, and returned to the table. She was not there, so he thought she must have gone to the toilet herself as ladies do and poured himself another wine. He was looking around wondering where the girl was when he noticed the window on the restaurant side of the toilet was not as high as the toilet side, and he realised that she would have been looking straight at it and would have seen his arse flash in the window and done a runner. We were pissing ourselves.

The other one of note is when he took a nice lady out for a date. They got dressed up all fancy and went high flying trying to impress her. They had a really good night, and when returning her to her place, she invited him up for a nightcap. So up they went. When they got inside, she showed him the bar and said, 'Fix us a drink, and I'll slip into something more comfortable,' and disappeared into a room. He thought he's in, so he made the drinks, stripped off bollocky buff, and lay on the couch waiting for her. She came out of the bedroom wearing a light pair of jeans and a top. She saw him lying on the coach nude and went absolutely psycho. 'Get out, get out, you creep!' she screamed. He jumped on to his knees, begging her not to kick him out. 'Please, please,' he begged. 'I won't take long.' She grabbed his clothes and threw them out the door. Oh my god, we were absolutely pissing ourselves. The way he told it was just mint. I will never forget those after-shift story days. Some better than others, but overall taking the edge of a really cramped living and working environment.

The job itself was pretty intense. A lot of the boat landings on the platforms were breaking down and unsafe. We had to put these big steel boxes called cofferdams on the legs of the platforms, pump all the water out, and make sure they were sealed and safe. Then the Filipino welding crew would get in, chop off the landing stubs, and weld on new ones. Then we would put the landing back on. If the weather was rough, we would be continually going in and out of the water blocking up leaks in the seals. Twenty feet down inside these cofferdams with the temperature in the Middle East, the Filipino welding boys put up with intense conditions. This particular job had no worthy stories apart from the fact the vessel was too small for the number of equipment and personnel but would set me up with another three contracts over the next couple of years, and I would meet other people that would curve my winding road.

While on the Qatar job, I had a letter from my mum saying my brother was about to leave South Africa after six or seven years there and bring his family home through Europe. I thought I should go there before he leaves and started looking into it. The deal at the time with Hydrospace was you had to do your three months to pay for your flights, but if you did six months straight, you could get the return airfare in cash. I decided I would do six months, and instead of heading back to Singapore/Bali, I would go to South Africa. Before we sailed, I did some homework and set this in motion. Our office travel agent put me on to a travel agent in town, and she looked into my options.

The debris removal job finally was mobed on a vessel called *Gemini 5* at the beginning of August. At the right tide, the captain backed the vessel up hard to the Dubai Creek wharf. We drove the crane on and welding big pad eyes down to put huge turnbuckles on to hold the crane in the location and then moved the rest of the surface gas spread on, and off we went. I remember on one of my gas dives, when I must have been around the eighty feet water stop on my way back to the surface, I was lying down on the bottom of the wet bell when all of a sudden, heaps of fish arrived out of the murky visibility. I was looking at them when all of a sudden, this huge shark appeared. As I shit myself, I realised it's OK, it's a whale shark, and as it slowly ambled past my vision, I was able to enjoy the presence of the wild, what a shame, the visibility wasn't better. It circled past one more time ten minutes later and then headed away into the gloom.

Not long after, there was a bang on the head, and there was Brent. He had come flying down the bell wire with a mask and fins and had his head up in the top of the wet bell catching a breath. Holy shit, I think I was around the sixty or seventy feet stop at the time.

We traded thumbs up, and he waited, hoping the whale shark would come back. After five minutes, he gave up and waved, and I watched him disappear towards the surface.

We just had a day shift crew and some old and new faces. One of the new guys was an Australian ex-cop called Wayne. There were a couple of English guys I hadn't met before. One of them ended up refusing to dive because he reckoned the supervisor was an idiot and was trying to kill him. He refused to come out of our cabin for a few days, and lucky for him, the weather picked up, and we went in. The travel agent had said that I couldn't get a visa in UAE to go to South Africa because of apartheid. But I could go to Mauritius on my way and apply for one there.

I said, 'Sounds good. Let's organise that.'

We sailed back out to the field but not before I sent Christina a letter inviting her to join me. We had gotten along pretty well in Bali, and I thought I hadn't had that magic with other girls I'd been with, so let's give it another go and see if it's for real. Over the next month and half, the job just ticked over. We were in and out of town, and each time, I was a bit closer to being organised to head to Africa. I had heard back from Christina. We were to meet in Mauritius. I would arrive the day before her and then pick her up at the airport. Everything was done on one-way tickets, which you could do back then, but it had some drawbacks as we would find out.

Back on the job one afternoon, we were picking up the basket off the seabed because it was full. The diver was settled doing his chamber time, and the rest of us were watching the crane wire, waiting for the basket to hit the surface. It finally arrived, and the driver slowed down to let the water drain out. There were three or four big tyres tied off hard up against the outside, with scaffolding, steel boxes, valves, etc., on the inside. There were lengths of half-inch rope running down, obviously with something heavy hanging on it. The crane driver had taken the basket as high as he could so was slewing over for us to tie off the rope on the side of the vessel so we could land the basket on the deck. There were mud and shit dropping all over the place. Made worse by the swell, the basket was swinging around and jerking.

I was watching the rope get closer, about to grab it, when, whoosh, the English guy next to me just disappeared. I looked around, and a huge tyre that had been tied on the outside had broken free and slammed my workmate into the deck and up against the crane wheel. The crane driver slewed the load away, and we pounced down to get the tyre off our friend. It was bloody heavy, but we managed to get it off him enough to drag him into a position we could administer first aid. He was in a bad way; three teeth smashed out, probably broken jaw and collar bone were obvious. He was coherent but dazed, looking at us like 'What happened?' We moved him again, making sure we didn't do any more damage, but we needed to get into space so we could check for serious injury. Then he started going into shock.

There was another Hydrospace vessel working on the other side of the platform, and we knew Ahmed, an Arab American diver medic, was on board. Our supervisor called the vessel, while I jumped in the Zodiac and raced over to pick him up, filling him in on the injuries we knew about on the way. Ahmed helped get him stabilised as the rest of us got the boat ready to head into Dubai and get our friend to hospital. This was my first real introduction to when shit goes wrong and how fast it can happen. Later that night after he was evacuated to hospital, I was sitting on the back deck having a smoke, thinking, *How close was that? That could have been me.* We were standing shoulder to shoulder. I got covered in shit; he nearly smashed to death. I never saw him again, and on my return from Africa six months later, I was to find out that when they reset his broken shoulder, they pinched nerves or something, and he only had regained partial use of his arm. Whether he ever got it back, I never found out.

So my time in Dubai this trip was coming to an end. Everyone was saying, 'What are you going to Africa for? It's dangerous. They are blowing people up.' It made me a bit anxious, but I was up for the challenge. My brother and his family were in Durban, but Christina and I also had a friend from home who was living in a place called Port Shepstone, wherever that is. We were going to find out.

Finally, my day arrived, and I headed to the airport. This would be different because I was off into the unknown again. I had that buzz of anticipation with the anxiety of the destination. But above all, I was looking forward to catching up with Christina again. It was over six months since she walked through the airport door and disappeared.

Chapter 7

Into and Out of Africa

Note: In this chapter, I say a black guy or black lady did this or did that. This should not be taken as racial discrimination because it is not. I don't know if they were Zulu, Xhosa, Cape Coloureds, or any other of the hundreds of tribal nations they may have come from. But they have a different character, and that is the reason they are separated in this script. Both Christina and I had a lot of experiences with the black nationals of Africa, the Dutch white South Africans, and the English white South Africans, and we found them mostly beautiful and very friendly. But as with all countries, there is a bad side. We had a Christmas Day where Christina met a bad side, but he is still referred to as a black guy only because he wasn't white. So don't turn it into something it isn't. Thanks and read on. There is some funny shit in this chapter. There are black guys and white guys. But they are all Africans because we are in Africa, and it is their home.

My flight to Mauritius took me through Nairobi, and I landed there late afternoon. My connecting flight was 8 a.m. the next day, so with a bit of mucking around, I managed to get a twenty-four-hour visa and went into the city and found a place to stay. By then, it was dark; a bit dodgy, I thought, so I found a restaurant, went to a bar for a couple of drinks, and just went back to my room. From memory, I wasn't that comfortable there. In the morning, I hit the airport at just after 6 a.m. The check-in counter was closed.

I said, 'What has happened to the flight?'

The guy behind the counter said, 'That's it on the tarmac just about to take off.'

I said, 'How could that be? It says here departs 8 a.m. Why wasn't I told last night when you organised my visa?'

A manager came out. He was very apologetic, but that wasn't going to solve my problems.

Oh, no, Christina was going to arrive in Mauritius with no forward flight, no money, and no idea why I would not be there. I was freaking out. I said, 'Sir, you are going to have to have someone meet my girlfriend when she arrives or she could be sent back to Australia, and that will be a major drama.' He promised he would do that.

She was arriving the next day. I had no way of getting in touch with her, so I was stuffed. To make it worse, it was three days before the next flight. The manager organised accommodation and a taxi. He rebooked my flight and promised to have my girlfriend met when she arrived.

By mid-afternoon, I was walking around Nairobi; not really anything happening there. I found a tourist shop and looked for something to do the next day. I could have gone to the coast at Mombasa, but I decided to go to the rift valley and take in a Massai tribe village. Glad I did that because it was pretty amazing. The road out the next day was pretty uneventful until all of a sudden, it was on us, this huge ridge dropping off as far as you can see, like a normal river valley back in New Zealand but a thousand times bigger and way more majestic. The distant ridge was hazy, but the floor below was clear. It looked like a scene out of one of Wilbur Smith's books, one of which I had just finished reading. After a short stop to take in the sheer size of this valley, we ambled off down the dusty road to the valley floor.

We pulled up at an old colonial homestead surrounded by beautiful gardens, got out of the bus, and were given a bit of history of the area. We then walked down this path around the side of a hill and into the local Massai tribe village. You guessed it, just like on *National Geographic* but real. The mud huts were pretty weird, and even though it was mid-morning and still warming up, they were warm and stuffy inside. The men were very tall but looked taller with their headgear on. They had a little tourist show, and we were told a bit of background into their lifestyle and shown some of their dances. They are nearly purple. They are so black, and their colourful homemade jewellery really stand out. Kids were either running around or just staring at us, holding on to their mother's legs. We were led back to the homestead and had tea and scones in the garden out the back. On the way back, we went through a safari park, but on that particular day, there weren't a lot of the amazing animals that we would come across later in our trip. I was back wondering around killing time in the city by late afternoon.

The next morning, I was on the flight to Mauritius when we had a good little bit of excitement. There is a little island north of Madagascar called the Comoros, and I didn't know we were going to land there until it came over the PA. At the time, we were getting lower and lower. I was looking out the window, when all of a sudden, the plane did a big bank to the right. I was looking straight out my window. The plane wing looked nearly in the water. When we, all of a sudden, straightened up, a cliff face flashed under us, and we landed straight away. Bloody hell, that was awesome. Two old ladies behind me just about had heart attacks, ha ha. We got the brakes slammed on, and we're thrown forward into the seat in front. Then at the end of the runway, he was turning around and put his foot down. Everyone was getting thrown around the plane like we're in V8 supercar race. I was loving it, thinking this captain is a nutcase, but the poor old ladies behind me were absolutely freaking out. Unfortunately, leaving the island wasn't as eventful, and we finally landed in Mauritius.

It took me ages to talk my way through customs, as you would expect. They took my passport off me because they weren't happy with my story and said I had to come back in two days' time. I wasn't allowed to go anywhere until I informed them where I was staying. Once I got through, I found Christina there with security. They had recognised her from her own drama two days earlier. I found out where she was staying. We went back together and told customs. I got my passport back and was told where to go to get the visas for South Africa, and off we went. Unfortunately, my bag never made it. That was a major blow because now I had no clothes. But I expected it to show up, so off we went to trade stories and have a major catch-up. It turned out she was put in a holding room because the airline guy that was supposed to meet her was late. She was finally allowed to leave but had to give up her passport as well and had to stay in the closest hotel, which, funny enough, was the most expensive. It was bloody nice, though, and we enjoyed it.

We hung out in the morning. They had horseback riding, so I decided to take a horse for a gallop, something I hadn't done since a kid on my uncle's farm. Around lunchtime, we got this taxi driver that she used her first day to take us into the city to get my visa on the go. I was a bit stressed that it was going to take two weeks, but there wasn't anything I could do about it, so we organised our driver to pick us up the next day to do a run around the island and look for cheaper accommodation. He said he would bring a more suitable vehicle the next day. We had a prearranged price for a day hire. So the previous day, we had been chauffeured around in a six-cylinder Peugeot. So when our driver turned up in a V8

Statesman, I had to laugh. Here I was thinking he would bring a more economical vehicle being fixed price, but, no, we were styling it. Well, so we thought. Both vehicles were old but still classic. So off we went.

Our first destination was Tamarind Bay. There is a good surf break there, but it is 'flat ass' when we arrived. We checked out the hotel, the only accommodation in the bay, and it was bloody expensive, so we moved on. To this day, I wish we had just stayed there because it is a world-class wave, and I never got to surf it.

We drove through the city of Port Louis and out the other side heading north to Grand Baie. It was about this time that we were starting to get over our driver's driving style. He would put his foot down, get up to a fast speed, and then put it in neutral, coasting until it nearly stopped. Then he would drop it into second and chug-chug back up to fast and then do it again. It started off funny, but we soon lost our humour. Sometimes, he would put his foot down and then take it off, put his foot down and then take it off. It was driving us nuts. After pulling into a petrol station, he stepped it up a gear, heading out of Port Louis. The traffic was lighter, and he started actually turning the engine off at the top of hills. We would coast down with no brakes or power steering. At the bottom, he would put in second gear, turn the key back on, and drop the clutch, chug-chug, probably burning more fuel than he just saved. It was bloody madness.

We finally arrived in Grand Baie and quite happy to get out of that bloody car. We found a cheap hotel that we could stay in. The receptionist was a pretty local lady and stood out because of her extremely long fingernails, and she was cleaning and painting them as we walked in. The room was a box with a bed and a toilet/shower. But the price was right. We had a chat with her about her lovely nails; they were like a pig's tail, every one of them. Apparently, it was a local thing. God knows how she got anything done. No way could she pick her nose anyway.

We went and had a beer and a wine and prepped ourselves for the arduous journey back in our classic chauffeur-driven V8 Holden Statesman. It was no better, but we finally made it. Two days later, we used another driver to move up to the little hotel in Grand Baie. There wasn't that much to do there if you were trying to keep the costs down, which we were. My main objective was South Africa, and I needed to keep as much money in the bank as possible. We were happy to just hang out on the beach. There was a restaurant on the beach, and we would have a drink there in the evenings.

One day, I spotted this couple snorkelling around, and they had set up on the beach not far from us. When they finished snorkelling, I went over and asked if he would mind if I borrowed his gear. They were French, and although he picked up a little of what I said, he called over a creole local he knew that could interpret for us. I went out for a look around, quite pretty reef but not a hell of a lot of fish. There was a little jetty that kids jumped off, and I was a bit alarmed to see a couple of stonefish hanging around the rocks underneath. They are not good if you stand on them. But I left them alone because they were under the jetty and not really in a walking area that the kids would use to get out of the water. When I gave the French his mask back, we started asking the usual questions, with the Creole doing the interpretation.

When I said we were from New Zealand, he said, 'Zoo Zeelan, where dis place?' Now the French had sunk the *Rainbow Warrior* in Auckland harbour in retaliation to years of protest over the nuclear testing on Moruroa atoll. One person was killed. I would have thought every Frenchman in France would know about New Zealand, but obviously not. So I explained it was two large islands off the east coast of Australia. His girlfriend smiled as we laughed because she knew no English at all. Christina had come over, and we were slowly getting through some dialogue, thanks to our Creole friend. I found out they are from the southern area of France in the mountains and do a lot of skiing and come to Mauritius most years so he can enjoy his other passion of scuba diving and collecting shells. They ended up inviting us to their villa the next night for dinner. We accepted and organised time and got the address.

The next day, we thought we would go to the restaurant and have a bottle of wine before we went; it was early arvo and no one around. It was bloody funny. The waiter came over in his penguin suit with the wine, poured us a drink, and then went and stood to attention ten feet away under the shade of a tree. Every time we had a sip or two, he would be straight there, topping our glass up, bless the dude. It was actually annoying, but he was so sweet we didn't say anything. We left him a tip and headed off to our French dinner.

We walked in with a nice bottle of wine and did the customary greetings, and he disappeared and came back out with his Air France book.

'Uh, where you say Zoo Zeelan? I cannot find.' And he handed me the back page of his book that has the world map with all the flight destinations.

I pointed to Australia and then down. 'Holy shit, it's not on the map.' He absolutely pissed himself. His girlfriend even started laughing. He was so funny. I said to Christina, 'Hey, they have Tonga, Fiji, Samoa. No New Zealand.' We laughed as well.

Guess they didn't like us, eh? They would have hated us even more two years later because we beat them in the first World Cup rugby final. Well, that set the tempo. Our poor Creole friend had his work cut out keeping up with us. At about 5 p.m., we all walked down to a small fishing harbour where we walked along the boats until he saw some fish he liked. As with most little harbours at this time of night, it was a hive of activity. We bought fruit and veggies as well and went back and had a lovely meal and a good laugh and really enjoyed their company. We traded addresses and promised if we ever ended up in anyone's area, we would make contact. They were off the next day to the southern end before flying back home, so that was the last we saw them.

A couple of days later, we went on a charter boat out to a beautiful little island about an hour away. There were about eight or nine other couples on board. We all split up and just hung out by ourselves at first. We had this lovely stretch of beach to ourselves and at about two o'clock met in a shaded area not far from the boat where we had a campfire. A local guy played guitar in the back ground, and we had an afternoon party with some drinks and local food. It broke up the time and was worth going. A day or so after that and we were in Port Louis picking up my passport. We carried on down south closer to the airport and found a place to stay for the night because we were flying out the next day. We met a South African lady in the bar that night, and we would bump into her again four months later on our trip down to Jeffreys Bay. We also met a Rhodesian guy who was pretty interesting because it was now Zimbabwe and sounded really dangerous. He said it wasn't as bad as the outside world was making it. But that's not to say there were some atrocities. The next day, we flew into Durban.

Now to this day, I'm not sure why, but I had not told any of my family that I was going to Africa. The idea was to surprise John and Susan. It seemed a good idea at the time and would have not been a problem but for the fact that Susan's mum was over for a visit. It was Friday afternoon when we walked up the driveway, and they were all about to get in the car to go to the game reserves two hours north of Durban. Well, all hell broke loose as you would expect when we walked up—a few tears and 'What the hell are you doing here?' and 'Why didn't you let us know?' etc. I remember Susan saying, 'Oh my god, I saw you walking up through the window and couldn't believe what I was seeing. It's really you.' They had the trip all booked. Luckily, Katie and Jon were young and small, so we managed to all squeeze into the BMW, and off we went.

Over the next two days, we visited the Imfolozi, Hluhluwe, and Mkuze game reserves, in the KwaZulu-Natal. And our first taste of real Africa. It doesn't matter how many national geographic programs you watch; nothing actually prepares you for the buzz you get in real life. Not just the big five; even zebras, the majestic giraffes, warthogs, herds of impala, kudu, waterbuck, and wildebeest, to name a few; packs of wild dogs and yipping hyenas. The waterhole with marabou stalks that are bigger in real life than you think; 1.2 to 1.3 metres high, often standing on one leg. From a distance, they look pretty, but up close, they are pretty ugly.

Christina and I totally cramped my brother's weekend getaway, but it was good to see them, and that along with the park atmosphere, I don't think anyone really cared. The Sunday morning, we came across the famous white rhino, our first sighting. They were across the valley. Then John noticed movement in the bush not far from us. We jumped in the car to get closer to where they would break out onto the road. Bloody hell, it turned out to be a female and calf, so we kept our distance. She was nearly the size of our car, and we didn't want to piss her off. We saw no lions or any of the cats for that matter, bit of a shame because they have a large lion population at one of the parks, Hluhluwe, I think.

So we got back to Durban, and John was back at work. He was working at the castle brewery in Amanzimtoti. Before he left for work, he told us the rules for catching a bus. We were on the Bluff, the southern side of Durban harbour, and we were going to go walk around the city. Catching a bus was the best option.

'So there are two types of bus stops. The one on this side is for the blacks, the one opposite is for whites. Don't stand at the wrong one—they won't pick you up.' It seemed pretty easy, no worries.

He went to work, and Susan took the kids to school. It had been raining but slowed down enough for us to head off. We walked along to the bus stop, completely forgetting about the black side and the white side. A bus came along. It had the number we were supposed to get on. I was waving it down. It not only flew past us, but he made sure he hit the puddle and totally took both us out in one muddy splash. As the back of the bus disappeared up the road, we could see lots of laughter in the back window looking back at us. Ha ha, we looked at each other and laughed ourselves. *Welcome to apartheid*, I thought, and we went back and got changed.

I said to Christina, 'Shall we try the white bus next time?' She agreed.

We finally made it into Durban and walked around looking in the shops. We walked into a surf shop, and I asked a guy behind the counter if he knew any good surfboard shapers because my board was starting to look beaten up, and I thought I'd replace it.

Straightaway he asked, 'Kiwis, whereabouts are you from? When are the All Blacks coming back? Who's in the Cricket team?'

We copped these same questions every time we asked anyone for information. The reason being that the Kiwis were the only country left in the world that would play them in any sport, with Australia cancelling all sports a year or two earlier because of apartheid.

Anyway, the guy made a phone call and then told me if I came in the next day with my board, he would take me to see Spider Murphy, who at the time was Shaun Tomson's shaper (a legend

South African pro surfer). We said goodbye to the little crowd that had formed around us and carried on our tour of the city and up to the main beach. What a lovely town with beautiful beaches. We managed to get back to John and Sue's without too much drama. He and Susan pissed themselves when we told the morning bus story.

John dropped me off at the closest surf break to his house early in the morning, and I had a surf before taking my board into town to see Spider Murphy. He was a really nice guy. After the standard Kiwi questions, he asked about my board and what I liked and what I didn't. We kept the same shape and length, but he put a bit more foam in the nose, which he said would help fix the only issue I had with it. He reckoned in three to four weeks, he should have it finished.

Christina and I went down and hung out on the beach in Durban for the rest of the day. I must mention that although we had not talked to many blacks since our arrival in South Africa, the ones we had communicated with were friendly and very helpful. We did not see any of the tension we were led to believe existed at the time. And the ones that loved their sport also asked all the questions about the Kiwi rugby and cricket teams.

The next weekend, I went off with John on Saturday morning, and we went looking for a car to buy so that Christina and I could get around and be a bit more mobile. We came across a VW Beatle in reasonable condition for 900 rand. All I had to do was get it licensed. On Sunday, I called our friend Mark who was living in Port Shepstone, an hour drive south, and we had a catch-up, and he said he would get up and see us soon, and I said we would stay in Durban for Christmas with my family and then come down to stay with him for a couple of weeks. There was a music festival in a couple of weeks, so we arranged to get tickets for Mark and his South African girlfriend, Rolley, and they came up for a long weekend stay. It was pretty good seeing our old friend from home. We dragged my brother off, chasing waves with us, and the ladies hung out looking after the kids. The concert was pretty good with a few really good local bands. A band called Ella Mental really stood out, and I ended up buying one of their albums the next week. It was sad to see them drive off down the road, but by then, it was only going to be a little over two weeks, and we would be staying with him.

John organised a long weekend off so we could go to the Kruger National Park. Once again, we loaded up the BMW, and off we went. We headed out of Durban through Swaziland, and I'm pretty sure we stayed at Lower Sabie Camp that night. We must have pushed to get there before gates close at 6 p.m. We got up early the next morning and went for a local drive around before breakfast, catching hyenas sleeping on the roads. Their pups look so cute, but, man, do they get ugly as they get older. We got some good photos of warthogs, hyena cubs, marabou stalks, etc., at the waterholes. We came across lots of giraffe, zebra, and then our first hit of elephants. Christina and I were blown away. It was pretty warm. We had the windows down and the sun roof open. We came around a corner, and this big adult elephant was pretty close to the road. We slowly sneaked along, getting closer.

I said to John, 'I'll stand in the sunroof and get a close up.'

He stopped the car. I was focusing the camera as he was trying to squeeze in the roof as well. Then young Jon started screaming because he was freaking out; it was so close. Next thing, the elephant started throwing his ears and heard Jon's screams louder. The elephant charged us. My brother was stuck in the roof but managed to get on the gas just as the elephant was about to smash the back of the car. It moved so fast I never got anything focused well enough for a photo. John was copping abuse from everyone but me. It wasn't funny, but, shit, it was funny afterwards, ha ha.

So we decided to have breakfast and let everyone wind down before the big drive right up to the Olifants Camp alongside Olifants River about two-thirds up the park. So after breakfast, we started our cruise through the veld, keeping our eye out for the big five, especially the cats; they are very hard to see. We had a few herds of elephants, kudu, zebra, and buffalo. We were out in a pretty flat area, and all of a sudden, from behind some bush, this huge male, with tusks right down to the ground before sweeping back up, was in front of a baobab tree. Talk about the photo of photos. He wasn't super close, but my zoom brought him right up. The second photo came out perfect with his ears spreading out to listen to us.

On the day, he was just a big elephant, but years later, I spotted him in a *Reader's Digest.* It turned out he was one of the big tuskers of Kruger. His name was Tshokwane (pronounced 'chockwana', I think), and he was in the *Reader's Digest* because of a death charge he did on a well-known wildlife photographer, Daryl Balfour. Daryl only survived because one tusk was hitting the ground before the other one that was hitting his chest. He was unconscious, and the elephant walked away. Tshokwane was found dead from wounds received from a fight in 1998 at an estimated age of fifty-five years.

So as we ambled through the veld on our way to Olifants Camp, we were on the lookout for the cats. John would say, 'There's a leopard tree,' and we would scour it to make sure one wasn't hiding in there. We never tired of the herds, and there was always something to look at, large or small. At one stop on an open savannah flat, John thought he saw a cat. We stopped for five minutes in anticipation. I noticed a large elephant poo rolling intermittently about five metres away. It looked so weird. As soon as we established the fact that there wasn't a cat, I got out to investigate the rolling poo. Oh my god, there was this dung beetle pushing this poo with his head, his wings making a noise like an amplified bee, and as the poo started to roll, he went over the top with it, keeping the momentum before hitting the ground, running around the other side, and starting it all over again. He was a noisy little bugger, and he was on a mission. It was quite bizarre.

We arrived at the camp mid-afternoon, checked in, and sat in a large lounge area with a cold beer and enjoyed this absolutely incredible view of the African veld. The camp is located on the top of a cliff over the Olifants River. You could see for miles the odd giraffe above the height of medium trees; they looked so *Jurassic Park*. Eagles and hawks were floating on the thermals over their territories. Another family came in and were sitting around, and we were swapping notes on what we had seen and where we had been. We told them we had seen heaps of elephants but no cats. They said they had seen a couple of prides in the area but had not seen one elephant. He said there was a pride of lions just down the road where the road drops down to the river valley.

John and I decided to grab a six-pack of beer and try our luck. Christina, Susan, and Jon had had enough, but Katie was keen, so off we went. We got down to the river base and pulled over because we must have missed them. At that time, this huge eagle with something in its talons landed on top of an old tree stump over the top of a couple of hippos. Man, those hippos are big. One climbed out of the water while we watched. Then we noticed there was a baby still in the water. I took a couple of photos.

John said, 'Come on, we better find these lions. It's getting late.'

We drove slowly because we knew we must had driven past them. We came around a corner, and there were three cars parked up where we had stopped originally on our way out. It turned out what we thought was a log was actually a female asleep, and until she started moving, there was no way you would have guessed. A large male sat up and shook his main, and that was about as exciting as they got. It was a bit of a let-down. We hung out until we were the last car, so we could start yelling at them and play up a bit to try and get them to arch up. We were having a bit of a laugh. Katie was telling us off. All we achieved was they went further into the woods. Bugger.

We returned to the camp and prepared a braai (barbecue) for dinner. It was right on dusk, extremely picturesque, and then all of a sudden, all hell broke loose. Trumpeting and smashing and then people running to the cliff face, and we all followed. Down in the valley alongside the river right below us, two elephants were having a standoff. How bloody awesome. They charged at each other but smashed down and trampled the small trees and bushes in their way so they had a mini coliseum. Now they were at opposite ends stamping and trumpeting. Then they charged and hit head-on to one hell of a bang. I couldn't believe it when they lined up for a second, but late in the charge, the one to the right veered off and charged through the bush to leave the victor with a smashed-up backyard, but at least it was still his, I suppose. Wow, that got the whole place buzzing and was a fitting end to an amazing day.

The temperature cooled, and the smells of the bush got stronger after the last braai was finished. We sat outside John's bungalow and finished off a nice wine, talked, and reminisced about the day's adventures and made a rough plan for the next day. Christina and I headed to our bungalow, and not long after we turned the lights out, there was someone tapping unconventionally on our door.

Christina said, 'Who the hell would that be?'

I said, 'Buggered if I know.' I got up and asked, 'Who is it?' through the door. No answer.

I opened the door, and it's a bloody dung beetle or a relation, and it's flying around our light above the door. Holy shit, they are solid. As I turned the light off and shut the door, I thought, I wouldn't want one of them to hit you in the face when you're on a motorbike doing 100 khs; that would bloody hurt.

Next morning, we did another pre-breakfast circle, hoping the lions had made a kill during the night. We spot a lot of buzzards circling, and when we got as close as we could, we could see a male lion on a kudu kill, but we couldn't get that close to him. He was roaring every now and then. There were a few hyenas trying to get his breakfast off him. While he was chasing them off, the buzzards would jump in and get what they could, and he'd have to chase them off. We watched for a while, and in the end, he gave up and let the hyenas and buzzards fight over it.

We drove along the river again and stopped to watch some hippos and then made our way back to camp. Over breakfast, we just enjoyed that stunning view from the Olifants reception lounge, finished our coffees, and loaded up for the drive back down towards the Sabie gate. Our first thing of interest was a pack of wild dogs. There were about twenty of them. We were stuck about four cars back from the kill. By the time we had moved up one car, the adults of the pack were sitting on a rise to our right, and about ten young ones were fighting over what was left. All of a sudden, this lady just walked past my car window. I automatically pulled my camera up and focused on her. I was thinking, *If she gets hit, I'll get it.* My brother couldn't believe she walked out to the front of the leading car and took photos of these dogs going apeshit over what was left of a small buck. Lucky for her, they paid no attention, and we finally moved on.

A couple of kilometres down the road, there was a huge family of monkeys on the road, and when we came around the corner, two adults charged the car, but I had seen two babies run and followed them with the camera. They jumped up on a trunk of a fallen tree, turned, and cuddled each other as they looked back at us. I got the photo, and it came out as cute as it looked. The two adults stayed their ground until the family was safe, and then they let us pass. Not far from there, we came across another pride of lions. By now, it would have been midday, and they were pretty much just crashed out. There were three females and two young males. We watched them for a while and took a couple of photos. Then we noticed there was one more farther back, a female, staring at us. It was amazing how she was blended into the bush until you actually saw her; you really do have to have sharp eyes. We moved on.

Around the next corner, not even one hundred metres away, was a VW Kombi van parked up. There was a guy with his head stuck under the engine cover at the back. John pulled up and asked him if he was OK and told him about the lions. He didn't seem too fazed, and off we went. I think it was the Numbi Gate when we got out for a look around and a stretch. I walked over to this big car. It was a V8 Lincoln and had a sign next to it with a short story. The front of this car was smashed in like a big V. The engine was pushed through and wedged nearly between the two large bucket seats. A white rhino had charged it and walked away. The sign was a warning that you will not win, so don't try.

We left the park. We had done a whirlwind trip. We had seen a lot but had not really had time to really enjoy the park and what it has to offer. I hoped that we would get a chance to come back, but unfortunately, we never did. As I write this now, I still hope that one day I will do a proper safari and spend more time, maybe do a night one or maybe even a camping one. The reason being that until you see these absolutely beautiful animals, I don't just mean the big five, but even zebra, giraffes, monkeys, baboons, herds of buck, and buffalo in the wild for real and right next to you, you do not realise how amazing they are and how much of a buzz you get out of having them so close.

Leading up to Christmas, my surfboard arrived, and because my brother had a trip organised with his family over Christmas, we headed down the coast to Port Shepstone. It may have been that day when the reality of apartheid hit with the Amanzimtoti bombing on 23 December. Mark and Rolley lived in a place two streets up off the coast, with a really nice ocean view, often catching whales blowing off not far out to sea. So we had Christmas Day with Mark and Rolley, and from memory, in the arvo, we were playing a card game called bugger it. Christina went out to the backyard to check the washing on the clothesline, and all of a sudden, we heard this almighty scream. Mark and I went running out there, and there was this black guy with his dick in his hand twenty feet away on a walkway that passes the house. His eyes were bulging, and he was jerking himself off. Christina was freaking out. Mark threw a rock at him. He came out of this trance he had been in and ran away. Although for Christina that was pretty traumatic, Mark and I were bloody pissing ourselves. Christina is such a weirdo magnet.

Anyway, through them, we met a few locals, and being a small coastal area, I got to know a few of the local surfers as well. Mark was a high-voltage power technician and had a work truck with about ten blacks working under him. They were funny blokes. He said they were a nightmare when he first started, but now they get along all good. One day, at about ten o'clock. he turned up in his truck with all the boys on the back. He dropped down the high ab legs and started lifting these big rocks off the back of the truck, over the fence, and onto the grass at the bottom of the hill. I asked what they are for, and he said the boys are going to put them around the three small trees he had planted. We went up to the house. He chased out three of his boys that had gone in to chat up his amour, who was inside doing housework, and then told them where he wanted each rock. The three of us sat down with coffee and watched as they got into their little groups, muttering away in whatever dialogue they were using; I think they were Zulu from memory.

Mark started yelling at them to hurry up. Christina barked at him for being horrible, and he explained that that is the only way they work. If you're not stern with them they just walk away and go to sleep under the tree. Anyway, they jostled into position and then started this really neat singing chanting rhythm. They built it up to a climax, and then at the peak, they lifted the rock and put it back down half a metre up the hill. Then they would start the whole process off again. It was really neat watching them and listening to them, and we cheered them when they had them all in position. They were pretty happy themselves. Then Mark disappeared inside again and came out chasing a couple of his boys that had sneaked back in to chat up the amour. They all jumped back on the truck, and off they went.

One day after a surf, I stopped in to have lunch with Mark out in the bush. When I turned up, half were asleep under a tree, and half were mucking about. They got a fire going, cleaned a shovel, and cooked a ring of boaravour to perfection for us.

While dining in a restaurant in a small town called Margate, the manager who had spent a bit of time talking to us about the All Blacks and the Cricketers asked Christina if she wanted a job managing the restaurant so that he could have some time off with his family. She agreed as long as she spent a week with him and his wife to learn the ropes. Bloody ripper, Christina. So she's looking after a restaurant, and I'm surfing most days. We were having a pretty good time. It is a busy area over the summer being a holiday destination for people from Pretoria, the Drakensberg ranges and the inland farming areas. Very pretty part of the coast with lots of good surf breaks.

One Saturday, a friend of Mark's had organised a river rafting trip for the three of us down the Umzimkulu River gorge. The river is the largest on the South Coast of Natal, and the gorge is very beautiful. We got dropped off inland, and after mucking around trying to make a decent big raft out of all the tyres we had, we just tied two each together, and off we went. The river wasn't in full swing, so it was just an absolutely beautiful slow cruise down through the gorge, and about four hours later, we got picked up. It is surrounded mainly by farms, so we were never going to see any major wildlife, but we did get to see a few eagles and hawks.

By now, the original plan was to be heading back to the Middle East for me to go back to work and Christina back to Brisbane, but now she had a job, we decided to head to Jeffreys Bay as soon as she finished. For a farewell, Mark decided to do a Hangi, a tradition Maori meal. So the couple of weeks leading up to it, we were collecting what we hoped were volcanic river stone. We had a real funny Saturday arvo with a big fire. We were putting the stones on one by one, and one by one they were blowing up. 'This will be one,' we would say only for it to explode five minutes later. Then we ran out of stones; it had been a stormy onshore day. Then all of a sudden, the wind stopped. We had just opened another beer.

Mark said, 'Hey, shit, the wind is going to change.' Then blow me over, the wind changed and went really warm offshore. 'That's a berg wind' (a hot wind that comes off the Drakensburg ranges), he said with excitement. 'There's going to be waves at Shark Bay. Let's go.' Shark Bay is a little sand beach off the side of Umtentweni Rocks, a good fishing and large swell surf spot.

We grabbed the boards and headed off to the south side of this big rocky point. Sure enough, there were three-foot waves with a straight offshore, and it was looking like fun. Out we went. Sitting out the back, I looked inland towards the ranges where this warm breeze was coming from, and the sky was just insane, black and angry looking. As Mark and I were taking in the scenery, this local guy turned up. He and Mark had a catch-up, and he introduced me.

In the meantime, this purple/black front was getting closer; you can tell it's pissing down under it because as it moved over towards us, this picturesque church steeple poking up from dense bush just disappeared. Then there was lightning with the following rumble of thunder. This was turning into a spectacular little surf. Within five minutes of the church disappearing, the rain hit us. It went black, and it was like a waterfall. It was so heavy that your hand disappeared before it went underwater from the raindrops bouncing off the sea. What was really radical was the lightning. The rain was so heavy, and the lightning was making our hair stand out. Every strike you could feel, and they were really close. We were that mesmerised by the intensity; we weren't even catching any waves. Then I saw one strike explode some rocks on a point only a hundred feet away. It was a bloody deafening crack and rumble, and I could feel the electricity standing my hair out like it was trying to grab it.

About ten minutes of this, and it started to abate. Then the black sky started to crack into blue spots, and then as if to say goodbye to us, a rainbow came out. We still hadn't caught any waves for about twenty minutes. We were just so taken with this show of beauty, fury, and then beauty again; it was amazing. Then life was back to normal. We caught a few more waves and went home and told Christina and Rolley over a wine and a beer. We also told them about our rock explosion day, and we were wondering what we were going to do about the Hangi, when Mark said, 'Let's go for a walk later down the train yard. There might be some shit down there we can use.'

A week or so later, our stolen pieces of railway iron did the job perfectly. The Hangi was a smash, and the locals were pretty impressed. John and Sue had come down from Durban, and our last weekend in Port Shepstone was memorable. We said goodbye to a lot of really nice people we had met. Two days later, we loaded up our put-put VW Beatle and were on our way down through the

Transkei. We got into a place called East London, on the southern border of the wild coast, as the Transkei is commonly known as. We found a nice caravan park close to a good surf break and set up our borrowed camping gear. There are monkeys everywhere here, and we quickly found out you have to lock everything in your car, and I mean lock your car as well, which I didn't do and woke up with the car door open and our food gone. I couldn't believe the little bastards; one was running off yelling at me because I shooed him out of the car. We had a laugh, but the next night, I locked the car as well.

We spent a couple of days here while the surf was good. The water was a lot cooler here, and you have to wear a steamer. We had a good laugh with some other campers the second morning as they suffered the same fate as us with the cheeky monkeys. They had a four-door, and the monkeys had actually opened the back door and lifted the whole esky out and had it scattered all around the back of the car; it was bloody funny. They are all up in the tree, holding your food, squawking at each other, and laughing at you, I reckon. The couple was South African but said they had never had that anywhere else. It turned out the park is well known for it. Monkey Mafia.

So we head towards Port Elizabeth, but under instructions from Mark, we stopped in at Port Alfred to do a surf check. As you drive in, you drop down into this lovely little fishing village. The north side is a bluff covered in dense native bush, and the south, cleared farmland. There is a big jetty with batches lining along the bottom of the south side with waves breaking down towards the beach in the centre of the bay. There was surf, so we decided to camp a night there. We set the camp up and checked for monkeys. The place looked clear, so I went for a surf. While surfing, I was treated to another little purple cloud outbreak of rain. After fifteen minutes, it cleared, and while a rainbow streamed out, I heard this hooting of a whistle and couldn't believe midway up in the bush a steam train came chugging around the cliff face up through the valley. *Shit, there's a bloody time warp,* I thought.

That evening, while we cooked around one of the barbecue plates, a lady goes up to Christina and says hello. Well, it's the lady we met on our last night in Mauritius. We partied with her and her friends, and she told me the train I saw was a tourist train that went up into the ranges and was worth the trip if we wanted to go inland. I was keen to hit Jeffreys, so with no waves in the morning, we packed up and headed to Port Elizabeth, did a bit of a drive around, got some supplies, and moved on to Jeffreys Bay. We checked into the camping ground in town, and because we had been rained on the night before and the fact we would be here for a week or two, we booked an on-site caravan. It was a bit old but comfortable with a view out to the ocean. For being a world-renowned surf break town, it was pretty quiet. I soon found out that changed when the surf turned on, though. Far out. As soon as it goes offshore, there are people with surfboards everywhere.

On 29 January, we celebrated my birthday by having dinner in a restaurant in Jeffreys. We were the only people in there, and during our meal, the waitress came out and told us the space shuttle had just blown up after launch. She turned the TV on, and we watched in sadness as it was played over and over before she said, 'That's enough, hey,' and turned it off. That launch was of note because it had the schoolteacher on board. We still had a good night because we got invited to a local party by a friendly crew we met at the pub. Some of the local surfers told me where to go on curtain-size swells, etc., and they told me about seal point out at Cape St Francis, and the best bit of info was when the swell went flat out there to go south to Mossel Bay.

'There is a good surf break in front of the caravan park, and it is consistent. When it gets too big there, you come straight back up here because it will be big enough.'

Another guy chirped in and said, 'Yeah, if you go down there, divert to a place inland called Oudtshoorn. They have a little safari park, an ostrich farm, and some really good caves, and it is worth your time. Stay at least a night.'

I had a few small four- to five-foot days with a taste of what this surf break can be like, long, fast, and lots of fun. One nice day, we headed around the next bay south to Cape St Francis. We stopped in a big car park just out of the town, which I guessed would be where the famous Bruce's Beauty is, a surf break brought to life in a 1970s surf movie. We got out for a look, and with it being low tide, Christina spotted all these green-lip mussels on the rocks. She started ripping some of while I headed to the car for a bag. By the time I was back, she had half a dozen, and because I don't eat them, she said that was enough.

There was a little half-foot wave barrelling down this rocky point, and I said, 'Come on, I'm hanging for a surf. Let's go.'

As we walked back to the car, a Land Cruiser tray back, with the driver side suspension compressed to the max because of this huge African guy in a khaki uniform, pulled across in front of us in a whirl of road dust. His door flew open, and he fought his way out. The car lurched back to normal as he came out of the dust and snarled at us.

'What you got in da bag?'

A bit set back by this part rhino, part man with the bull attitude, I timidly said, 'Oh, we just picked up some mussels for lunch.'

'Oh, Kiwis!' he bellowed, attitude change straightaway. 'When are the All Blacks playing who's in the team? What's happening with the cricket team?'

He wanted to know everything, and he wouldn't let us go. He invited us up to his father's ranch in the Drakensberg, etc. I was itching to get surfing; it was bloody hot in the car park. But I didn't want to be rude; he was actually a nice guy.

Anyway, he finally grabbed the bag, looked in, and said, 'You must go and get more.' Apparently, you could take a dozen each. We said we had enough because I don't eat them. He wished us a pleasant holiday and watched us leave.

We had a laugh as we bumped and banged along the gravel road out to the point of the cape. The point has two breaks, but the inside one was going off that day. I couldn't believe I had it to myself. I could hear hooting and yelling every now and then, and in the pub that night, the locals told me they were surfing a really good beach break in front of a caravan park in between the point and Bruce's Beauty.

We swapped surf stories, and one said, 'The swell will be gone tomorrow night, so if I don't see you, head to Mossel Bay, and don't forget Oudtshoorn, and don't forget, as soon as it's too big at the caravan park, get your arse straight back here.'

So he was right, and after a small surf in the morning, we headed south. We kept seeing this sign 'Grootboom' every twenty kilometres. What the hell is a Grootboom, we wondered? Well, we finally found out just after going over this amazing viaduct bridge.

I said to Christina, 'Far out, let's stop here and go back and check that out.'

It turned out the Grootboom is South African for 'big tree', and at this roadhouse tourist centre, they had all the info on the making of the bridge, which was spectacular, and the history of the huge baobab tree. It was a seriously big tree especially for a baobab tree, but I'm afraid to say it has nothing on the big kauri in the north island of New Zealand called Tane Mahuta. Now this roadhouse is pretty much the start of scenic drive called the Garden Route. And it is absolutely beautiful, winding through a native forest and bursting out onto the coast. We turned left and decided we would stay at this campsite and go for a bush walk in the morning before embarking on another day in the Beatle.

In the morning, we weaved up the valley, crossing over a stream numerous times with the sounds of birds and the smells of the forest. It was a really nice exercise well worth the time. We continued on and took the turnoff to Oudtshoorn. About twenty kilometres out of town, we got pulled over by the cops. A white guy got out on one side; a black guy got out the other.

I wound the window down, and as he walked up, I said, 'Hello, sir, what's up?'

'Oh, Kiwis. When are we playing the All Blacks? What's happening with the cricket team this year?' Blah blah. He drilled me over the two teams, while the black guy went around the car a couple of times, shaking his head. I was thinking, *This isn't looking too good.*

He stared at Christina's tits and then went and talked with the black guy for a minute, came back, stared at Christina's tits again, and said, 'How long are you staying in South Africa?'

'Oh, we've got about a month left. We're running out of money.'

'Guess it's a waste of time giving you a ticket, then, eh?'

'Oh, I guess,' I said.

He said, 'Tell you what, do yourself a favour—go into town and buy yourself four good tyres. It will help you get back to Durban because there's a good chance you could have a serious accident, OK?'

I got out and looked and thanked him for the advice; they were pretty bad. So that's what we did as soon as we found accommodation. Next morning, I picked the car up, and we went to the Cango Caves. Man, they are beautiful and well worth the effort. The tour through them is really well done as well. On the way back from there, we went into the Cango Wildlife Ranch. This is another must do—close up with some wild animals that are basically in a refuge care so are a bit more friendly than wild.

The top thing to do, though, was hand-feeding cheetahs. Far out, that was insane. Christina and I both being cat lovers, we hung out in there for a while. Three fully grown cats were standing pretty much chest height to us. Then the warden handed us donkey liver, and they started purring like motorboats; it was unreal. I decided not to give them some and had my arm up in the air, keeping it away. They thought it was a game. One buckled my legs in a tackle and dropped me to the ground, and another just put my whole hand in his mouth. I could feel his tongue pulling my fingers apart until he had the jackpot. I was on the ground, and they were all over me stopping me. I had to push them away to get up. Absolutely insane.

On our drive out, we saw a zedonk, a zebra crossed with a donkey. How bizarre. I wonder if he is still alive.

Now, Oudtshoorn was the centre of two ostrich booms, 1865–1870 and 1900–1914, and there are amazing mansions from the day scattered throughout the township and the farms. We went into one of the farms, possibly the safari show farm, and two or three of the rooms of this amazing house were like museums. Then we were taken out to a big barn and stood on an egg to show us how big they were and how strong. Then a group of about twenty of us went down to a coral with a little amphitheatre. A couple of black guys brought out an ostrich, and our guide told us all about them. Next thing, this black guy got on one, with his legs crossed down the ostrich's chest so his neck was between his legs. He was dressed like a jockey, and he looked pretty funny. The guide told us how to ride them.

'If you want them to go forward, you hold their neck and push forward. To go back, you just pull it back.' Sure enough, the ostrich with the rider did this. Then he said, 'If you want it to turn right or left, you pull his neck the way you want to go, and at the same time lift the opposite wing.'

He turned left and then right and then ran around for a bit and stopped. Everyone clapped. The guide asked if anyone wanted to have a go. The place went quiet, so I jumped up and walked down. Well, bugger me, that was fun. I did all the same stuff as the jockey. I got off, and the guide asked again. The place went quiet.

Then Christina said, 'I will.' There was a stir in the ranks as Christina made her way down.

I said, 'Go for it, babe. You're going to love it,' and laughed.

The rest of the group were watching intently. They put the ostrich in a V style that had a step up to it and put a bag over its head. Christina climbed on.

'I'm already pissing myself.' She was so funny.

They backed the ostrich out of the V and took the bag off its head. Christina screamed. The ostrich took off with Christina screaming. It was so bloody funny; it even had the rest of the group pissing themselves. Luckily, they had four jockeys around to throw a bag back over its head. Finally, got Christina off. Tell ya what, man, that was priceless. The whole group thought Christina was a heroine and shook her hand and thanked her for the entertainment. We then watched a race between six of them that looked pretty funny. The guide asked us to come back every day because it was the most fun he had had in ages, and he reckoned it would be good for business, ha ha.

So the next morning, we headed back to the coast and pulled up at this really neat caravan park on a point in Mossel Bay that has this really nice right hander right out the front of our tent. Three to four feet and heaps of fun. After a good surf on our first day there, we toured around and came across the Post Box Tree. In the early days, vessels going back and forth would leave mail in the tree. If your vessel was heading west, you took mail to Europe, and if you were heading east, you took the mail that was heading to Asia. If I remember correctly, it was located on top of a hill overlooking the bay. We may have only spent three nights there, but in that time, Christina took a challenge to carry me on her back along the road in front of the surf break slash camping ground. She did bloody well, and all the cars that went past were honking their horns, ha ha. Legend.

So that night, I was kept awake to the pounding of surf; it was a crisp sound that meant it was offshore. I couldn't sleep with anticipation. With the crack of dawn, I had my wetty on and headed out the channel and started my way out to the point. There were heaps of white water and lots of turbulence. I saw a seal on its back eating something, shellfish probably; it looked pretty cute. Then there was a splash to my right; I looked. There was a splash to my left; I looked. I was a bit spooked, but I think the seal jumped over me for fun.

I sat in the line-up, but as it got lighter, I realised it was really washed out and not really working. Every now and then, about three hundred metres out in the bay, there was this big peak with a left and right. Then a set went through when the sun shone on it, and it just looked too majestic. I paddled straight out there and got about three or four rights, which were the better waves; it was about eight feet. Four local guys came out and asked me if I had come out by myself and looked at me really strange. One broke his board. Then they all left. I got a couple of more and headed in myself. We packed up camp straightaway and headed back to Jeffreys. I was to find out later that I had paddled through Shark Alley, surfed Outercom by myself, and got back through Shark Alley not even knowing luckily how big the white pointers are in that area. They actually do shark tours and cage diving in that area. I should have bought a lotto ticket; but then again, maybe that was my lotto ticket. I got about five absolute screaming rights. Only a surfer knows the feeling.

When we arrived at the main car park at Jeffreys Bay, it was packed, but I lucked into an empty space. A six-foot set of about five waves peeled off from the point. It was pumping but had a crowd on it. While I was putting my wetsuit on, a guy asked me where in Durban I lived. He had seen the Durban number plates but lit up when he realised we were Kiwis, and we chatted to him and his friends until I headed out. I had my best surf there that day. There were a few bigger sets. It was a bit crowded, but out of the three to four hours I was out there, I got plenty of good waves and pretty much had a taste of why it is a world-class wave—very fast, very powerful, and you get barrels, sometimes long ones, the jewel of any surf.

After my surf, we sat watching it for a while. Then I suggested we stay at the caravan park out at Cape St Francis instead of the Jeffreys Bay one. Christina agreed, so we bought some food at the store and headed out there. As we set up the camp, the Durban couple that had talked to us at the surf break car park walked past heading down to look at the beach break. After a chat about the surf, they invited us to visit them at their camp later if we wanted. We said we will drop in, and after we cooked dinner, we took a couple of beers and a bottle of wine.

We were introduced to Glen and Noeline, and Tex and Hannah. They were very friendly and funny, and we had a good laugh. They were heading back to Durban the next day but were going to stop at a surf break called Lwandile, in the Wild Coast, about two hours' drive off the main road south of Port St John. They asked us if we would like to join them. We both agreed, so we loosely hatched a plan for the next day. While doing that, there was a change in the wind. Then all of a sudden, it started blowing, not just blowing but blowing hot—I mean like standing in front of a heater.

Tex said, 'It's called the berg wind, and it's the warm air blown over from the central plateau on the other side of the Drakensberg ranges.'

This was way hotter than the wind we experienced in Port Shepstone. In fact, this was hot like a blowtorch and a lot stronger. We shut the campfire down and organised a morning surf check before decided what to do with the day. It was a hot and steamy night in our little tent, but the next morning was cool and onshore, making the decision to pack up and head north easier. We drove straight through to East London and set up camp at the surf break out of town where the monkeys steal your food.

Next day, we did the big trek to the beach head at Lwandile, Wild Coast. Tex had a Toyota Hilux four-wheel drive ute, and we had to pack all the gear into his ute and drive about a kilometre south from where the beach batches lined the coast to a little river at the base of a large hill. It was a cute little spot with a surf break peeling down from the point of the hill to the bay where the river mouth was. It was onshore at the time, and we needed two trips to get the camp set up. We got a fire going and had a nice campfire braai for dinner. We got woken up in the middle of the night to a major rainstorm, and because we were at the base of a hill, a mini river of rainwater was running right through the centre of our tent. We got soaked. The rain stopped, and we finally got back to sleep. I awoke early pretty much first light. I had my head poking out the tent, checking the sky.

'Thank God it's cleared up,' I said to Christina as she went back to sleep.

Within a half hour of light, I started hearing a wailing sound that seemed from miles away. It would come and go but got louder over the next hour or so. I had just come back from looking at the surf and for dry firewood, when on top of the hill, I noticed a basket moving along towards the coast from inland. It got bigger. Then a head appeared under it, turning into a big black lady holding the hand of a kid. She looked down and stopped walking. Another couple of ladies and a few kids appeared, and they looked down, obviously discussing what they were seeing. As they proceeded down our side of the hill, I told Glen and Tex what was going on, and they came out of the tent, followed by Noeline and Hannah. I called Christina out, and we all treated them with a 'Hello, good morning.'

They made a beeline straight to Hannah, who was a very white blonde, and they were pouring all over her with big smiles and jabbering to each other. It freaked Hannah out a bit, but they were harmless, just intrigued. The kids spotted Glen's soccer ball and Frisbee, and Glen did a deal with them that if they started our fire, they could play with the ball. That got them fighting over firewood, and it was funny watching them get it all organised. One of the older ones took off to the beach. The ladies gave what appeared to be instructions to the young ones and waved goodbye. They were heading up the valley to work in a maze paddock around a bend in the little river. By the time the pot was boiling for a morning coffee, the older boys had come back with a couple of crayfish they had caught in the rock pools along the water's edge of the hill. So guess what we had for lunch.

Around the middle of the day, the swell had picked up a bit, and the wind was feathering a nice four-foot wave about halfway along from the point into the bay. It was quite a long ride with a couple of good fun sections, and Glen and I had it to ourselves because Tex didn't want to surf. We had a good afternoon in the waves and then played soccer with the kids until the mothers came back and took them back to their village. That night, it rained down twice as bad as the night before, and Christina and I ended up moving our bed into Tex and Hannah's tent. Luckily, the days were warm and dry enough to dry our gear.

The wailing across the morning hills was just as beautiful the next two days. The kids were in charge of our fires, and we gave them food and played soccer with them in the afternoon until we left. We had found out that the wailing in the mornings was the mothers that rose later were singing out to the mothers that left the village early to ask if they had their kids with them, and of course, the mothers that were already halfway were replying whether they had them. It was a beautiful sound and really gave the mornings a magical touch.

With no surf on the third day, we packed up the camp and headed to Port St John and stayed in a caravan park where we splashed out and shared a villa. Tex knew of a blowhole out on the coast, and after walking across a shaky swinging bridge to a rock outcrop and up and over the top, we came across about a three-metre swell running up the coast. We could hear this sucking and blowing really loud as we got close to the top of a share rock face angled about thirty degrees down to a ten-foot vertical drop. The swells were pushing into a gully. Then two seconds later, this blowhole about half a metre wide would throw a geyser about fifty feet in the air. It was bloody unreal. Then it would go into sucking mode as the surf drained back in front of the next wave. Then, bam, the next wave would hit, and when you put your hand out, it would hurt; there was so much power in it. We were lucky to get the spot on such a big swell because it was performing with a roar. We were mesmerised and entertained for at least an hour before the possibility of getting good waves up the coast at St Michael's was too much, and we headed off.

By early afternoon, we had pulled up at St Mikes, and the surf was cooking around six to eight feet. Tex joined us out there, and it was after that surf that he explained why he didn't surf with us at Lwandile. He told me of a really good surf break just south of where we were that rivals Jeffreys Bay for perfection. Two years ago, they were there with a group of friends, and one of his friends was hit by a white pointer right in front of him. As you would expect, it has left a lasting impression on him, and he can't bring himself to surf in non-netted surf breaks.

My friend Mark from up the road in Port Shepstone joined us out there, and we surfed till dark. Glen and Tex had friends locally and stayed there. We returned to Mark's place and promised if we didn't see them in the surf the next day, we would contact them when we arrived in Durban to do a catch-up before we left South Africa. We thanked them for inviting us on their trip back. It was truly a beautiful sidetrack to what would have been just a return drive.

After a week with Mark and Rolley, we returned to John and Sue's in Durban. We went into Noeline's hairdressing shop for a haircut and organised a visit to their place up north of Durban in Umhlanga Rocks, where I had my last surf in Durban with Glen. We had a lovely dinner and stayed the night at their place and said our goodbyes the next day.

About a week later, we departed South Africa and headed back to Dubai under the false information that Christina being a U.K. national through birth would be able to enter the UAE. We were about to find out how wrong that was. We had been in Africa for over five months. We had seen and done stuff that blew us away. We had met beautiful people, black and white. We had caught up with friends and family. We had a holiday we will never forget, and the memories will always be strong. But without work, there are no fun tickets, so back to work I go.

The plan was to arrive in Dubai, find out when the next job goes out, and fly Christina off back to Australia before I head offshore. Unfortunately, that plan did not work. They refused Christina entry into Dubai and locked her up. It was late Friday afternoon, and with Friday being a holiday, I had no way of contacting anyone from the office.

I was told by someone at the airport that the hotels often sponsor tourists so they stay at their hotels, so as soon as I got to the guest house, I started calling hotels. The last and most expensive hotel I called was the Hyatt Galleria. The night manager said that they sponsored couples as long as they stay at the hotel. I checked if they had a room, told the man of our situation, and when he said it would not be a problem, I hung up in total relief, called a taxi, and headed straight there to do the paperwork. While filling in the paperwork, he realised that we are not married and said it was impossible and that he assumed we were married. Thank God he relented when he realised how desperate I was. He signed the sponsorship, and off I went to the airport to get my poor lady out of lockup.

We were both happy to be off in the taxi, and I asked what it was like locked up in the airport. Typical of Christina's nature, she had used the time to check out other people's culture fashion. Using sign language and pidgin English, she had discussed the use of henna art on an Arabic lady's hand, and they complimented each other's jewellery. But she did say she could kill a wine, though, to de-stress, ha ha. So could I, and so we did after we checked into our extremely expensive room on the fifteenth floor. The next day, I went into the office and was told by the travel agent I should have called him; he would have sorted it out, blah blah. Too late now.

There was a job going out in a week's time. I couldn't afford to pay the hotel for that long. I called Mum and organised the US$3,000 I needed to pay the hotel and airfares for Christina's return. It was possibly a week before that money would show up, but luckily, one of Lance's friends lent me the money on short term. Christina really enjoyed her short four-night stay in Dubai, walking around the gold souks and markets of Dubai and Deira, the art of a different culture, and she loved the sun and the heat. The farewell at the airport was extremely hard. We had been together close to six months, and life was just fun with her around. To lighten the mood, I farewelled her with a promise to meet again in Bali, probably in four months. Then she was gone.

Chapter 8

YOU CAN'T HIDE RINGS FROM CHRISTINA

When I returned to the guest house, the burnt-out shell of the saturation system that had been on the *Smit Maassluis* when it was hit by an Exocet missile was stored under the stairwell. As I looked around the chambers, I thought to myself, *I'm glad I wasn't on that job.* If Christina had not gotten the job in Margate at the restaurant, there was a good chance I would have been. The *Smit Maassluis* with a dive crew with a lot of my friends was on its way into Kharg Island for a saturation diving job for Hydrospace International when it was hit by an Exocet missile, killing a young Australian diver called Wayne Spicer. Luckily for them all, the superintendent Matt had decided not to commit the divers into sat until they had the vessel set up in the field, which would have been a few hours later, or there may have been more fatalities. As it was, two Australians and one Kiwi were seriously injured. Most of the crew had their ears blown out by the concussion.

Aubrey, an English friend, showed me footage of the vessel on fire on the back deck as they ran for cover as Kharg was being attacked by fighter jets. The missile had gone through the HydraTite shack where Wayne was working and blew up the gas racks next to the sat system. Tony, my first supervisor from my first job offshore;

Robby, a life support technician; and John, a diver, were badly hurt from shrapnel and concussion and were rushed to the closest hospital. My friends told me that they were in a hotel not far from the hospital waiting on news.

Jim, an Australian whom I was yet to meet, was up early and decided to go for a walk to the hospital and see how the boys were. He told me this story a few years later when I first met him. He said it took him a while to find Tony and Robby with not knowing any Arabic and no one speaking English, but they didn't know where John was and hadn't seen him for a while. Jim started walking around looking in rooms, trying to communicate with staff. He was fearing the worst when he spotted someone pushing a bed with a very sick patient on into a room with a closed door. He decided to walk in and by chance came across John. The room he was in was the dying room, he said, and it stunk of death. They put the patients in there because they can't help them anymore. Jim pulled his bed out back into the main area and put him alongside Tony and Robby. He managed to get on the phone to the hotel, waking up Matt. Matt was straight onto the company, and they got the three of them medivacked by chopper to a hospital in Bahrain, I think, and probably saving their lives, especially John's.

So this last paragraph has been someone else's story, and I have only relayed it here. I hope it is a reasonably accurate account. We all know stories grow wings and morph into monsters. John is thankful to everyone that kept the three of them alive. Tony apparently still brags about nearly having his balls massacred by shrapnel but living to tell the tail. But John quit diving, and I came across him years later in Perth, but we didn't talk about it. Billy laughs about how all the Brits and Aussies got their ears blown out, but the Maoris didn't because of their big noses, ha ha, typical Bill. True or not, who knows. I had worked with Wayne for three months before I left for Africa. He was a nice guy. RIP.

Over the next four months, I was just going from one job to another, the odd drama here and there. I remember the first time I shit myself, ha ha. We were doing a seabed scrapping job, dropping a basket to the seabed and filing it up with rubbish. I was carrying a couple of paint tins and went to throw them in the basket when this huge cod—well, it seemed huge at the time—had decided to make the basket its house. I threw the tins in at the same time I saw it. It charged straight at me. I shit myself and ran away, ha ha. What a dickhead. It actually wasn't even that big. I just got a fright. Harden up, you pussy.

A month or so later, I was on the mud brace of a platform in 175 feet of water looking for an anode that had been dropped, and we had to recover it. I was at the leg and struggling to breathe. I was narced big time. I could hear every vessel in the world. The visibility wasn't very good, but everything was changing colour, and I knew I had to pull it together. I stopped moving and closed my eyes. I concentrated on slowing my breathing down to get control of the narcosis. I opened the free flow, but all that did was steal gas from my demand valve. I told the supervisor I needed more gas. He said I had everything. I had to disagree. I told him to wind up the regulator and give me more. He gave me more, but it made no difference. The noise and colours started to back off. I was sweating in the hat.

I managed to find the anode, hook it up, clear it off the seabed, and leave bottom. All the way up, I was struggling to breathe. I got to the surface, ripped my gear off, and got thrown in the chamber to decompress. When I got out, they had found the problem. It was caused by a charcoal filter that had blown on the compressor and pushed charcoal through the dive panel down my umbilical and clogged up the demand valve on the hat, so I wouldn't have even been able to use my bailout if I needed to.

This is a big lifesaving rule here—*do not panic*. There is a good chance that if I had panicked, I would have been in all sorts of trouble. Looking back on this situation, I was quite lucky I didn't panic. When I got to the seabed, I thought I was narced because I had gone down too fast. But it was most likely caused by struggling to breathe. When you work really hard in diving hats, you start to overbreathe the capability of the hat to give you the gas you demand. This creates a knock-on effect; the more you need, the less you can get. You have to overpower your will to suck as much air into your lungs as you can to actually do the opposite and slow your breathing down. It is bloody hard. By slowing down, you can actually get more gas through the demand valve. Then you can get back control of your breathing. If you panic, you lose control and possibly consciousness, who knows? Hopefully, your standby diver gets you before the final curtain call.

We cleaned all the gear out and got it all up and running again, finished the job, and demobed. The next project was a job in Iran in the war zone again, double bubble (twice the day rate), just don't get hit by Exocets. We couldn't keep a low profile because the barge we went up in was the Tak Pull 750, a big barge with a big crane, pretty easy to see. We were right on the Iran/Bahrain border but under the flight path for jets hitting Kharg Island from Araq apparently. We spotted jets flying high over us most days, but three weeks later, we finished the job and arrived safely back in Dubai. It was just over three months, so I decided to head back to Bali. I got it organised and went into the Dubai gold souk in Deira and bought a ring that Christina had been drooling over when we walked through. I was held up leaving Dubai because of overbooked flights, and it took me three nights waiting at the airport before I scored a seat.

When I finally arrived, Christina had beaten me by a couple of days and had a losmen organised off Rum Jungle Road. She picked me up at the airport. When we got to the hotel, I sorted my board out ready for a surf. While she was having a shower, I got the ring out and was waiting to propose to her, when an American couple she had met started yelling out to her at the bottom of the stairs.

I walked out, said hello, told them she was in the shower, and told them who I was, and they started pouring a drink from their icebox. I took one offered to me, and we chatted until Christina walked out. We carried on for a short time. I think they may have realised we needed time to ourselves, and off they went. They were a funny couple, and we spent a lot of time on and off with them. They were from the Hollywood area. Al even came to our wedding, although he missed it by two days as he got delayed getting lost in Sydney visiting other friends he met in Bali.

Anyway, getting back to the non-proposal, Christina jumped on me and said, 'Are you proposing to me?'

I said, 'What?'

She said, 'I found the ring.'

Ha ha, so I never actually got to do the down on one knee because her eagle eye for jewellery spotted the ring even though it wasn't out in the open. Blew that one. Anyway, I said if she was going to travel around catching up with me wherever I was, I didn't want her to keep getting locked up. We made a rough date, late February 1997. That'll give Mum time to organise it.

We spent nearly two months in Bali again and moved around a bit and really noticed how much it had expanded. Rice paddies at the Legian/Seminyak border were now turning into losmen and large hotel complexes. Some of the secret surf spots like Bingin that I used to surf by myself now had losmen and warung on the cliffs. Yung Yungs now had a private complex over the top of it. Uluwatu and the Bukit Peninsula were slowly increasing in places to stay.

The roads were getting better, and we were starting to lose that adventure style of motorbike ride that we used to have just going for a surf. I do miss the motocross ride we used to have from the

Uluwatu Temple road into the surf break. It was a hassle, but it was also fun. You used to go on the beach at night on your bike. Sometimes, if I was up the Kuta Beach end, I would take the beach back to Legian/Seminyak, practice wheel stands and do doughnuts and have a bit of fun on the way back home. Sometimes, we rode from Legian to the beach temple at Chungu on the beach. The crowds were increasing, but when the swell was on, the waves were still pumping. Christina would spend all morning walking around finding amazing things outside the tourist trash. I would surf till midday if it was on. We would catch up for an afternoon beach session and then spend our nights together catching up with friends. What a life. All of a sudden, it was time to go. She flew back to Brisbane, and me, back to Dubai. Another airport farewell.

Chapter 9

THE FIRST RETURN HOME

About three weeks after arriving back, we mobilised another boat landing contract off Halul Island, Qatar. This time, we had two cofferdams, and we were on a small self-propelled barge called the MV *Carol*. We also had a new superintendent, an Australian guy called Anthony; his nick name was Roo. We got along pretty good. He was pretty organised. We sailed from Dubai with pretty much the same welders and riggers from the previous contract. Richardo, the Filipino welding foreman, and John John, the Indian rigging foreman, were on my shift again, and Roo put me in charge of the cofferdams, rigging, and repairs. There was a bit more room on the *Carol*, but it wasn't handling the weather. We were smashing the cofferdams up, putting them on and off.

They found a barge in Qatar called the *Jawharah*. After three weeks of smashing the cofferdams, we went into Doha and moved all the gear over to the much bigger barge. It had a huge crane, which fixed some problems but created some as well. The barge was a mess, but it tidied up good. Within a couple of days, we were back in the field. The *Jawharah* was not self-propelled but was towed around by tugboats. It took longer to set up in position, but we were able to work in rougher conditions.

There was a Canadian guy on the other shift called Pat. He was a nice bloke that I had met in Singapore. Anyway, one night while we were down on weather, he had decided to coat all the rigging with blackjack, a sort of graphite and oil mix, and he had brushed it all on. Oh my god, what a bloody mess that made. I'm laughing at the memory as I write. We bagged him for ages for doing it. He was really tall, and one morning, they were preparing to swing a cofferdam over to a platform. The weather was borderline rough. They had set the transfer rigging up on their shift, but by the time they were ready to pick the first cofferdam up, it was shift change.

Tall Pat was the transfer rigger on his shift, and short arse me was the transfer rigger on my shift. The transfer rigger's job was to ride the cofferdam over from the side of the barge to the leg, and as it swings in under the overhang, you connect the cofferdam rigging onto the overhang rigging, come down on the crane, transfer the load, and take the crane rigging off so it can then swing out and back to the barge. Well, there was a bit of swell running after some strong wind the day before. I jumped on the top of the cofferdam, and over we went. We set up against the leg, but with the swell, it was really tricky getting the height right. This is where the big crane had a drawback. It was swinging up and down a lot more, and the crane winch doesn't react as fast, so a bit of a double blow. We sat off the leg a bit when we realised that it was looking tricky.

On the radio, I said to Roo that we will have to time this right between the sets of swell. Once we commit, we will have to go the whole way. So we set up ready, and when the break in the swell came, I swung the crane into position, I put the cofferdam hang off rigging onto the chain fall hooks, but I couldn't get the crane hooks off because they were a bit too high, and I missed them. The swell hit again, and I had to drop to the top of the cofferdam and hang on as the crane rigging and the platform rigging fought over which one would hold the weight. I was on my stomach holding on for my life, looking down at the platform leg and cofferdam banging and crashing. The crane rigging was going over my back, down past my head, and then whipping back as the load would transfer onto the crane. The cofferdam would shudder with the transfer. I had to stay there until the swell stopped long enough for me to jump back up and try again. It took me three attempts before I managed to get it off, and they slewed the crane away. I was covered in blackjack head to foot, front and back. It was bloody scary shit. We decided that we would not put them on in that sort of weather again, and we didn't.

One night, the weather was getting up, and we had to get the walkway off before it broke the hold down rigging and went to the bottom. I took John John and his right-hand man, Mohammed, over in the Zodiac to derig the walkway hook up the crane and swing it off. I rode the walkway back on the crane, so John John and Moh were stuck on the platform. The weather was getting up quick. We could see the fear in their eyes when I told them they had to make their own way back. We needed to hurry up and pull away from the platform. It was dark and getting scarier, and John John couldn't start the outboard. Moh was up on the platform holding the bow rope, waiting. Both being from India, they couldn't swim. They were petrified, and John John was nearly thrown out of the Zodiac.

I decided to throw a rope to them and said, 'Catch the rope, and we'll pull you back.'

John John caught the rope and straightaway started pulling himself back to the barge, leaving his mate behind.

We're yelling at him, 'No, wait for Moh.'

He's saying stuff to Moh, in Indian obviously. We slacked the rope. Moh managed to pull the Zodiac back and jumped on. We pulled them over as they swung behind the barge. They were yelling profanities at us as they walked up the deck. We were absolutely pissing ourselves. God, that was a funny night. You just can't do that stuff anymore. They have taken all the fun out of the job. I would love to sit down with Richardo, John John, and Mohammed and have a couple of beers and a catch-up. They were good guys, hard workers, and I'm sure if I could speak their language, I would know a lot more about them. The Indian riggers and Filipino welders were not that good with English, so communication was hard. Lots of sign language.

We had a large crew on this job, and Roo had decided we needed to do a lifeboat drill during one of the rough weather days. It was a total stuff up. None of the Asians made it to their lifeboat stations. Next day, Roo had made all these tags with big letters *A B C D*. Each letter was a lifeboat station. The cabin you were in downstairs related to your lifeboat station. All the Asians were given a letter that coincides with the cabin and lifeboat. We did walk around and put people on the lifeboats so they knew where they were supposed to be. Problem solved, he thought.

Before we had a chance to do another lifeboat drill, we got hit with another storm. We were actually in transit from one platform to another when it hit us, and the tugboat had only dropped the first ten-tonne gravity block anchor for the barge set up. It was too rough to pick up the next one, so they dropped another storm anchor off the bow, and we were just going to ride it out where we were. At about 3 a.m., the vessel alarms went off. I thought, *This is a good time for a lifeboat drill*, and as I walked out on deck with my life jacket, I saw the platform fly past our bow, right were my life boat station was. We were moving at about three to four knots, which is fast considering we had anchors down. It was New Year's morning, and the wind was howling. We missed the platform by about ten feet. Only the expats were at my lifeboat station. All the Asians were in the middle of the barge as far away from the water as they could get. They were holding their little plastic letters, showing each other and nodding. None of them had understood anything Roo had said. Thank God we didn't capsize that night.

I went up the bridge to see what was going on. Charlie, a hard-case Scottish guy, was standing in the back, watching the barge captain and Roo discuss the situation. Charlie saw me, smiled, turned to a blackboard behind him with a list of the platforms we had to work on, and grabbed a chalk and put a stroke through a number as he said, 'Guess we can cross that one off our list.' We laughed and went down and made coffee.

The next day was still blowing a gale. We managed to drift right through the field without picking up any pipelines or hitting any platforms. At the time, I thought the waves were huge, like ten to twelve feet, but after living in Western Australia and surfing ten to twelve feet and bigger, I guess it was only six to eight feet, plenty big enough to sink that barge if we had been unlucky. When the weather calmed down and the barge was set up on the job, I said goodbye to everyone and flew by chopper into Doha and then made my way through Dubai, Singapore, and into Brisbane, where Christina had been living since her departure from New Zealand in 1984.

We hired a car, and she took me up to her favourite hangout, Noosa Heads. She said, 'It is so beautiful that you have to see it before we leave,' and she was right. What an absolute paradise. We stayed with some friends of hers and then headed back to Napier to help Mum and Dad—well, Mum really—finish organising our wedding. I hadn't realised how much I had missed our friends, but life went on as if we had never been apart, and we just slotted back into the life I had left behind.

Napier is a pretty little town on the southern end of Hawke's Bay on the east coast of the North Island. Nicknamed the Fruit Bowl of New Zealand because of its numerous orchards, the bay is a large valley with very fertile soil. The harbour is one of the largest exporters of wool in the Southern Hemisphere, and the twin cities of Napier and Hastings, about eighteen kilometres inland, are known for their art deco architecture after an earthquake levelled most of both cities in

1931, and a large proportion of the city buildings are still standing. In 2007, Napier was nominated for a world heritage site and was the first cultural site in New Zealand to be so, though it didn't meet the requirements to be listed in the end.

The beaches around the city are stony, but the beaches out of town but within a twenty- to thirty-minute drive are lovely white sand and surrounded by sheep and cattle farms with rolling hills and patches of native bush. The rivers are a lovely escape from the coast with some beautiful fresh waterholes to picnic at. When it rains, it pours, but when the sun is out, you really are in a pretty country town. There are three river mouths that on their day produce epic waves, with the Wairoa river mouth being the secret gem. Not far north from Wairoa on the north end of the bay is the Mahia Peninsula, only a two-hour drive north from Napier, and you have about twenty-five surf breaks within a twenty-minute drive once you arrive at the first spot called Black's Beach. My friends and I had learnt to surf there when we were all doing our apprenticeships, and Mike and I had gone halves in buying a block of land on a northern beach called Mahanga. We had two caravans and a shed on it, and it was called the swamp. I ended up buying Mike out when he had moved to New Plymouth, and now my other mate, Mark, owns it, and he has but a proper beach house on it, and it still is a magical little spot away from the city, a getaway to wind down and relax. So glad it is still in our family of friends.

Hawke's Bay is surrounded by the Kaweka Range to the north and the Ruahine Range to the south, which sucks a lot of the clouds, leaving the coast basking in sun. Both ranges are well known for hunting and hiking. There are two pictures in my memory that jump to mind when thinking of my hometown. One is the view when you drive up the last steep hill coming from Taupo, just over the crest, and, bang, I think you are at a thousand feet, and sweeping down into the distance over forestry and farmland is the Napier Hill and harbour. Rain behind you, sunshine before you.

In your mind, the thought 'I'm home.' The other picture is when you are coming from the southern beaches of Ocean Beach and Waimarima Beach, you cross over the Tukituki River and drive alongside the Te Mata Peak foothills, your view through the river valley to the ocean towards Haumoana river mouth on the right, and left of that the Napier Hill cliff face that overlooks the wharf in the distance. On a sunny day, it really is a picture to paint, and it will remain in my memory forever.

We were married in our local church not far from where I first went to school. With all our family and friends around us on 28 February 1987, and as you would hope, it was a day to remember. Our honeymoon was actually staying at home to enjoy our friends and family as long as possible, because through Roo, I had organised Christina to be sponsored by Oceaneering in Singapore, and we were going to move there. So we bounced between our friends' houses, our batch on Mahanga Beach, and Christina's family home in Tauranga. Al, the American we met in Bali, turned up for a few nights while we were staying at Damian's place on the beach at Ahuriri. That was a nice surprise. We left our friends and family as husband and wife in early May 1987. Christina was pregnant. Best we start a new chapter.

Chapter 10

PREGNANT IN SINGAPORE

We were invited to stay at Roo and his family in Hong Leong, not far from the Oceaneering yard, Anne and their two children, Karly and Nathan. It took about two weeks to organise for Anne to help us find our own apartment not far from their villa complex; in fact, just down the road, very handy and very close to the Hong Leong markets and food circle. Not being a very high-expat community, the food was very cheap and mostly lovely.

Christina being a good cook and therefore liking to cook decided one day while I was working on a welding project that she would cook chicken for dinner. God bless her. Off she trotted midday to the market and asked a lady if she could have a chicken, please.

'Ah you want chicken ah.' The lady had a big smile and brown crooked teeth.

'Yes, please.'

The lady spun around grabbed a live chicken out of the cane basket cage, spun back, and whacked with a meat cleaver the head off. Christina screamed and nearly jumped out of her skin at the same time.

'Oh my god,' she told me later. 'The poor bloody chicken, one minute it's sitting there laying eggs. Next, its head's off, and the boss lady is pulling feathers out.'

She got such a shock she said she'll come back on the way out. She said the worst thing was it was still warm in the bag as she walked home. I don't think she bought another chicken there. I laughed when she told me, but it took her awhile to tune into the local way of life.

Oceaneering had a hyperbaric welding repair project on the go, and I was in the workshop preparing to code up for the job. This was very handy because although I could weld, I had never learnt pipe welding and never did a lot of welding in my apprenticeship. Singapore is hot enough, but when you start welding, temperatures can only go one way. There was about nine of us in the yard all doing our best. Three or four were really good, and they helped us learn the techniques needed to master the codes. One was Hugh, who was Bill Ensor's younger brother. Bill was the guy I first worked with in Oceaneering yard in Kwong Min Road back in 1984.

When Oceaneering won a contract for dive support in Miri, Malaysia, they sent the Smit Tak vessel *Morey Harstad* alongside in the Tuas harbour area of Jurong. I think we spent a week cutting stuff off and preparing the deck for a saturation system and ROV system. One notable memory was an afternoon that was swept with thunderstorms. Lots of puddles everywhere. Tiny, a big hard-case Kiwi, was fabricating on the harbour. The rest of us had been on the vessel until the big lift crane was set up to lift part of the saturation system into place. We all headed down the gangplank and watched alongside, taking the piss out of the local riggers as you do. All looking skyward, next thing, bam, I was in the water, fifteen feet down between the vessel and the dock. I looked up, and everyone is creased up, pissing themselves. I climbed up the safety ladder to find out Tiny had noted I was standing in a puddle, so he touched me with his electrode to give me a jump. He didn't think I'd jump that far. He was welding with 4 mm rods so would have had 180–200 amps ramped up on the welding machine. I actually had no say in the matter. God, I hate divers sometimes, ha ha. We ended up going on shift work to get it finished for the contract start. I still don't think we were paid enough for that. The vessel sailed. We went back into the yard and pipe practice. In the meantime they had changed the coding for the job, so we had to learn a different style. Stove pipe it was called from memory.

What I remember most were the burnt fingers and the lunches we had at the Jurong Bird Park. The bird park had large beer glasses the size of a jug, ice cold. We would drive up there with about six of us in the back of the ute, get about three or four down for lunch, and stagger back into the workshop. Funny enough, our best welds were in the afternoons. I spent a couple of days with Roo getting a chamber in the other yard ready to do the hyperbaric test pieces in, and we had started practicing at thirty feet on an argon/air mix. We had to wear an AGA mask, and it was hot as hell in there. What I noticed was the gas environment seemed to help stabilise the weld pool and made it easier to work. Before we were allowed to start the hyperbaric qualifying, we had to pass two surface pipes ASB9 setups. We all passed and moved to the other yard for another week of full-on pipe qualifying at forty-five feet. Every pipe we did was scrutinised by the client and engineer reps.

Around this time, Roo had gone back to Dubai and Christina's visa was up for renewal. I was in the office filling out the paperwork, and knowing that Christina was now possibly three months pregnant and starting to look like it, I said to Lucy, the lady in charge of the sponsorship, that she was pregnant. She went psycho at me for not telling her earlier. I just played dumb. When she calmed down, she said I had to go to the New Zealand embassy and get a letter to state that if our child was born there he or she they wouldn't try to apply for Singaporean citizenship. We went in, and I was surprised that they would not give us that letter. And that was basically the end of Christina's sponsored stay in Singapore. Another airport farewell with Christina's return to Napier.

We had only two weeks left on the lease, so a couple of the welders moved in to save them driving all the way back to Sembawang. A couple of days after I moved out of Hong Leong, we were all passed to the next stage of actually setting the test pieces. For this, we started using heating elements to get the pipe to the required temperature before welding. With Roo gone, Hugh was running the dive panel as well as the welding machines. We were using the same earth penetrator for the heating elements as the welding machine. For some reason, while I was on my hot pass, which is the first filling run after the root weld, I was at about the eight o'clock position, and my amps surged. I managed to pull off before I blew through.

Tiny was my assistant to do the grinding. He said, 'What the hell was that?'

We asked Hugh; he didn't know. I hadn't done any damage, so we carried on. As I was doing the cap at about four o'clock coming up to three o'clock, it did it again. Hugh spotted the surge off the heating element welding machine and turned it off. Unfortunately, the damage was done. My cap was two millimetres too high, and he questioned the hot spot on the inside of the pipe where I nearly blew the hot pass. That was me—failed. All that hot and hard work gone down the drain. I was really annoyed at myself for blowing that opportunity. A lack of experience meant I didn't pick up on what could have been an obvious problem. But at the end of the day, fate is a funny thing. Because I messed that up, Roo got me back up to Dubai because they were mobing another boat landing project. While I was in Dubai, the welding job went out, and the boys nailed it and made good money. I would work with Ben, Kevin, Tiny, Jack, Neville, and Hugh again over the coming years.

In July, I was back on board the *Jawharah* with Richardo, John John, and Mohammed and a lot of other familiar faces amongst the welders and riggers, plus a lot of my diving buddies from the previous project. Roo was setting the barge up but handing it over to a Canadian superintendent called Larry. Larry was OK, but he and my shift supervisor, Jack, didn't get along, and it gave us low-life divers something to laugh about. Not a lot of note happened this trip, so the heat between Larry and Jack kept us entertained. Jack was a real arsehole to the welders and riggers, treating them like dumb labourers. The captain and the crew of the barge were not much better.

This time of year is extremely hot in the gulf, add to that a big steel deck and not a lot of wind. We were all copping it and used to do one-hour rotations off the deck for a break from the heat in the hottest part of the day. When supplies arrived, cases of soft drink would be dished out between the ship's crew and the dive crew. The welders and riggers never got any. I thought that was shit but typical of the attitude towards the lower-paid workers.

Anyway, one hot day, Larry was down on deck, and he and Jack got into a major spitting match. My mates and I were watching from a distance and laughing. We didn't like Jack either, and in the end, it was draw straws on. Did he sack him, or did he quit first? Larry's version is run-off motherfu—er'; Jack's, of course, is he quit. We liked Larry's version. So with Jack gone, I was made supervisor; no pay increase, mind you, just more authority. I must admit I soaked it up.

The vessel that came into pick up Jack was also dropping off supplies. At about 10 p.m., I was heading up to the bridge. As I went past the captain's cabin, the door was open, and there I spotted a big stack of soft drinks. I quickly assessed the situation and managed to get six cases out and down into a dark hiding place. They stayed hidden for a couple of days while I gauged the reaction. Blow me down, I never heard nothing, so just before shift change one night, I pulled Richardo and John John aside and told them I had six cases of soft drink for them to share between the two shifts, but they had to keep it quiet because I stole them. Their eyes lit up. They thanked me, and I showed them where they were.

Over the next week, the change in their work mode was noticeable. Usually when we pull the cofferdams off and land them on deck, when I'm finished with the diving and the barge is being moved to the next location, I would have to go around both cofferdams and check for damage to the seal faces and then get Richardo and show him, and he would organise the work. Then I would have to check the rigging and do the same with John John. Not anymore. As I'm sorting out the dive station with the divers, and they would both come over, tell me the issues, and ask if I wanted it sorted, and then they would come and get me to inspect it all when it was done. Cool. I had definitely been lifted up a peg in their eyes, and everyone was generally happy.

We finished the last platform, demobed the barge in Doha, and said goodbye to all our Filipino and Indian friends. We sailed on a supply vessel with our dive equipment back to Dubai. During the trip, Larry pulled us aside and said he had some beers in the dive shack and would meet everyone after lunch. We had a few beers, a good laugh about run-off Jack, and other stuff. Then Larry mentioned the fact that after Jack had left, he couldn't believe how much faster the weld times were for the stub replacement. It turned out that for the last three projects, the standard time for the butt weld was four hours. The last two platforms, those times were halved, two hours, start to finish; both shifts, same weld times. I told him about the soft drinks and the general way they had been treated and the difference afterwards.

Years later, in a harbour called Chik Wan in China, I came off a vessel called the *Rocky 2* for Subsea 7. I was heading home, but the engineers on the beach needed a hand for a couple of days in the harbour mobing a barge with a riser and two spool pieces. They needed to be loaded and welded down and quite a lot of prep work. They were a man down, so I said I would stay back and help them. I had about twenty Chinese welders, riggers, and labourers. It was pretty funny actually because they looked like rags walking around. They really didn't like being in the sun. There were men and surprisingly a few woman welders. Shame I couldn't speak Chinese because they couldn't speak English, so communication was difficult. Anyway, when we nearly had this barge done, the engineer in charge was off into town for something and asked me if I wanted anything.

I said, 'You have another two barges to mob for this project, don't you?'

He said, 'Yeah.'

I said, 'While you're in town, get a whole lot of chicken and rice and couple of cases of cold soft drinks and give it to this crew as a thank-you. It'll be worth it.'

He returned with it. They were pretty impressed, and you could tell by the volume of talking and laughing that that didn't happen to them very often, if at all. The engineer said it didn't even cost US$50. A year or so later in Singapore, he recognised me and thanked me for the idea. He said it made the next mob a lot easier. Too easy, eh?

Anyway, back to 1987 in Dubai, we were sent out to crew another ETPM job—easy time plenty of money—and had the DB401 working in the DPC field, laying pipe and then installing risers and tie in the spool pieces. Towards the end of the job, I ended up working the same shift as Aubrey. He was my supervisor, and he came up to me as we were finishing the project and told me I had done some good diving. I thanked him because it meant a lot to me. When we first met, he had been one that was hell bent on getting rid of me and said he wouldn't dive if I was his standby. Now he would have me on any job. That was good for my confidence.

It was the end of August. My residence visa was to expire. Norbert, the Hydrospace boss, said he would renew my visa, and when I got my passport back, I returned home to Napier. I never worked back in Dubai again—well, so far anyway. Apparently, it is a different place now compared to then. I fly through all the time on my way to Aberdeen where I work now. One day, I will stop. Maybe.

Chapter 11

A BABY BOY AND A BREWERY

The flight from Auckland to Napier on my return was overbooked, and I ended up sitting between the pilots once we were airborne. What a bonus after the long trek home. It was early morning, and we left Auckland with sunny skies. There wasn't a cloud over the whole North Island. We could see Mount Egmont on the west coast, and to the East Cape and the Volcanic White Island in the Bay of Plenty was the only wisp of either smoke or cloud. It was a spectacular scenic drive, and the pilots let me stay up front for the landing. Far out, I never thought we would be coming in that steep. I was thinking, *Pull up, pull up*, ha ha. We landed smooth as.

A very pregnant-looking Christina was there to meet me and take me back to what would be our home for the birth of our first child. She had rented a lovely little 1930s one-bedroom house on the hill opposite the botanical gardens. It was old but cute, about the size of two matchboxes but with a bath overlooking the gardens. 'That was what I scored it for,' she said. And it was a spectacular scene from a deep hot bath that got a lot of use.

I picked up a job at an engineering company. Two weeks later, I looked at my first pay cheque and thought, *Holy shit, how am I going to survive on that!* That two-week wage I earned in three days offshore. There were a couple of guys that I knew from where I did my apprenticeship. The meat works had shut down, and work was tight. I started off in the welders workshop but didn't do so well there, and after getting told off by the foreman, he shipped me over to the mechanical workshop. Whenever he saw me, he looked the other way. I didn't care; I wasn't on enough money to care.

The surf was up one day. I organised with Damian that if it was still good at lunchtime, let's piss off to Waipatiki Beach for a surf. I called Christina from the workshop. All good. Damian picked me up from work, and we did a runner and got out to the beach, and an hour later, it went onshore, bugger. On the way back, we stopped into the Westshore Hotel for a beer. There was no one in there except us. After a couple of beers, the phone rang.

Damo said, 'That'll be for you. Christina's in the hospital.'

'Ha ha, yeah, right.'

The bar man looked around. 'Hey, mate, are you Damian?'

Damian took the phone. Christina's in the hospital. They had been looking for us for a couple of hours. He took me up, and I took over from Tracy, one of Christina's friends. Christina was swearing at me a lot over the next couple of hours. I started to sober up. So when the nurse was out of the room, I jumped on the laughing gas until she quickly came running back in. Not sure how I would have survived the ordeal without it. I mean, the abuse was totally uncalled for. I think Ryan was born not long after I was told off the second time for using the laughing gas. It was probably obvious because every time she came in, I was smiling and Christina was cursing. It was 4 November 1987 when Ryan joined our team. When I returned the next day, Christina was glowing and very impressed with herself and happy to have the little boy finally out.

About three weeks before Christmas, I spotted the boss of the engineering company handing out envelopes to some very depressed-looking guys. I could see by the body language that they were termination letters.

When he was alone, I walked past and said, 'How are you?'

He looked at me, looked at his little stack, and then said, 'Oh, could I have a word?'

I said, 'Are you walking around sacking people?' He looked a bit shocked. I said, 'Have you got one for me? Good. It will save me quitting.' He was a bit taken back and asked why I didn't like working there. I said, 'I don't mind working here, but the money is shit, mate. I'd rather be on the dole and go surfing.' I thanked him for the job anyway and shook his hand. He said he wished the others were that easy. I laughed and walked off. We had two weeks' notice. They had taken on extra workers to get a workload out to meet a deadline. I felt sorry for the other guys.

On my last day, the foreman for the machine shop whom I got along with really well rocked up at afternoon smoko and dragged me out to his car. He opened the boot. He's got an esky with some cold beers and all this treasure he'd found while scuba diving around Papua New Guinea when he worked in the mines over there. He had some amazing shit and said some of the portholes took a couple of months to get because they were so deep. A lot of shipwrecks from WW II. So we swapped stories over a few beers. I said 'see ya later' to the guys, and off I went.

Our first Christmas with a child was spent with family, and Mum loved it as mothers do. My brother asked me what I was doing, which was doing a few shutdowns now and then in the logging and pulp and paper mills for a guy that I used to work with at the freezing works.

He said, 'Why don't you set up a sole trading company and apply for a job with Lion Nathan Brewery? They are revamping the old Leopard brewhouse in Hastings. The manager of the project is a mate. I'll set you up with an interview.'

'OK, I said.

So Phil, John's mate, was overseeing the modification of the Leopard Brewery, basically changing from an old traditional style of brewing to a new style called high gravity. In essence, it changes what would have been, say, a thirty-thousand-litre tank that would ferment into thirty thousand litres of beer into ninety thousand litres of beer—basically concentrated. This new system opened the door to the craft beer error we have now. Anyway, it meant a lot of changes to the factory. Now, Phil had a team of stainless steel fabricators coming down from Auckland but wanted a local workhorse to help do all the prep work, steel work, and general labour.

I said, 'I'm your man.'

And he agreed, and so that was me, working twelve hours a day, eight hours on Saturday and Sunday. Pretty good money with a case of beer thrown in every two weeks. Once I got into the swing of things, I really enjoyed it. The Auckland crew were a good bunch of guys. I learnt to TIG weld stainless steel and got pretty involved with the whole job. My main area was the tank farm, and once I had completed installing two new thirty-five-thousand-litre tanks, I had a lot of stairways and walkways to put in, as well as pipe up all the cooling system.

Phil and I were looking over the project one afternoon, and he said, 'There's too much to do here. I need you to start the brewhouse. I need the roof off ready for the new brewer.' A few days later, he came up to me and said, 'I've got a guy coming to see you tomorrow morning. He's a foreman for an engineering company. Show him around and tell him what you need and what you want to get the tank farm going.'

'OK,' I said.

Next morning, I was welding some pipe, and the foreman from the welders bay that kicked me out and into the machine bay at the job before Christmas walked in and got the shock of his life. I got a shock myself when I realised who it was. Then I had a little laugh to myself at his discomfort when he realised whom he had to deal with. But I shook his hand professionally and took him around the area and told him whom and what I wanted, and he only had to deal with me a couple of times after that.

Lion Nathan and Dominion Breweries were both taking on this modern way of brewing and were shutting down some companies and revamping others. So the people at Leopard were really happy they were staying in business, and they fell over themselves to keep us happy. I really enjoyed that job and was there for over six months, about a month after the Auckland crew went home.

We were living in a rental house on Napier's Marine Parade, and it was a good spot. By then, I had dropped the hours down and was getting a bit more time with my young family. We had money in the bank again, and life was just cruising along. I got a phone call from my old boss Ian from Singapore, who was now in Tauranga.

'What are you doing?' in his boss voice.

'Hi, Ian, finishing off a construction project.'

'I need a diver. Do you want a job?'

'What's the story?'

'I've got a paua licence down at the Bluff, and I need some divers on the boat to knock it out."

'Where the hell is the Bluff?'

'It's down the bottom of the South Island, you dumb shit.'

'Oh, OK, um, why not? This job is about finished. When do you plan on kicking off?'

'I've got a couple down there now. So as soon as you can get organised, we will lock it in.'

'OK.'

So after discussions over a bottle of wine and a bottle of milk for young Ryan, we came up with another plan, and we moved into another phase of bumpy old life. Christina's parents lived in Tauranga, which has a lovely beach city called Mount Maunganui, which is pretty much where Christina grew up. The plan was we rent a place up there so she can hang out with her parents for a change, while I go down to the Bluff and knock the job out. Goodbye, family and friends in Napier, and hello, family and friends in Tauranga. After we got settled in, we had dinner with Ian and his wife at the yacht club and finalised the travel. I got some gear and flew to Invercargill. Where's that, you might ask, as did I? And this is the answer I received. 'The Bluff is the arsehole of New Zealand, and Invercargill is thirty miles up it.' Ha ha.

I got picked up by the captain of the boat I was working on, and we went to a house in the hills overlooking the Bluff Harbour. The weather is pretty full on, and it is hard to get out to get fishing. The deal is you cannot use anything but a snorkel, no tanks. You carry a specially-shaped knife and a bag, and you go up and down, up and down. When your bags full, you wave out to the Zodiac man. He comes over, and you dump the bag in the boat and then go and bust your lungs again until it's time to go home. Because the weather is so bad, it's really hard getting to good places to dive, so it is bloody hard work, and I was useless at it. In the three months I hung in down there, I got chased by seals and swept off reefs to be nearly lost at sea and basically had a hard time earning a living.

One of the guys working with us was from Dunedin, and when the weather was closed in, he took me there for a weekend. That is a pretty town with some real early settler heritage. I got a bit of surf there and hung out with his mates. Then all of a sudden, we hit a nice weather pattern. Two days of sunny light wind and low swell, and we were able to get out and get into some good ground. The first day, we hit a place called Centre Island, which, as you would expect, is between the South Island and Stuart Island. There was still a two- to three-metre swell running, but we found a bay that was not too rough and extremely picturesque. We got a long day in, and at the weigh in, we had pulled in 1.5 tonnes, plus Ian got money for the shell.

The next day was mint. We got down the west coast of Stuart Island and got into some bay, and it was all on. We came back with two tonne of chucked paua (chucked is when it is taken out of its shell; it is a pain in the arse, and we were chucking it all the way home, but that is how you sell it or did in those days). We also had a few crayfish to add to the day's catch.

I had a major ear infection from using the local swimming pool to build up my breath-holding fitness and decided to fly home and see the family and a doctor at the Mount. The flight really brought on the infection, and by the time I got to a doctor, I was going psycho. I told him my job, and I needed my ears back ASAP. He was going to give me a packet of antibiotics and ear drops.

I said, 'How about some heavy stuff like penicillin in a needle to kick-start it?' He said it was beyond that. I said I need all the help I can get, so he got it sorted.

The nurse said, 'This is going to hurt.' When she looked at the dose, 'What did you do to deserve this?' I laughed, but she wasn't wrong.

I limped out but had to get Christina to drive because I couldn't operate the accelerator. So the Mount is another of New Zealand's little gems, and Christina was enjoying being there but had some weirdo hanging around that was making her uncomfortable. The place we rented was not the scene she likes, so I made another one of my executive decisions.

'Let's pack up, and I'll take you to the Bluff with me.'

Next thing, the house is in the car, the boards are on the roof, we loaded Ryan in the back and drove from one end of the country to the other. I figured by the time we get there, my ears will be good enough to persecute them again. Well, I had never driven in the South Island before, so it was a bit of an adventure. We managed to get through Wellington and across on the ferry to Nelson for our first night stop. It was a long drive down the west coast between two mountains on what I think they call the Desert Road.

The next day, in the top of the South Island was a major difference with the coastal drive through Kaikoura along the coast through tunnels and farmland to Christchurch, almost seeming you are in a different country to the day before. Surfers are lucky here. They can be surfing in the morning and skiing in the afternoon. One thing about driving in New Zealand, there always seems to be a mountain range in the background. We stopped in Christchurch for the night and caught up with some of Christina's relations, and the next day was another planet, not just another country; large flat paddocks of brown grass and straight roads with the standard mountain range in the distance.

Christina and I were discussing how dry it was when the old trusty 1960s Holden special I had bought off my old man decided to go quiet. I looked at her. She looked at me. I put the car in neutral and coasted as far as we could while looking around the empty wilderness. Holy shit, no farmhouses around. I looked over the back at Ryan asleep in his car seat. Oh shit, for some reason, the situation feels that much heavier when you have a child to worry about. If it was just Christina, we would have laughed, had a joint, and gotten out and started walking. But I got out and didn't even lift the bonnet because I knew it was open heart surgery to some extent. I remember being worried as the time was late afternoon.

Then a car arrived in the distance heading our way. They gave me a lift to the next farmhouse. The farmer towed me to the closest town's garage, and then we booked into a motel and hoped over dinner that the next day's surgery wasn't going to give us real bad news. I told Ryan that it was a 1969 Holden engine. 'They are solid, young lad. It sounded like the timing chain, and I hope that's all it is.' He agreed and then threw up his milk, but that was OK because it was on Christina's shoulder, not mine, ha ha.

So the next day, the mechanic confirmed our fears and hopes, and said the parts are on the way and the old girl should be purring again by lunch tomorrow. Our unscheduled stop meant that we skipped Dunedin and straight to the Bluff with no fuss. You would have thought that Christina had landed on Mars. She is a beach babe, lying around sunbathing most days with just a bikini and a kaftan. Not in the Bluff, she reckoned. She was better off on the beach at the Mount looking over her shoulder for the weirdo.

The family we stayed with were very accommodating, but the weather just shut in, and Christina was not impressed and thought everyone had two heads and was really pissed off I dragged her down there. To top it off, Ryan got sick, and then to top all that off, we were having dinner with everyone and the house owner's brother was down from Invercargill. Christina asked if he had been in Auckland or anywhere else in the North Island, and he looked at her with disgust and said, 'What would I want to go there for? We have everything I like here.' I must admit he was a bit rude, and I don't think he was joking. Well, I didn't get a root that night, and I think it was a while before I got another one.

The weather never gave in. Ian turned up with bad news about the price of paua dropping and he had to let me go. I said, 'No worries. How about getting a word in for me in Singapore, and I might head back over there?' He said sorry for mucking me about and that he would make some calls.

I went back and told Christina we were leaving. She started bouncing off the walls with excitement. I said, 'Any chance of a root while you're happy?' She told me to piss off until the sun comes out. So house back in the car, boards on the roof, Ryan in the car seat. Goodbye, we are out of here.

We stopped at Dunedin on the way this time. I had to show her a few of the spots I had seen previously. We decided I would fly them out to Napier from Christchurch, and I would try and get a surf on the drive back. I pulled up at Kaikoura, but it was just a bit small but peeling off nicely. It looked cold, so I decided to hit Nelson and the Ferry. I just made the ramp on the last ferry out. I had a few beers and a sleep. When I got into Wellington, I had decided to go straight to Cape Palliser on the bottom of the east coast of the North Island. I woke up out the front of a house I hoped were some surf mates. No one was around, so I went looking for waves. It was small but looked like it was building. My mates had come in from the morning cray boats, and in the arvo, from about 2 p.m., Crap Point, a really nice left hander started breaking and by the late arvo was a nice four to six feet. I stayed the night with friends and headed back into Napier.

Christina had been looking at options to rent, and we moved into the best one at the time. Not long after that, I needed to get the money happening, so the decision to hit Singapore and look for a job instead of waiting for one at home was taken. When the time came to go to the airport and say farewell, I felt horrible, and my legs seemed to weigh a tonne. I said bye to friends, hugged everyone, Mum and Dad, and then Christina and Ryan, picked up my bag, and walked out. I totally lost it on the walk to the plane. Waterfalls were coming out my eyes; I couldn't talk or look at the hostess. I sat in my seat and tried to get my shit together.

A friend, Shane, was on the flight behind me and said, 'It's OK to cry, Spike.' I lost it again. I think to this day that was the worst farewell I have ever experienced. I don't know why, maybe it was the first real farewell to my own young family, I don't know. They never got easier; I just got harder to it, I think. Nothing has changed even now. I hate going to work. It's so overrated.

Chapter 12

THE ROAD TO INDIA

So I decided to stay at the Mitre Hotel in the city just off Orchard Road. It was very popular not just with divers but with a lot of other oilfield workers. There was always a diver or two there, and it was reasonably priced because it was getting run down. Not sure why the brothers that owned it didn't do it up; there were always people staying there. It was a neat building set back off the road amongst the trees with a big grass area off the front where the driveway stops at the entrance. During WW II, it was the allied officers' mess until the Japs took it over. I had been to a few good parties over the years, and sometimes, dive companies would call and ask the brothers if there were any divers there when they needed one in an emergency.

Once I dropped my bag down, I called around to get my finger on the pulse. Not a lot going on until Roo called one day and gave me a number for a company called Walter Williams in India and said he had just been talking to a lady called Sue who called him looking for divers. So I called Sue, and next thing, I was off to what was then Bombay. Man, you know when you are getting off the plane in Bombay. You know when you're a kid and your old man takes you to the rubbish dump for the first time, well, it could be argued that it is worse than that. I picked up my bag and made my way out of the customs area. There were people everywhere, and the place was humming, not just the smell but the noise, like bees on steroids.

I found a guy holding a sign with my name upside down, He was reasonably well dressed, wobbled his head as Indian people do when they welcome you, and motioned me to follow him. We stepped out of the airport, and everything intensified, noise, smell, and just everything—people, cars, car horns, buses, bus horns; it was bloody mad. I thought, *Jesus, has everyone come to the airport for the day?* But, no, it's like that all the way for nearly two hours in the car. There were over nine million people in Bombay at the time, and I think they were all between the airport and the beach where the hotel was, which I think was called Jamera.

I acclimatised to the smell and the heat but was bamboozled by the people and traffic, bikes, motorbikes, rickshaws, trucks, cars, and buses. Don't forget the tuk-tuks, all going anywhere they wanted with a loose meaning of road rules. I think the rule is do whatever you need to get where you're going, but try not to hit anything while you're doing it. Better mention the taxis. The black-and-yellow Premier Padmini taxis are everywhere and are iconic to Bombay. They are all the same. In fact, I think they bought one and then put it through a copy machine. Same shape as a 1960s Hillman or Humber. The hotel wasn't flash, but it had a bar, and I needed it—few beers, sleep, and wake up for an adventure tomorrow.

In the morning, I met a few other guys, and we were bundled into a car and taken on a two-hour drive across the city to an office where we met Sue, a Kiwi I was to find out later, and her secretary, Yasmine, a local lady. We filled out contracts and got told to go down to a restaurant on the corner where someone will pick us up and take us to the harbour to take a bumboat out to the vessel we would be working on. By the time we reached the vessel, we were all stuffed. It took ages going through customs and immigration down on the docks where you didn't know if someone was a worker or a beggar. I had never seen so much squalor in all my life. There is shit everywhere, and there is someone sleeping in the shit everywhere. It's bloody mind-boggling. One thing I learnt in Bombay—if you think you have seen it all, walk another hundred yards, and you are guaranteed to see something else that will rock your world.

The funny thing is, amongst it all, *if you look*, you will see smiling faces, colourful women, well-dressed boys and girls in school uniforms, and like kids anywhere in the world, when they see you looking at them, they turn to their friends and make smart remarks behind their hands and skip away laughing. But you have to look—look past all the madness that is the canvas of the Bombay picture. I sat on a wall in the harbour thinking this and staring down at the water when my eyes focussed, and I thought, *Shit, I hope I'm not diving in here.* I could go on and on for ages about that first trip out to a vessel in Bombay Harbour, but let's just get to the boat and say the trip wasn't much different than the one on the road.

We got on board the *Eastern Installer*, settled into our cabins, and met our shift teams, and the next day, we sailed out to Bombay High, one of the bigger fields offshore. The vessel is a DSV purpose built for diving with a built-in sat system. We have a full saturation dive crew plus us, the air dive crew. I knew a couple of people from Singapore and Dubai, and we settled in to work. I went down around the sat system the first time and looked into the chambers, got shown inside the dive bell, and thought, *No way, that looks pretty scary and intense. I don't like the look of that.* I remember a week or so later, when I was down there, I walked past a porthole; it's like a window. There on the outside was a cigarette and a lighter. I found out it was one of the divers in sat, and that window was where his bunk was. He could look at it every day and say to himself, 'I'm going to have that when I get out.' Is that mad or what?

Most of the work was sat diving, so we just mulled around on deck sending shit down to them, hooking things up on the crane and stuff. We got to launch the bell, and that was the highlight of the day. We did a couple of air dives to install a riser, but not a lot else happened. Stew was the superintendent. He didn't have a lot to say to us, but Pete was our supervisor, and he was pretty laid-back. We all got along well, and the days went on. Someone had some local whiskey and hash, so we used to get smashed after shift.

We met a couple of English guys that lived in Thailand; both called Mark. I worked with them both over the next couple of years until one passed away in Thailand. He had been bitten by a dog and left it too late. By the time they worked out he had rabies, it was too late, and he passed. The remaining Mark gave me the news. But for now, he is still alive, and we are having as much fun as you can on a boat in Bombay High.

As usual with companies that pay your airfares, they expect you to do a minimum time to recover some of the costs, and they expect you to hang around for sixty days. The first job went maybe three weeks, but they had another job lined up on a different vessel, so they put us in a hotel for a couple of nights. We managed to get to Leopold Cafe the second night. That was pretty cool; lots of backpackers, and the food was OK. Let's face it, they have been making curries that will blow your arse to bits and set it on fire for not hundreds but probably thousands of years, so when in Rome.

Over the curries and really bad Goldfischer beer, we heard the stories of the local clubs, mostly a place called the Slip Disc Bar. Apparently, the roof is so low everyone has to stoop over so they don't smash their heads on the roof beams. I actually never got there. But don't worry, I managed to find some equally entertaining spots in the years to follow. At the time, I was quite happy sitting in Leopold watching the world go by and the beggars get shooed away and contrasts of people and the colourful clothes. Don't forget the occasional cow—yeah, cow, or two. Don't ask me how you get a cow in the middle of the city, but we are in India. And I learnt not to question anything you see. Just look twice and touch it if you can. It will be real. After dark, a mate had scored some hash, so a couple of us went off down a side street that was dodgy. There were people everywhere just lying all over the place, and it was a bit scary, but after that, I went for a walk down to the coast to where the gateway of India and the Taj Mahal Hotel is.

We returned to the hotel pretty late, and the taxi drive is worth a mention. For some reason, they turn the lights off when there are no other cars on the road; no idea why, but bloody hell, that sobers you up. You get used to it after a while, but far out, they don't really drive that fast, but the street lights aren't very bright to start with, so every now and then, you forget about your burning arse and worry if the other guy driving at you with no lights on has seen you.

We survived and the next day went out to another vessel called the *Boa Canopus,* another purpose-built DSV. The superintendent was a real character, bit of a legend around the industry in this area; his name was Monsoon Boone. Mark from Thailand and I were on the same shift again, and we had some pretty funny moments with Monsoon, especially when he lost his voice from yelling so much and had to whistle to get our attention. Then this grated growly sound would come out.

One day, when shit was going wrong and it was pretty serious, Mark and I were rigging up this big buoy that we were installing when we heard this really bad whistle like a kid learning. We looked up, and there was Monsoon in his flip-flops and board shorts, holding this bit of rigging that was slowing pulling him over the side of the boat. Mark went running up to him, imitating a dog because we didn't actually realise how much trouble he was in. Anyway, he couldn't yell at us anymore, but he was pissed off, but we managed to save his arse. We laughed with him about it later. He said he hated us.

I'll have to tell you about the job we are doing so you can understand that although this was very dangerous, it was bloody funny at the time.

So we are installing these mooring buoys for vessels to wait on outside the field. There is this big anchor on the seabed with an engineered length of chain. We would send a twenty-tonne winch down to the seabed. The saturation diver would lock out, go over, find the chain, and hook it onto the winch. The winch picks it up close to the surface, and we transfer the load to a fixed thirty-tonne wire sling. The crane lifts the buoy into the water, and we tie it off next to the vessel. Then we get this big sheave block set up on the crane that is attached to the bottom of the buoy. When it's all ready, we jump two air divers and hook the other end of the sheave to the top of the chain. The winch is connected to the sheave block, and we slowly pull the buoy down until it is deep enough to connect to the chain. Sounds easy, right? Now you know why Monsoon has lost his voice, ha ha. It was complicated.

Anyway, we were on our third one and getting better at it when the bloody winch broke down. Normally, who cares—get the mechanic on to it and we go and have smoko, which we did. Mark and I were out on the back deck, and next thing, we heard this gruff voice going, 'Fuck, fuck, fuck.' We went running over to Monsoon in his flip-flops and saw that the thirty-tonne sling was so tight it's starting to tilt the vessel over, and the thrusters were starting to arc up to counteract the force. The bloody tide came in so fast in India that it had caught us out. Luckily, Mark and I had the crane driver in the crane, and we got him swung around and hooked into another link and took over from the job the winch was supposed to do. We reckoned Monsoon would have polished off a bottle of vodka that night. Anyway, we finally installed all the buoys with no loss of life and no vessels sinking. We headed in for a demob and remob for another project.

MY FIRST SATURATION DIVE

We said goodbye to Monsoon, and a few divers, a new superintendent, and a couple of supervisors arrived, and we sailed out for the field. To start, we were mostly air diving, and they only put one team in sat. When we had that part of the project finished, we went into sat mode, and the job was to cut an obsolete pipeline up into lengths that the vessel could retrieve to the deck of the boat. I got called up to Ian's, the superintendent's, cabin and got asked if I can Broco cut, and if so, did I want to go into sat? I said yes. He said he would put me in with Brent, one of my friends from the Dubai days. So Brent took me under his wing again and made sure I had what I needed to go into a saturation diving living chamber and that I had the necessary diving gear as well.

We blew into sat with another team. In those days, there were two divers per team, usually four in a chamber. When you locked off from the system to go to the seabed to work, you took turns at being bellman first and then diver first. Our first bell run, I went bellman. Brent came with me into the bell to do all the pre-dive bell checks and that way show me where all the safety critical valves and equipment are and gave me a quick run-through of the procedure. We locked off, and when we got down the bottom, I dressed him in, and off he went to get the job up and running.

I was left sitting in the bell, and I used the time to go over and over where the valves where, etc., and anything else to keep my mind off the fact that I was down in a saturation diving bell off the coast of India in about seventy metres of water, and soon I was going to have to put a hat on and go out there. At least my arse had stopped burning, but I think my pulse may have been up a bit. Eventually, Brent came back, and we swapped out. To tell you the truth, I can't remember a lot from that dive except the fact that I didn't feel I did very well. I cut a couple of sections of pipe. I remember it was muddy, and the vis was shit. But I wasn't that happy with my performance.

We eventually did our time and returned to the system, had a shower and food, and then went to sleep. I slept pretty well. When we woke up the next day, it was to the bad news that the vessel had blown an electric motor that had something to do with the thrusters, and we couldn't dive anymore so we were decoing. Bugger. That could have been my big break out of air diving and into the premier of money earning in the industry.

It wasn't as bad as I expected it to be, being shut in a steel tube about 1.8 metres in circumference and about four metres long with three other people, everyone talking like Daffy Duck, and getting food through a steel tube and having to ask for everything. Whatever you need, you push a call button, they ask what you want, you tell them, and they do it.

Ding dong!

'Yeah, what do you want?'

'Could I have a shitter flush, please?'

'Yeah, coming up.

Ding dong!

'Yeah, what do you want?'

'Um, can I trouble you for a pot of hot water, a pot of tea and some stickies?'

'Oh, come back on the last, didn't get that!'

'Yeah, some stickies, you know, biscuits or something.'

'Oh, stickies, why didn't you say? Do you need any milk?'

'Oh, no, we have milk.'

'Right oh, coming up.'

And eventually, the medical lock gets sent down, and in the lock is a pot of tea, a pot of hot water, and something to eat. For three days, we just lay around in our bunks reading books and listening to music on our state-of-the-art Walkmans. *On the big money.*

So we got out and were told it will be a few days before the vessel will be repaired. They had bumboats going to and fro, so we spent a couple of nights out in town getting up to mischief. The Kingfisher beer was so bad you actually got a hangover before you got pissed, so we started drinking Old Monks rum. I'm not a rum drinker but got used to it. When we sailed, we had another set of divers fresh up from Singapore. We were back out to continue the pipe retrieval, and when the sat teams came out, I wasn't on it. I thought I must have been bad so decided to go and see Ian. He was a nice bloke and basically said I was lucky to get in last trip because there wasn't much experience on board, and he reckoned I did OK. He said, 'I have experienced guys on now after the crew change,' and he has to put experience in first. He said, 'Don't worry, you'll get back in.' So that was me back on deck with the rest of the air divers smoking and drinking after shift and making the most of the warm weather.

As we moved from project to project, one of the supervisors was changed out, and the new guy happened to be on my shift. His nick name was Digger, and he was from Perth in Western Australia. We were chatting one day. He was a mate of Roo's as well. I told him I was back in New Zealand but wasn't ready to stay there and didn't know where to relocate to. He said, why not Perth? The oil and gas were about to pick up there, it has good surf, and he painted a pretty good picture, so I made another executive decision and sent Christina word to prepare to move again.

Around the end of March 1989, I finished my first season in Bombay High and flew to Perth knowing that Christina and Ryan were flying out of Auckland five days later. I stayed at Digger's place, and Shadida, his wife, made me very welcome and helped me get around to buy our first car, a 1973 Holden Kingswood, for $900 and sort out a place to stay. I booked an on-site van in a caravan park for a week not far from the beach.

Christina and Ryan arrived. Picking them up at the airport was unreal. It may have been close to three months, and Ryan had grown, but Christina was beautiful as ever. Perth is Christina's type of place with white sandy beaches, very clear blue water, and very hot sunny days. We looked for a place to rent and found a little unit up off Scarborough Beach and moved in the next week. I started looking for work but was enjoying the time down the beach even if it was a bit hot for me. Through word of mouth, we found friends from home and one of Christina's friends from her days in Brisbane and my mate Lance from Dubai that had moved to Perth. So we had a little crew that we could hang out with. There were also some divers I knew that lived in the west, so I kept in touch with them for opportunities in diving.

Dave, a friend from Napier, scored me a job delivering the green wheelie bins in the south city suburbs that brought in enough to pay the rent. Money was tight after a while, and I remember having to ring Craig more than once over the first three months to borrow enough money to buy baby food and/or nappies in between small pay cheques. I ended up getting a job with a hydraulics engineering company, and about three weeks later, a mate, Steve, called from offshore on the North West and said he had a job lined up for me if I gave his boss a call. I did that that night. Next day, I went into the union office in Fremantle and joined up, and a couple of days later, I had finally broken into the diving industry in Australia.

I flew up to Karratha and by helicopter joined a McDermott construction barge, the DB 17, out of Thevenard Island off the coast of Onslow. I caught up with some friends from Singapore and the Middle East. I'm pretty sure Pat was out there. I ended up on night shift with a small crew working out of a workboat stacking small grout bags under the pipeline where they had blown to much reef up. It's like an aquarium up on the North West Shelf, and every dive was good visibility and lots of fish. I think I was out there for two to three weeks, which once I was paid got us out of the occasional money borrowing that I had had to do. We moved out of the box on the beach into a little two-bedroom cottage overlooking a park with a short walk to Scarborough Beach, and life got a little easier.

It was about six months between diving jobs, so no wonder we were so broke. About this time, Roo had come down from Singapore to visit family and had lined me up to see a guy called Jim Philips, who ran Franmarine Diving Services out of Fremantle. Jim and I got along really well, and whenever I was home between jobs, I would call him and help out with local harbour work, which kept the wolves away from the door and meant I could still go surfing whenever I was able. We would clear the monofilament from the tuna boat fleet returning north from their runs down towards the Antarctic Circle and clean sea chests, polish props and hull, and scrub huge container vessels, which is like mowing a lawn upside down surrounded by water on a little hydraulic brush cart. Some vessels were so big you got lost underneath until you came to either the end or the side, got some light, and got your bearings back. At the end of the day, driving home with a beer in your hand, you were absolutely exhausted.

We did a lot of wet stick welding on harbours and vessels and did quite a few salvage jobs over the years with another hard-case guy called Roger from D1D2 who teamed up with Jim for a lot of projects around the Fremantle and Rottnest Island area. They were fun days with Clive, our supervisor, Drew, Andy, myself the main crew with a few other faces turning up now and then between jobs. It wasn't movie star wages like offshore, but the bonus was you were home every night, so with Ryan growing up, it was nice to stay closer to home.

I got my first real taste of outback Australia when I got a call from Oceaneering in Perth to crew a small job on a drill rig move off of Onslow in December 1989. We flew into town on a six-seater plane with a couple of the guys I had met in Dubai in 1984, transferred to a chopper, and flew out to a rig to be told to go back to Onslow because they weren't ready for us. We got put up in a workshop guest house, about a ten-minute walk out of town. Of course, as soon as we dropped our bags down, we walked into town to the only pub. It was probably mid-afternoon, and I guess you could say I met my first ridgy-didge aboriginals. Man, that was like being behind the scenes of a *Crocodile Dundee* movie, bloody funny.

They were shit-faced when we walked in. There were a few whiteys but about eight to ten abos or coons, or whatever you would prefer to call them. They saw us, and by the time we had ordered a drink, they had all moved over towards us and were checking us out. We moved away for a while, but they kept checking us out.

When I went up for my round, this big lady that was dressed like something out of World War II and looked like she had been hit by a bomb leaned over to me and said in the aboriginal accent that is so aboriginal, "Aye, boy, you wonna fluck me?' I laughed and said sorry, but I was a bit busy at the moment. She said, 'Maybe latter, then, aye, boy?'

I smiled at the bar lady, grabbed my beers, and went back to hide in the corner and pass on to the boys my little story. We all had a laugh. Not long after, the bar lady kicked them all out and came over to apologise, and we had a laugh. It turned out she was the local cop's wife, managed the pub, and was the town sheriff while her husband was away out bush, which he was at the time.

A couple of hours later, a few local abos (sorry, that's the local lingo) that work around town came in after work and joined in the bar activities. We played pool and had a laugh with them just like your normal country town folk. So you could say within a couple of hours, I had met two very different sides of the country aboriginal community— one functional, and the other not so. It was a very interesting time over those couple of days we spent waiting for the job and returning home. And I will never forget that first four hours in that country pub in the outback of Australia. I remember thinking how insanely barren the North West of Australia is when you are on land, yet put a mask and snorkel on, and, bam, totally different—it is teaming with life. A two-colour landscape, red and blue.

We had our first Christmas in Australia. Then I scored a couple of weeks for Oceaneering down in Bass Strait working on the platforms. The water was rough some days. It was teaming with tuna, and sometimes you could nearly walk on the water; there were so many circling the platforms. We were on night shift, and if the current was to strong and we couldn't dive, we would go and watch the platform operators that were off shift fishing for tuna. The seals were hanging around waiting to get them as well. We helped one guy pull his 110 kg blue fin tuna up sixty feet to the floor he was fishing off. They weren't allowed to fish off the lower floor, so they had these special lines made up with three big steel hooks that they would slide down the fishing line once they had the fish on the surface and too tired to fight anymore. The hooks would drop past the gills, and when you pull it up again, they would sink in, and then you had a half-inch rope line to pull them all the way up. Unless you were there, you wouldn't believe it.

My second trip out there, a diver called Roger from Melbourne had a Hawaiian sling with a lead weight on the barb end and a rope off the back. He was on the stairwell fifty feet off the water, and I said, 'What are you doing with that?'

He looked at me like I was a dumb arse and said, 'I'm fishing.'

I carried on down thinking he's lost the plot. Twenty minutes later, I see him walking along to the gutting table with about a fifty-kilogram tuna. Guess I was a dumb arse after all.

The whole time I was out there, I scanned the place for the white pointers everyone always talked about; they are bloody everywhere, they say—well, everywhere but where I was looking. I never saw one. The tuna fish seemed to be thickest when the current was running, and the current used to scream through sometimes the same direction for days, only slowing down at the change of tides. And it changed from platform to platform. So we moved around a bit. When we did dive, there were never as many tuna, which was a shame; it would have been pretty amazing diving through those layers of fish with the small ones on top getting bigger as it got deeper.

There was a hell of a lot of seals, though, and sometimes they were fun to watch, and sometimes they scared the shit out of you. One night, I was pushing the dive stage past the twenty-metre level, and all this fluorescence lit up on my right shoulder. I turned to look what caused it; nothing there. I turned left, and looking straight into my faceplate was a seal bigger than me and two inches from my face. It gave me a bloody fright; nearly shit myself. Then I laughed at how funny he looked. Huge eyes and big whiskers. Sometimes when you're swimming from one place to another, they would grab your fins for fun. Cheeky buggers. After a second two-week stint in Bass Strait, I was back home getting acclimatised to the wind and heat of a Perth summer. Then I got a call from Stena in Bombay.

Chapter 13

SATURATION DIVING

In the middle of March 1990, I was back in Bombay joining the *Essar Stena 1* with a mixed nationality of Kiwi, Aussie, Brits, Canadians, and some local Indians. Most of us had all worked together before. We had the usual night of playing up down the tourist strip and heading to the vessel with the standard Kingfisher headache and some funny stories. It was a big team with saturation and air diving crew. I was on the air team with a couple of guys I hadn't met before, but we had heaps of fun playing table tennis after shift. The boat was huge.

Pedro, a Brit, and I would have a few drinks and then play table tennis. Pedro was ex-Royal Navy and used to beat me, 21–2, 21–4, 21–3, game after game.

I said, 'You don't have to win every point, you know.'

He said, 'Yes, I do.'

Ha ha, bloody wanker, so I made myself get better, but I don't think I ever got more than eleven points on him before he would win.

After about three weeks, we both blew into sat but in different teams. My bell partner was a Canadian called Doug. The system had four living chambers, two wet pots, and a TUP, which led to the bell. Doug and I were in chamber 4 by ourselves. Doug was nowhere near as helpful as Brent had been. Brent had always given me good advice and encouragement. And honestly, when you're in this learning curve doing this type of work, the difference with your own self-assurance is amazing. It makes you more relaxed, and that gives you more time to think about what you're doing, and that, in turn, means you don't make so many mistakes. Less mistakes means less stress, and that gives you a full circle of control and comfort. Doug was a lot more close to his chest, told me enough to get by, and would bark when I did something wrong, roll his eyes, and, I got the impression, probably laughing at my insecurity.

According to my logbook, we were stored at fifty metres and dived to fifty-five metres putting on riser clamps and working mid-water on my first dive, so not really much different to air diving except we were gone from the system for nine hours. So I would have done four to five hours in the water, and you can bet your arse after getting back to the system having a shower and a feed, I would have slept like a hibernating bear.

So the days ticked by. From what I remember, we mostly had reasonably good visibility, and most of the bell runs were just working away with nothing to say. But there were a couple of things that happened. The first is a funny one about hermit crabs. We were doing pipeline spans, and I was on the seabed waiting for the supervisor to make a decision, and out of the corner of my eye, I saw an orange peel—you know, when you peel an orange in a circle. Well, it was walking along the seabed. I went over, and there was this hermit crab that had decided to shed a decent shell and climb into this as its new house. I couldn't show the supervisor because in those days, we had no cameras on the hats. But we had a laugh when I told him. Well, the next day, I was doing a video survey of the same area, and I kid you not, there was a bloody banana peel walking along the seabed. Sure enough, another hermit crab or possibly the same one, I don't know, was going vegan as well. Thirty years on, I've never seen it since.

The other memory I have of that first major sat job was when I had to do a video survey of a pipeline that a barge had possibly done some damage to. We started at the J tube, which is the transition piece from the riser to the pipeline running away from the platform. I locked out, and the visibility was pretty murky. There was a tonne of baitfish so much so that they were getting squashed in these useless black dot gloves that we used to wear. It was bloody horrible. By the time they sent me down the video camera, I had to take the gloves off and turn them inside out to get the squashed fish out and put them back on. In the end, I had to give up because it was constant; I just had squashed fish in my gloves the whole time. But that wasn't the main drama; no way, it gets better.

As I was going over to establish the J tube and get ready for the video, two large barracudas turned up—I'm talking about over a metre long, and because of all the baitfish around my light and the shiny stainless steel around my hat, they started stalking me. As I was slowly walking out from the platform filming the pipeline, all of a sudden, I would get hit in the head by one them flying in attacking the baitfish. Over the next three hours, it was sheer hell as I was attacked front and back. They would fly past the light and straight into me. All the commotion brought in a couple of sharks. They were only small, but they were still sharks, and sharks were very scary to me back then because you didn't see many. Well, needless to say, there was a lot of swearing as you would expect. Eventually, the sun came up, and it got lighter down on the seabed, and the baitfish went off to annoy something else, and finally, the walking in hell was over. My logbook says I did 611 hours (twenty-five days) under pressure and I did eighteen bell runs. It was my first real working sat.

Doug and I got along OK, and when we stepped out of the chamber, the vessel was in Bombay Harbour. We all ended up getting on the piss in one of the cabins, and then Pedro and I went down to play table tennis. He was so pissed I beat him 21-5, 21-7, 21-3.

I laughed and I said, 'I don't have to thrash you, but I'm going to anyway,' ha ha. Good bloke Pedro.

So the next day, we went into the office to pick up our pay and plane tickets. Andy, the boss, saw me and started going off at me. 'The language you used in that video was appalling. The superintendent has spent three hours overdubbing it. It's a bloody disgrace.' I said sorry, and he stormed off. I looked at Sue, his wife and secretary, and Yasmine, Sue's Indian secretary, and they laughed and said they thought it was pretty funny watching me get attacked over the three hours. I said, 'Yeah, pretty funny looking back but wasn't funny at the time.'

That afternoon, instead of joining the party team in the tourist strip, I went for a walk to look for a set of earrings for Christina. I came across shop after shop of jewellery and spent two to three hours buying some really amazing bracelets, earrings, rings, and necklaces for really good prices because I bought quite a lot from each shop. It was the start of a trend I would carry on with in a lot of countries I visited. I would get home, and Christina would paw over everything, pick out the stuff she loved mostly for herself, and then pick out presents for friends that had helped her while I was away. Then she would sell the rest at nearly half what you could buy them for in the markets in Perth. Usually, I would get close to the money I spent back—meaning, Christina's and her friends' gifts were paid for. We found over the years that if you kept the prices to $20–$30, they would run out the door. Some of the heavy, beautiful bracelets but pricy took a bit longer to move. Necklaces also took longer, but rings and earrings, I couldn't bring enough home. The best quality and most amazing jewellery were in Mexico. That stuff was solid and absolutely beautiful.

So returning home, life went on, and over the next eight months, I mainly worked locally for Jim with an occasional offshore run up north. I met my first big grouper on the bottom of the *Vicksburg*, a jack-up drill rig offshore from Onslow. I was cleaning along the welds on the spud cans (the feet of these giant legs). They were covered in mussels, so there were fish everywhere getting a free feed. The mussels were so big that I brought some to the surface and opened them up. The colours inside were amazing, and I picked the best, cleaned it up, and dried it out to take home. When open and together, it was like a pearl butterfly about 300 mm across. It got a lot of comments over the years until it finally disappeared.

Anyway, back in the water, all of a sudden, I was slowly getting pushed into the leg by this spongy weight. I turned around, and it's a huge grouper. God knows how much it would weigh, but it was twice my size. I had to keep pushing it away to continue work. It was funny it seemed like a game to him. With the jack-up being so high off the water, it took a while going down on the stage before you hit the water.

One day, I was about ten feet from hitting, and I came to a sudden stop. I looked up to see what the issue was. There were three of my mates looking over the side. I looked down, and there was an eight-foot tiger shark right underneath me. Holy shit. They carried on down as soon as it was out from under me. They said later they were laughing, waiting for me to scream when I hit the water. I hid as far back in the little stage as I could, but it just carried on until it was out of sight. Needless to say, my eyes were going everywhere that dive.

One night on the *Vicksburg*, I was outside looking over at the flare stack, watching a pod of dolphins playing around, and I noticed they were being stalked by a three-metre shark. It was just lazily shadowing everywhere they went. I decided that the myth that if you see dolphins there are no sharks around may not be the case.

Over the next twenty-five years of working the North West Coast oilfields, I would grow to love the interaction and look forward to the harassment of the sharks that live in this area. Funny enough, originally, they used to stand off in the edges of our sight as if they knew how far we could see, but as the oilfields grew and we became more frequent, they got bolder, and sometimes it was fun and sometimes it wasn't. And we grew to notice their different moods and when to be more aware. You could tell when they were feeding. Like electricity in the water, your senses changed with the fish around you. Everything starts to move differently, jittery, and even if you can't see them, you know they are hunting, and the fish around you are darting here darting there. You can't see why, but you know why, and your arse gets twitchy, and you're not just running around; you're now in stealth mode trying to keep large structures in close proximity in case you need to hide. And as the years go by, you get used to that as well. There are a few good shark stories on the way over the next few years, so I'll move on.

In December 1990, I received a call from Sue in Bombay. (Funny, you know, in those days, people used to ring you; now they just send e-mails. I do miss the phone calls). Anyway, they were crewing a job in Cameroon in West Africa and asked if I was interested.

'Hell, yeah,' I said.

'OK, I'll be in touch with mobilisation info.'

We had to get a thousand needles jabbed into us and all that, and could you believe it, but two days before Christmas, we flew out of Perth to Bombay. We all converged at a hotel and were given our flight and joining instructions, and then like a gang of deviants, we headed back to the airport. We were heading to Douala in Cameroon via Nairobi in Kenya. The flight out of Bombay was delayed by three or four hours, and we missed our connecting flight direct and had to wait overnight to take a flight through Addis Ababa in Ethiopia, where we would spend Christmas Eve, and on Christmas Day fly into Douala. This was really cool, a nice little tourist trip on the way to work. We landed and finally arrived in the hotel by lunchtime, and a small crew of us embarked on a look around.

The Addis Ababa markets are supposed to be the biggest in the world, someone said, so off we went. And that was pretty amazing and pretty hot. The drivers stopped on a hilltop lookout on our way in so we could see how big they were. And they were. They stretched for miles, and I think we only covered a small area. We moved quickly through boring areas, and slowed down through the interesting ones, making sure no one got separated and lost. The colours of the materials, beads, and jewellery were all noted and talked about as we moved through the tight walkways pushing past vendors and buyers with an occasional noted tourists like ourselves, although we did stand out as there were six or eight of us. I don't think anyone bought anything; it was all just looking.

We moved into the fruit and vegetables and then came into the spices and herbs, and by the time we managed to find an end to a tight alleyway, our noses were burning with the intensity of all the different aromas. We were hot and thirsty, called it a day, and went back to the hotel for a well-deserved swim and a beer. The other half of the crew were already drunk around the pool, so we dived in and joined them.

At dinner was the discussion of 'Where shall we go? What shall we do? It's Christmas Eve.'

Most the answers were 'I'm not going anywhere, too dangerous with government forces patrolling the city keeping their eyes out for troublemakers.' They were having trouble with someone probably anti-government at the time; they probably still are.

A couple of the team were keen to go out. 'It's Christmas Eve. There's a club up the road. Let's go for a look.' So I joined in.

It was still light when Roger, Doug, Sheldon, and I walked out of the hotel and down two blocks to a nightclub. Roger had decided to bring a bottle of Red Label Johnny Walker with him, but he wasn't allowed to take it in and had to leave it at the counter. Everyone was friendly, and after the usual 'Where are you from,' 'Why are you here,' and a few laughs, we trundled down this stairwell to a dark bar full of cigarette smoke and African-style rock music. It wasn't super crowded. We found a table and got the beers over and settled in. We were pretty much just crowd watching until Doug brought over some women he picked up at the bar, or should I say they picked him up.

Anyway, a bit later on, it's getting a bit boring, and one of the girls suggested going to the Hilton Hotel because there is a high-end nightclub there. 'Shit, yeah, you should have said earlier.' We walked out. Roger got his Johnny Walker back. We jammed into a taxi, and off we went. We went in, but the door was shut. The bouncer said it was a midnight curfew and the doors were now closed; no amount of persuading would open the door. We should have come earlier, he said. Oh, shit. So we went to get a taxi. No taxis. Why not? Midnight curfew. No way. We were stuck in the car park of the Hilton Hotel. It was twenty past midnight and no way of getting back to our hotel.

Roger was passing around his Johnny Walker when this Peugeot station wagon pulled up next to us. A guy fell out of the driver's seat and staggered over with a bottle of Black Label Johnny Walker, saying "Merry bloody Christmas," chinked the bottle with Roger's, and sculled a big mouthful.

His mate got out, and we were all cheering and sculling when one of them said, 'We going to party. You join us.' No was our original answer, but they said if we go with them, they would drop us at the hotel afterwards, and after a few more sculls, we decided it was the only way to get back. Doug wasn't going to leave his four women behind, so with the driver, his mate, and their girlfriends, plus eight of us, we all crammed into this Peugeot station wagon that had an extra row of seats in the back, where I lay along the laps of the four squashed in the back seat.

With a scull of whiskey, the driver took off and headed out the gate. *Bam, bam.* What the fuck was that? Sheldon, who was sitting on the middle row left side, said it was the security guy shooting at us to stop us from leaving. Holy shit, the mayhem started. The driver honked his horn and put his foot down, and we disappeared up the road as fast as a car with eleven people could go. There was a main intersection with an army patrol in the distance, and three hundred metres before that, he swerved right down a dirt road that went up into the hills dotted with what looked like houses. Over the next hour and a half, we went from place to place, banging on back fence gates. We got out a couple of times for a piss and a look around and another scull of whiskey. The driver was really pissed now, so his mate took over, but I think he was worse.

After our third near car accident, we had stopped on top of a hill overlooking the city. The moon was up high, and it looked quite tranquil. The guys said they have one more place to try. We had finished the whiskey. We climbed back in the car. It was starting to smell of burning rubber because the drive shaft was spending a lot of time spinning against the chassis. We went down a hill full tilt and flew up the other side around a corner, and he slammed the brakes on, turned the lights off, and stopped on top of the hill. The car really stank now. I was looking over the shoulder of the girlfriend who had had enough. Down below were two main roads with an intersection with a few soldiers looking up our way. All of a sudden, he put his foot down. We lurched off the top of the hill, bouncing down this dirt track. I hit the roof about four times, knocking the wind out of me. I looked down through the windscreen and at the main road we were racing towards. There was a soldier with an AK-47. The driver hit the lights and his horn. The soldier dove out of the way as we hit the road and turned left. The other guy was leaning out the window, yelling, 'Merry fucking Christmas!' as we snaked our way up the road, dust, and burning rubber. We were waiting for guns to go off.

Next thing, he hung a right, and we disappeared up another back road into another suburb of large wooden houses hidden amongst the trees. We stopped at someone's gate. A German shepherd came running around the car.

The driver talked to a guy, got back in, and said, 'Just up here, one more place.' We got there; no one answered, and they finally gave up the hunt. 'Sorry, man,' they said, 'we cannot find a party.'

We all said at the same time, 'Oh, never mind. Could you drop us at the hotel?'

'Yeah, man,' they said.

And off we went down onto a main road, turned this way and then that, and finally the hotel. He swung into the driveway and stopped at the entrance and, bang, three AK-47s stopped anyone from getting out. The soldiers looked into the car, saw us, and motioned us to get out, no one else. We clambered out, put smiles on, and explained to one that looks like the boss the situation that got us there. He nodded and told us to go inside. We shook the two drivers' hands, said thanks, wished them Merry Christmas, waved to the girls, and got into the hotel before anything turned bad.

I went up to my room, which overlooked the entrance. I had a case of VB I had bought at duty-free, so I cracked one to celebrate surviving the ordeal. I looked out the window, and there was Doug talking to the head soldier. I went down to make sure he wasn't getting in trouble.

'What are you doing, Doug?'

He said, 'They are still holding the girls.'

I said, 'Leave it, man. They'll be all right.'

The boss soldier was saying, 'Go, go.'

I said, 'Come on.' But he wouldn't give up.

They finally let them get out as I watched from the window. They searched them. Then the car started up, and they were allowed to leave. I laughed as the smelly broken car ambled out and disappeared up the road. Merry Christmas.

I hung the rest of my carton out the window to keep it cool and crashed out. What a radical night. Still alive and loving it. Christmas Day, the carton of VB was gone by the time we checked in for our Ethiopian Airlines flight. We boarded the plane and then got an hour delay on the tarmac; by which time, Sheldon had organised us all Bloody Marys until we had drunk all the vodka on the plane. The hostesses were awesome putting up with a crew of young divers and their support crew. We took off, fell asleep, and got woken up for Christmas dinner mid-flight. While we were eating, the first-class hostess that had given us a bottle of vodka earlier came down with the first-class trolley with steaming hot turkey and asked all of us if we wanted any. The rest of the passengers' eyes lit up, only to be ignored after we were fed. Bloody classic. I think the three hostesses enjoyed our Christmas fun that day.

So we finally arrived on board the *Stena Wellservicer,* the latest DSV working in the North Sea. It was like being dropped off in a Mini and then getting picked up by a Mercedes. After doing vessel inductions, we were told the sat teams. I got a bit of a shock to see my name down in one of the teams with a friend Mark and a Scottish guy called Dave, or Davey as everyone called him. This vessel was set up for three-man sat teams—meaning, two divers lock out and work together, getting a hell of a lot more work done than a single diver. As we sailed out, we were run through the system and shown the set up and what was expected of us and blew into a six-man chamber with another team of divers. We worked a shift pattern, and when it was our turn to dive, Davey went bellman so he could show us the ropes and get the ball rolling. It was pretty good having another diver out in the water with you; definitely got a lot more work done and had some fun at the same time.

On our return, our team was in the chamber by ourselves because the other team was out diving. Davey being bellman had the last shower and cleaned up the wet pot. Mark and I were sitting at the table when Davey climbed through and joined us at the table. He ordered a pot of hot, a pot of tea, and some milk.

The LST came back on the comms and said, 'Sorry, Dave, what was your last?'

'Milk,' he said in his strong accent.

There was silence. Then the LST came over. '"Sorry, Dave, I didn't get that. Could you tell me one more time?'

Dave said, '*Milk*, how now brown coo,' in his heavy Scottish accent.

Mark and I pissed ourselves at the way he pronounced 'cow'. The order came into the chamber, and we made our drinks as he started a story about him and a couple of mates.

'I was in India last year, and me an' a couple of mates bought some precious stones, used dry ice spray to numb our cocks, slice a cut, slide the stone in, and we only had to do three stitches and a bit of Loctite and good as gold after five days.'

We decided Davey was a mad bastard, but, shit, he was funny. His accent was so strong half the time we didn't know what the hell he was saying.

The job was going pretty well, with visibility average, until one day, Mark and I were tying in a twenty-inch pipeline to a spool piece. We couldn't see our hand unless it was on the faceplate of our diving helmet. I'll never forget it because it was the first but not last time I had to dive with my hands, not my eyes. It took ages for us to do anything. When we started putting bolts in, I would keep one foot by the pipe, lean into the basket, get a bolt, move my hand along the pipe until I grabbed Mark's hand, and then would hand him the bolt. It was slow-going, and by the time we had it all bolted up and derigged, we were getting pretty tired. I was in the mud down the pipe trying to get a sling out from around it. My head was on top when the supervisor asked Mark to head down to a pipeline crossing and then come all the way back and make sure we have left nothing behind. He stood on my head as he went past. It was the only time we laughed the whole dive.

A few days later, we were out walking along following the boat while it was doing a survey with the ROV. All of a sudden, I seriously needed to have a shit—and I mean real bad. It had happened in India the previous sat, and I had tried to do it in my hand to get it out of my wetsuit, and it hadn't worked very well. I ended up stripping off my bailout and dropping my wetsuit. In India, I was out there by myself, and we had no cameras on the hats, so no one knew what I was doing. While the vessel was moving, I hatched a plan—I'll lag back a bit and get some distance between me and Mark, and when we stop at the next spot, I'll quickly dump my gear, have a dump, and get it back on.

The vessel stopped. I was already half undressed. I dropped the bailout and harness, ripped my hot water suit down, pulled my pants down, and just exploded with relief. Then all of a sudden, my umbilical went tight—the vessel was taking off again.

The supervisor said, 'Moving twenty metres ahead.'

'Roger,' we said.

I grabbed my bailout off the sea floor, jumped over a pipe, and struggled to keep up with my pants half down, my suit around my ankles, and my bailout under my arm. Message to self: make sure you go for a dump before going on a six- to ten-hour bell run. And, yes, every diver that is reading this would have a similar story.

We finished the Cameroon work, and they decoed three of us so that they could put in three others for a pipeline repair down in the Congo. I was lucky enough to get out of sat as we were still sailing down, and as we were going over the equator from north to south, they had a King Neptune party on deck for all those that had never been over it before. Mick, one of our supervisors, was dressed as King Neptune and governed the festivities. Obviously, an old mariner's thing. The weather was pretty nice. We were all on the back deck with a barbecue and cold beers. There were whales blowing off all around us, and it was pretty surreal actually. After a few beers and with the sun going down, I sat on the helideck watching the breaching whales and the sun going down and thinking, *How good is this?* I couldn't believe how lucky I was. The crew on the *Wellservicer* were really good and told us if we wanted a job in the North Sea, to look them up. And a couple did, and I should have too.

When we finally arrived back to the harbour off Douala, we left the Mercedes on not a Mini but more like an old Austin. Ha ha, we broke down three times heading in. What should have been a half-hour took nearly two hours. We partied at the hotel that night under strict instructions not to leave the hotel because of student unrest, and if we get locked up, 'no one will be here to save you.' So we promised we wouldn't, and two hours after they left, we were bored with the hotel, so we all went out clubbing, but everyone made it back, and we all made our flights home. It was a pretty neat trip for that job. Thinking about it, after the vessels I had been used to by then, the *Wellservicer* wasn't a Mercedes; it was more like a Jaguar.

Later that year, we had completed a Stena job on the *Seahorse*, a Stena DSV in Australia, and while on our transit back to Singapore, we got the shocking news of the sinking of the McDermott barge in the South China Sea. The barge had a sat system on it with four divers stuck inside and apparently only forty feet from the surface when the barge started sinking and had to be abandoned after being caught by a typhoon. They were on an emergency deco but unfortunately ran out of time. A good friend of mine from Dubai, Boyd, was the supervisor on shift when they had to abandon the barge and leave the guys behind. Apparently, Boyd was at the porthole crying sorry to the guys inside when they dragged him into the lifeboat forty minutes before it rolled over and sunk, killing the divers that were left behind. Sixteen lives were lost. It wasn't Boyd's fault, but he never forgave himself and apparently drank himself to death within three years. I was quite sad when I found out because Boyd was a good bloke and a good laugh. We had worked and played together a lot in Dubai. He was collateral damage created by people making bad decisions that possibly never faced the consequences, although the captain lost his life trying to save the vessel and personnel as well.

Chapter 14

THE SURF IS BIG DOWN HERE

So as money started to build up in the bank, we finally managed to buy ourselves a half-decent car that we could trust to get us down to Margaret River, the famous surf area of Western Australia. I scored us a red Holden Commodore station wagon, much to Christina's disgust: (a) she hates red cars; and (b) she hates station wagons. But I thought if we were going to chase waves down south, we needed the room. It was a good car and serviced us well.

Our first trip south was an eye-opener for the vastness of Western Australia. And we only went down the road in reality. Three hours after driving out of Scarborough, we drove into Yallingup and the caravan park on the beach. We scored an on-site van overlooking the surf. It was a setup that suited us, and we used the format for years, and I guess still do. I would get up early, chase the waves, and come back just after lunch at the latest if the surf was on. By then, Christina and Ryan would have been at the beach and returned for lunch. We would head off to check the coast, do the art galleries, a couple of vineyards, etc., and get a bush walk in. The area has some really neat spots to check out. The caves, of course, are worth doing at least once. The Kauri Forest, further south by Conti's, is a lovely forest drive if you get off the main road and do the bush track.

The main township of Margaret is really cute and worth a walk along, have a beer and a wine at the pub, and then amble back for the drive back through the wine country to the coast. The waves that hit that coast are plentiful and powerful. The average size is a lot bigger than most other places you will visit. But the main break at Margaret River's surfer's point is a real moody beast—one day, spirit lifting; another day, soul destroying. It can be majestic in the morning and ugly in the afternoon. When it's big and you've just come in, you can just sit in the car park and watch people face their fears. Whether it's surfing or kite surfing, it's a challenging surf break, and if you want to challenge yourself, there is no better place to practice. After our first trip down south, I had been forced to realise my board was not going to be big enough to handle the size and power of the south-west. I had already gone from my 5:11 that was shaped in South Africa to a 6:2 shaped back in New Zealand. My first surf at Margs went OK; it was big but not the biggest I had surfed, but it was powerful and fast, and I copped a thrashing a few times for not getting on them quicker.

I think it was over the following year that a French company called Coflexip bought out Stena. They had a new product that was perfect for the development of the numerous small pocketed oil and gas fields of the North West. The product was flexible pipe and was an asset that could be laid off the back of boats as well as barges, and when fields were depleted, they could be recovered at a fraction of the cost of conventional hard spooled pipe. Coflexip moved into Singapore and Australia, and Digger's prediction back in India started to come into fruition.

But around town, I had picked up a job for a South Australian company digging a trench for a water outflow pipeline off ocean reef on the northern suburbs. We were using a big digger that was converted into hydraulic from diesel and was a bit of fun. Pity it was winter with the cold, but the front veranda got filled up with some amazing shells, and I ended up in the local paper again. The previous time was climbing out in Fremantle Harbour after a sheep had jumped off a ship and we had saved it. Wet sheep are bloody heavy. I was doing a prop polish, and the poor thing landed twenty feet from me.

Around the same time, if not a little earlier, Matt and Roo had broken away from Oceaneering and started their own diving company called Divcon. When they started getting work around Asia, I would go up to Singapore and help mobilise their small sat systems that we would lift onto small oilfield service vessels and weld them down and get them up and running. They were fun days, and we used to get up to heaps of mischief, especially when Bill and Tony were around. Roo kept losing his driver's licence because Bill would be driving around in his car going through red lights and saying, 'Smile for the camera,' ha ha.

We were heading into Far East plaza one night. We were at Holland Village having some beers and went to get a taxi. As we walked past a money changer, I thought I'd change some US dollars. There was a Sikh behind the counter. I said, 'Are you a money changer?' He nodded yes. I gave him a $50 Singapore note and asked him to change it into a hundred. He wasn't impressed, but we pissed ourselves. He gave me a shit rate after that, but I apologised and left him some change.

Bill bought a cheap two-wave radio so he could listen to the Kiwi versus Australia Rugby International, and he would walk out of the bar and come back ten minutes later and tell us the score.

'How we going?' I said.

He said, 'I might have to take it back and get my money back.'

'Why?'

'It keeps giving me the wrong score,' he said.

We did some really good jobs, and I worked with a lot of different people. One job I flew over for was on a vessel called the *Balinator*. The job itself, I don't remember much; but the return to Singapore I will never forget. We arrived into Batam Island, a small Indonesian island not far off Singapore's coast. We were to get our entry visas for Singapore there. They booked us on the ferry because they didn't want to wait for the immigration to open. We got dumped off and told to wait. The trouble was the ferry they booked us on was the late afternoon one to make sure immigration got us sorted from working in Indonesia's waters. They dropped about fifteen divers and a couple of engineers at a cafe restaurant right next to a duty-free shop. By 10:30, there was no cold beer left, so we were buying duty-free whisky, vodka, rum, you name it. By 2:30 p.m., they had run out of Coke and every other mix you could add. There was no ice left on the jetty. There was no one else except us in the cafe. We were having heaps of fun, a few small play fights, with tables getting bold over, etc.

One time, I was having a piss, and the Norwegian engineer was in there with wide eyes, saying, 'I do not believe this.' I just laughed and went back out and helped pick up some broken glasses.

The restaurant started to freak out, but then we just bought all their food. They went off and got us some more ice and Coke. We finally boarded the ferry and departed. Then shit really went south. Halfway across, someone needed a piss. They saw Shane's gum boots and thought it would be funny to just piss in them. Shane started abusing him. Then Barry thought it was a good idea and grabbed his other boot and pissed in that. Then he went charging up the aisle, swinging his dick around all over the place.

I thought, *Oh, no, this is getting out of hand.* Someone else threw a chair at him. Tony was the supervisor. He was sleeping behind me. I looked at Phil, who was sitting beside me, and said, 'This is not good.' When I turned back to say something else, he was gone. *Good idea*, I thought and grabbed my bag and sneaked out the back and up to a back deck. There was Phil hiding in the dark. I said, 'The shit is going to hit the fan. I bet the cops are waiting when we arrive.' He agreed with a lot of worry on his face.

As we approached the ferry terminal, it was dark. We couldn't see any cops, but we held back to see if there was any drama. Nothing. We grabbed our bags. I woke Tony, and we got the hell out. We went from hotel to hotel but couldn't get a room anywhere. Tony called Roo, and we went and crashed at his place.

In the morning, Tony woke me up and said, 'What the bloody hell happened on the ferry last night?'

I said, 'Dunno. Why?'

He said, 'Roo is in the police lock-up in Raffles with something like thirty police charges against him.'

I said, 'No shit.'

Half hour later, we were told to get into the office and pick up our pay. Roo was out on bail pending an investigation, Barry was flown out on the first flight they could get him on, and everyone one else scattered. Roo's lawyers managed to get most of the charges thrown. Divcon had a sad on for all of us until they needed us again, and life moved on.

Chapter 15

A Home to Return to

I was working more frequently with Franmarine doing a lot of harbour work to fill in the cash flow and save some money. We were over the park one sunny afternoon and met a couple walking their dog. We had seen them a bit the last couple of weeks, and when I asked what he was up to, he said they were staying at his mother's house while they build a new one in Hillarys, a suburb not far up the coast. I said I wouldn't mind buying a house but didn't like what I could afford. He said the house he and his wife renovated and sold is up for sale again. He said the guy was doing a private sale and that he knew how much he paid for it, so I should just offer him that.

Christina and I talked about the options—buy here or move to the east coast to be closer to family in New Zealand. She said, 'You can move to the east coast. I'm not. I'm staying here.'

The next day, we went around and knocked on the door of this wood fibre house set amongst a group of trees that had a nice family aura to it. He said he was selling and showed us around. It was perfect really. All we needed was enough money. I went into the bank and found out how much they would lend me, which fell $10,000 short of what the guy told us he wanted and which was what he paid for it. After exhausting all avenues, I went around to the guy's house and asked him if he was interested in doing a deal. We were meant to have the house because he agreed that I could give him $110,000 to take the keys, and I had six months to come up with the last $10,000. I paid the last $2,000 a month early. But we would be very broke again for a while, while we got our feet and built the bank account back up. Now we have a home, and Christina turned it into a very homely home at that. Christina became pregnant.

I was still doing some long stints away in India and through Asia. Divcon had picked up a contract to supply the divers for a company called OPI that had just bought all Brown & Root's old barges and moved into Asia, and this was their first big project. I was never really on that many barge pipelay jobs, and, man, they can get boring. We mobilised the barge with an antique sat system similar to the one on the very first job I did and sailed off to the South China Sea off the coast of Malaysia.

The cooks were pretty good, but one was a pastry chef, and all we did was sit around while they laid pipe, smoked cigarettes, and ate pastries, and then smoked more cigarettes. By the time we were getting put into sat, I was sick of it and decided to give it up. I thought if I could get the jump of having twenty-six to twenty-eight days locked up, it could be all I needed to drop the habit. I gave all my smokes away. I blew in and about twenty-seven days later came out. Within twenty-four hours, I was buying another carton off the bond on the barge, and within three days, I was back to twenty-five to thirty a day and feeling shit again.

A couple of weeks went by, and we went back in for what should be twenty-one days. I thought, *Right, this time, I'll try again.* I didn't give my cigarettes away this time. We had moved in to install a couple of risers, but the barge was too big, and we couldn't reach the job. While we were doing other work, they had sent out a small Divcon system and installed it at the other end of the barge. When it was up and running, the four of us that were in this big antique system locked off. We got cross-hauled up the side of the barge thirty metres underneath. From there, we were in a position where we could lock out and get to the other bell that they had sent down with no one in it. I locked out, swam over, pushed the door up, did all the checks, swam back with the gear from the Divcon system, passed it to Billy, who headed over to the other bell, and I brought the hat back again to pick up Gavin and then Kevin. Then I took the gear off the antique bell and shut the door. When that was sealed, I swam back over to the Divcon bell. We returned to the surface and climbed into a system less than half the size of what we had just left. It was bloody horrible to start with, but eventually, you get used to it. We finally came out. I stepped on deck. I was not smoking, but within twelve hours, I'd had one, and by twenty-four, I was back to smoking like a chimney. Three days later, I was feeling shit again.

Another couple of weeks went by, and we got told we would be going in for a short four-to-six-day sat. Well, if I'm not giving up smoking after three to four weeks, I had no chance of stopping after four to six days so didn't even think about it. We nailed the work scope, and I was back on deck in six days. They had a shuffle of personnel, and the next short sat to do the last two risers, they had promised one of the supervisors a run. So Burnie, the air supervisor, went as gas supervisor, and I ran the air spread for the last two weeks. I really enjoyed that, and maybe it helped keep my mind off cigarettes.

The job was winding down. We were going to head home finally. After about fifteen days, I still hadn't had a cigarette. I thought once I get on the beach and start drinking, I'll get an urge, so I kept my smokes. We hit the beach and stayed overnight in a hotel around the Cherating Beach area. We partied all night, and I woke up the next day with no elephant shit in my mouth, which meant I hadn't smoked any cigarettes. I couldn't believe it. And to this day, I have never smoked a cigarette since. Thank God. I do a lot of other naughty shit, but thank God I don't smoke anymore.

Jorma, a friend I first met in Dubai in 1985/6, called me up one day to see if I was interested in going to a surf break north of Mindarie Quay called the Alkimos. Shit, yeah. So off we went and launched his boat at the Mindarie Marina, and about ten minutes up the coast, about 2 NM offshore is a reef that has a good wave on its day, picks up heaps of swell, but has a nasty sharp reef. It is often empty of surfers because it actually gets very nasty, and even the best surfers get caught. When you're unlucky, you can get shredded. The reef is so sharp it cuts your eyeballs just looking at it. And the left, which is the main wave, runs straight into it. If it's low tide and half out of the water, you have to have your wits or you will lose your skin. It has a nice right when it's big. With it being very unpredictable and so far off the coast, it cops a lot of wind. It is often empty or uncrowded. This day was about head high with four or five surfers on it, and it was pretty good. I was stoked to finally see a wave worth riding outside of the trip to Margaret River. The break got its name from a haunted shipwreck that lies on a reef inside closer to the beach.

You needed a boat, so one of the deals with Christina for staying in Perth was I had to get a boat. I finally found one I could afford, an old Penguin Phantom five-metre half cab with a Johnson 70 hp outboard called *Sandy Lee*. It went really well, way better than it looked. So now we were able to get out in the beautiful waters off the west coast. Because there are not many rivers, the water offshore is very clean. I would take Christina up to the Alki sometimes, and she would sunbake or sometimes fish while I surfed. It was usually too rough on the way home for her and Ryan, so we started doing trips up the Swan River, and that was a nice way to spend a day with a picnic lunch in the esky.

I had heard of the waves over at Rottnest Island, about fifteen kilometre off Fremantle, and after a job and we had some spare cash, we went over for our first Rottnest stay. It was midweek, and we were able to stay in the camping ground. What a lovely spot. Push biking is the only transport, and it was fun riding around the island. It doesn't matter what the wind is; you will always find a bay that is offshore with sparkling clear water. I was lucky enough to get the best surf break on the island on the second day we were there, so I was pretty happy because it is a classic powerful left and right peak called Strickland Bay. Later when I was brave enough to start taking my boat over, we would have some magical stays with a bit of fishing and surfing and plenty of crayfish. Buying a boat in Perth was probably the best thing I did after buying a house. We still have one, and it is always getting used.

Not long after we got a cat, a dog, and a boat, our second son, Jay, was born. It was heaps of fun because in the Aussie hospital, you could dial up the laughing gas from 50 per cent to 80 per cent, I think it was, so as soon as the nurse would leave, I'd dial it up, wait a bit, and then have about three quick drags of it, and dial it back before the nurse came running in. The hardest part was trying not to lose my shit when she burst through the door. Christina didn't seem to be as abusive as the first time, so overall, I think the birth went well from what I can remember. I do recall how she glowed with pride of her beautiful little boy the next day when I first visited her.

So the stage is all set with the players in play. Life trundled on. The red Commodore was changed out for our first Land Cruiser, a 62 series. We were now set up for family camping trips down to Margaret River. Ryan was at preschool, and we started to meet people of similar age that were actually true westies (born in Western Australia). I was trying to keep my long trips overseas down to one or two max a year. Kids just grow up too fast, and I was always missing birthdays, and getting Christmas at home was a 50/50, so when I was home, we made sure it was a big occasion.

We hired a friend's camper van and did our first trip north, through Geraldton, and stayed a couple of nights at Kalbarri because of a world-class surf break there called Jakes. By this time, I had come across a shaper that I knew from New Zealand that was shaping boards down south, so I had a quiver of two boards more suited to Western Australia. Jakes Point was epic for two days; talk about luck. The local chargers must have been at work because it wasn't even crowded. What it was, was perfect. The township is very small along the side of a river, extremely barren land, almost red, not a lot of trees around on the landscape, and what trees there were, were small compared to down south. The water is clean, and the night sky just lights up.

We headed out of Kalbarri and headed further north to Monkey Mia. Well, that is an eye-opener into how long you can have a straight boring road, I tell you. After driving around New Zealand, where Christina mostly has her hands over her eyes freaking out about the gorges and the trucks, this flat brown with shrubs is about as exciting as it gets. Although in the later years, when heading up to Gnaraloo Station in July, you can get miles and miles of blue and yellow wild flowers. I think it was a four-hour drive out of Kalbarri and into Monkey Mia. Even I was saying, 'Are we there yet?' Western Australia is so vast, once you are north of Geraldton, the distances between places just get further and further. Because I had no idea we were always arriving at dark or after, I never called to book anything, just lob in; so that was always dumb too. I was always setting our camp up after dark, knocking on park windows to book in because they were shut when we arrived. Funny enough, I still do that; must be my travel signature.

So we woke up to this very pretty camping ground on the edge of what really looks like a giant lake. Around midmorning, the dolphins come in and mingle with the tourists for an hour or so; it's pretty neat, and I guess if you had never seen one before, it would be amazing. The Japanese tourists would be there with their cameras and a knife and fork in the hope of sneaking a quick bite while the ranger wasn't looking (only joking). In the afternoon, I decided to shout the family on a cruise out in Shark Bay on a catamaran; I think was called *Shogun*. We had dolphins and dugongs, and it was well worth doing.

We stayed one more day. If you were a fisherman, there would be a lot more to do in that area; but for us, we just hung out on the beach for the day with the kids. It was wintertime, but the days are warm, and the nights are cool, made spectacular when the moon is low and the stars are out in the full darkness of night. Grab a beer or a wine, put a jacket on, and turn all the lights off. Bang, the sky jumps out like a silent movie, graced with the occasional falling star or space station. I think it was a thirteen-hour drive home from that camping ground—a drive that reminds you how far you have been.

Chapter 16

SURFING COAST TO COAST IN AUSTRALIA

Long before I left New Zealand, I had met an American couple that were on holiday and passing through Mahia while I was there having a break from my job at Whakatu meat works. We had been surfing together, and they ended up staying at my beach batch on Mahanga Beach. They were living on the big Island of Hawaii, and he was a pretty good board shaper. I had been in touch with him about a board just before I found Mark, my current board shaper. So Dean called me to see if I still wanted a big wave gun. He said he had a friend heading over to Australia and he would bring it over for me, and that's how I ended up with a really nice 7'4" big wave gun.

Steve and his girlfriend spent a week with us and travelled up and down the west before heading east and home. Not long after they left, we were down in Margaret River when I pulled up at main break, and it was pretty perfect. These huge lines were through the whole bay to the horizon, with peaks brushed with a mid-strength offshore. There seemed to be waves everywhere. It wasn't very crowded, and I watched with a bit of trepidation as I put my wetsuit on. When the sets were peaking, the half a dozen surfers that were out there looked pretty small. I waxed the Hawaiian gun and headed out. From the point, it looked bumpy from the wind, but once I got out there, it was actually clean on the faces and looked pretty friendly. It was a lot bigger than I thought and very intimidating. Two surfers had already gone in, and there were a couple of boogie boarders, and that was it.

I sat reasonably wide and watched the mood of the surf and then realised that one of the surfers that was sitting way inside of me was actually surfing the right. *No way*, I remember thinking. Getting caught inside by the sets that were coming through didn't look like a good option to stay alive. I finally got the balls to paddle in and take off. Man, that was scary and enthralling as I dropped down this huge face of water that was exploding to my right as I made the bottom turn left and flying back up the face. I was moving incredibly fast, but it seemed to be in slow motion as I made it around the first section, turned off the top, and dropped back down into the bowl, pulling back up midway to make the next section.

Even though you are going fast, you still need to pump the board to make sure you get past the sections and then drop down into the bowl and pull the bottom turn and fly back up the face to the top of the wave. I managed to make the whole wave and pull off the back at the end. It was easily triple overhead in the ten-to-twelve-foot range and way bigger than I had ever seen let alone surfed. I was buzzing with emotion as I paddled back out with a sense of conquering my fears and thinking, *This is easy. It's not that bad. I can do this.* And that set the tone for the next three hours of pushing myself in what was the biggest surf I had ever had.

The wind backed off. It got glassy, and a few more guys came out. I was just buzzing. I loved the way there seemed to be so much time between turns compared to small waves. Then it happened. I was sitting in the same area as I had been all morning when a hell set came through. We were all scrambling for the horizon, and as I paddled over this monster, there right in front of me was an even bigger one already pitching. I watched the lip hit ten feet in front of me as I bailed off the board and headed under as far as I could get. *Bam.* I don't know of any words to describe what really happened next when it first hit me. I got thrown around and pushed really deep. It went black, and I was getting totally ragdolled in pretty deep water.

After what seemed to take forever, I seemed to be coming back up, with a feeling of weightlessness and the water getting lighter. I thought, *Thank God I'm coming up. I'll be all right.* Then, *bam.* I was hit again. This time, I was sucked up and over in a vortex of water. Then, *bam*, I hit the rag doll sequence again, getting my leg yanked as I was dragged down into the black once more. Now I got no air in my lungs and was going the opposite way to where I need to go. I fought for a second and then realised I had to shut down, conserve my energy and oxygen.

I stopped getting ragdolled, and everything started slowing down. I needed to breathe, but it was still black, so I was still deep. I pulled my right leg up and got a hold of my leg rope. My board was above me, so I started to climb up using the leg rope to pull me out of the hold the water had on me. It got light. I was moving faster towards the surface when, all of a sudden, after what seemed like a week underwater, I blasted through the surface. My board was right there. I gasped in as much air as I could and bear hugged my board in case I got hit by another wave. There was no way I would have survived another ragdolling. Eight feet of white water on the edge of a ten-foot face pushed me up and over the shoulder, and thank God that was the last wave.

I looked around while sucking in as much air as I could, trying to get my breath back. Lying there on my board, I looked to where the car park was, looked out to where the main peak was, and worked out that I had just been underwater getting my arse kicked through the whole surf break. I was exhausted and just lay there as I was slowly sucked out towards the line-up. It was still perfect, glassy, with only about five people out. I thought, I can't go in on a hiding after I had had such an incredible surf, so I started paddling back out. I got a few more, being careful not to lull myself back into the inside where when the big ones come in, you have trouble getting out of the way. My last wave wasn't epic, but it was still thrilling, and I rode it nearly all the way back into the gap in the reef that you paddle out in.

I walked up the stairs into the car park with my head held high, a sigh of relief, and a buzz of accomplishment that would set me up for chasing big surf for the rest of my life. Since that day, I have surfed pretty big waves. A couple of surfs have been bigger than that day. All of them have had moments of near drowning. It is unavoidable. The longer you are out there, the bigger the chance that you will be hit by what I have come to call the lawnmower sets. These are a set of waves that come through way bigger than anything else, and they take everyone. Everyone cops a thrashing, mostly just hold-your-breath challenges, but occasionally you have a near drowning. They really test you. Margaret River is one of those places that doesn't have to be big to humble you and make you look like a kook.

It wasn't until I started to do saturation in Australia that I really started to get familiar with the sharks. There are heaps of them in the fields on the North West, mainly white and blacktip reef sharks, bronze whalers, grey nurse, and of course, the more elusive tiger sharks. Early on, they would always be out on our peripheral vision, as if they knew how far we could see. At night, it would be on the edge of our light; during the day, it would be a glimpse here and a glimpse there. Around the base of the platforms, there were lots more and, of course, a lot closer. They were weary of us; we were big and scary to them, so they kept their distance. And of course, I wasn't alone at always keeping an eye on them, out of a bit of fear to start with, but that soon turned to wonder and amazement as we got more acclimatised to them. Of course, they got more acclimatised to us as well and started getting closer.

Around the bottom of *Rankin*, one of the big platforms, was just teaming with fish, and of course, the size of everything was bigger than everywhere else. It's 120 metres on the seabed, and it may have been one of the first times I had worked there. We were actually working deep into the platform by the conductors doing preparation work for pulling in a new Coflexip riser. I had gone outside to the work basket to get some tools. Mike, my bell partner on that job, was twenty metres inside the jacket. The visibility was very clear, and I could see his hat light. By this time, we were doing three-man bell teams. We had cameras and hat lights, all very mod con.

Anyway, I had just jumped back up onto the mud brace when over the top of Mike's head was this shadow of a bloody huge shark heading away from me from right to left. I said, 'Far out, Mike, there is a huge shark just above you.'

He looked up as the tail went past him. I stood there watching as it turned and slowly started heading my way. I didn't move, just stared straight at it. It was a huge grey nurse, easy four plus metres with a big belly. It looked like a bloody truck. It kept coming straight at me. I didn't move. I didn't breathe. I didn't want to scare it off. As it came straight at my light with its mouth half open, I could see straight down its throat; bloody teeth everywhere. As it slid about six inches above my head, I put my hand up and stroked its stomach. It didn't do anything, just ambled on, no cares; it wasn't scared of us. *Curious,* I thought.

I was going off to the supervisor, 'Did you see that? Oh my god, did you see that?'

That was it. From that day on, I just loved having sharks around me, especially when everything was calm. When everything was jittery, it was a different thing. That means something is feeding, and when something is feeding, everything wants to get in on the action. When the sharks come in to see what the fuss is about, then they want some action. Then the whole dynamic in the water changes. You can feel it like electricity. Everything is moving fast. Because we have lights, they attract fish, so more often than not, shit happens around us. They love shiny things; any fisherman will tell you that. Well, we have lots of shiny things hanging off us, so we get hit a lot by fish, just normal fish, but when the visibility is shit, the bigger fish and the sharks come flying out of the dark, snapping their jaws at anything.

I was sitting on a pipe one time, with my partner Stew sitting behind me. We had about one and a half metres of visibility. You could feel the tension in the water. We had seen some big sharks up around the bell lights where the vis was better. They were two- to three-metre bronze whalers, and around on the seabed, we had the one-and-a-half-metre blacktip reefies charging around like fox terriers. There were baitfish everywhere, and the baitfish were hanging around our lights. The little reefies would come flying in and kick up all the seabed and make the visibility even worse. All of a sudden, a two-and-a-half-metre bronzy came snapping out of the mud straight at me. Stew pushed me to get away himself as it was heading up past my stomach, trying to chomp all the fish in front of me. My arms pushed its stomach about where its fins were, and its tail smashed me in the head as it took off.

The supervisor said, 'Jesus, that was close.'

I was huffing and puffing that much from the fright; I couldn't even talk. 'Holy shit,' I finally said.

Night-time was always the worst. I think the lights help get things going. Those little reefies reminded me of fox terriers; they couldn't help themselves. They would start causing trouble, and the big ones would come in to finish it off. Sometimes, when you're coming back to the bell—the bell is fifteen metres off the seabed—the fish are jittery, and you know that on the edge of your vision are these bloody predators that aren't scared of you anymore. You grab your umbilical and start climbing, you pull your legs as close to your arse as you can, and you get up to the bell and the safety of the clump weight as fast as you can. Then while you're getting your breath back, you look out, and there are these eyes, lit up by the bell lights, and they are circling and waiting for their opportunity. And it is actually quite exciting. Most of the time, the sea life ignore you, and you can just watch them; other times, you annoy them, and regardless of their size, they will have a shot at you.

One time, I'm on the seabed walking along a pipeline in the North West. Reg, the supervisor, asked me to put my pneumo on the seabed to get a depth of water reading. I grabbed my pneumo, which was a blue hose in my umbilical, and put it on the seabed next to the pipeline. Five feet away was a blue-and-black banded sea snake making its way towards me and decided to check the hose out.

I said to Reg, 'Hey, Reg, this snake is taking a liking to the pneumo.'

He said, 'See if he likes this, then,' and opened the gas up and blew the snake in the face.

The snake instantly reared up like a rattler and hit me three times in the chest as I was trying to back off. I fell on my bailout with my legs in the air like I was doing a dead ant. Reg was pissing himself, and I was abusing the hell out of him. They were solid punches for a little snake

Through the mid-1990s, I spent a lot of time with Divcon on or in these small saturation systems that were perfect for loading on and off oilfield supply vessels and charging around doing projects around Asia. I had arrived in Singapore to prepare a vessel for a salvage job off Thailand to recover Ming Dynasty pottery. A day after I had arrived, a friend, Kevin, had had an argument with a French barge captain at the airport over flight times and decided to tell the French man to jam the job up his arse and went back home to Sembawang. Guess who gets taken off the salvage job of the century and sent to a French barge in the outback of New Guinea? Thanks, Kevin.

I flew in to Port Moresby and stopped in a hotel for the night. The next morning, a couple of riggers and I boarded a small six-seater fixed wing and flew to an area on the South Coast called Kikori, a small village along the Kikori River at the base of a mountain range. It was actually quite a nice flight and landed on a small grass landing strip surrounded by native bush. About an hour later, we were picked up by a local guy who took us down to a very brown-looking river, and we climbed on a twenty-five-foot Whaler boat with the first diesel outboard I had ever seen. We headed off down the river slowly, and I just settled back to enjoy the view.

After going around a couple of bends, things started to get really impressive. The native bush got thicker and thicker. We would see dugout canoes paddling along, and we would have to slow to a near stop so we didn't swamp the canoe that often had whole families in. Things were getting very primitive, and it was reminding me of our camping trip at Lwandile in South Africa's Wild Coast.

After a while, we came around another bend, and I spotted smoke drifting up from the river's edge to our right. As we got closer, we could make out a small village with a dozen thatched roofs through the bush turning into small huts as we got closer and closer. There were dirt tracks and nice green grass areas in a clearing that looked like something out of a movie based a couple of hundred years ago. A couple of tracks led to a makeshift wooden jetty that looked like it was about to fall over, and pulled up the bank around it were dugout canoes of different lengths dragged clear of the river's edge.

I said to the others with me, 'This is a bit of a time warp, eh?' They nodded approval as we all took in the sight.

Not long after that, the river widened to possibly a kilometre wide for a while before narrowing right back in as we finally spotted the river mouth in the distance. We had seen smoke rising at a couple of other spots on the way but only seen a path down to the river's edge with dugouts pulled up as with the first village. About a kilometre from the river mouth was a platform that had just been installed, and alongside the platform was a French barge called the *Boss 355,* my home for the next couple of months.

We had a pretty good dive crew on board, and the deal was there is a pipeline running from an oilfield way inland on the other side of a mountain range that surrounds the Kikori village. They ran a pipeline over the mountain ridge and down into the river and all the way out to the platform. The platform acts as a pressure-decreasing station to feed the correct low pressure to an SBM that tankers that come along hook up to and fill themselves up with oil. Then off they go. So we were doing all the subsea pipeline hook-up. Working under the SBM was a nightmare at times because sometimes when the tide was going out, we would see driftwood the size of small trees heading out the river and straight at us. We had to keep a lookout because if something like that picked up your umbilical, you would be in serious trouble. We had to get our boys out of the water a few times.

One night, I came out on shift, and the barge was empty. There were only the French crew on and not many locals. I said, 'Where is everyone?' and got told that a few boats pulled up a few hours earlier, and after heated words, heaps of guys jumped in, and they were gone for a couple of days.

Apparently, what had transpired was that a village up in the hills had come down using the pipeline as a road and raided a river village, stealing a couple of pigs and chickens, possibly the one we sailed past, and then run back. The problem is the forest is so dense that it would have taken eight or nine hours originally, and now it only takes two. I would imagine that a lot of the villages will be pissed off with the pipeline. Anyway, we hooked up the pipeline to the platform and then started working on the SBM. They ran a smart pig down the pipeline to check for damage and unfortunately came across a couple of areas. One was right up by the main village, and a crew was sent up there to sort that out. I was kept on the barge, and we were sent to another damaged area right in the mouth. It was dodgy as we could only dive at the turn of the tides or the current was too strong. As soon as your head went underwater, you could not see anything, not even your hand.

For about a week, we were dropping onto the riverbed, finding the pipeline, and walking along, stabbing it with a knife until we hit soft foam. This means it's a field joint where the concrete is missing so they can weld the pipe together. Because they knew roughly what field joint the damage was at, once we found a field joint, we would look for the number. The number is painted on the concrete in white paint next to the joint. The only way we could read it was to have the plastic bag out of a wine cask. In Aussie and New Zealand, we call them goon bags, but they are the boxes of wine, sometimes or mostly actually cheap wine. Anyway, we had that full of fresh clear water. We would put the goon bag against the concrete, push our diving hat faceplate into it, and shine the torch into the side of it, and move it around to read each number. It was a painfully slow way of reading a field joint number, but it was effective. Eventually, we found all the areas that were supposed to be suspect, and luckily, they were all OK, so the smart pig wasn't that smart after all. We were bloody glad to get out of that shallow but bloody dangerous little job.

As all jobs do, this one came to an end. We travelled back up the river to Kikori and managed to score a few lightly cold beers in this stinking hot tin shed, while we waited for the six seater to take us back to the future. The next time I saw my mate Tony, who had supervised the expedition of the repair upriver, he was telling me how they had heaps of drama and had to have a crocodile watch. They ended up with a pet crocodile on board for a few days, ha ha. I sometimes wonder how those tribes have handled that change. Not everyone lives in the twenty-first century, and from what I saw on the Kikori River, a lot of people haven't even made it to the twentieth century. And you know what, it's fun visiting them, and you hope, for their sake, they stay there, if only we could leave them there.

The *Rocky 2* had a job in Bass Strait from November to December, and we had decided that we were going over to see Christina's parents for that Christmas. They had moved over from New Zealand to a place just south of Port Macquarie called Lake Cathie. The job was going to finish too close to Christmas, so I decided I would load the Land Cruiser up with the camping gear and surfboards and drive over by myself, drop the cruiser at John and Kitty's, and fly from there to join the vessel. Well, I thought the trip up to Monkey Mia was long and boring, but the trip across the Nullarbor is another dimension. Far out.

Because I was driving east, I left Perth at about 10 am. With only fuel stops for short breaks, I drove right through until about 3 a.m. I found a rest stop just before a township, had a beer, and crashed out in the back of the cruiser. I woke up at about 7:30. The sun was a bit low, but by the time I hit the gas station at the town, fuelled up, paid $5 for a shower, and had a cooked breakfast all at the gas station, the sun was out of my eyes, and I was refreshed enough to do another eighteen hours behind the wheel. It was quite an amazing drive in its own way. Some parts are very straight, and at one part, you drive along the longest straight road in Australia. I think it is 270 kilometres without a corner, not even a curve. Pretty amazing.

The biggest drama are the road trains, big trucks with three or four trailers. Sometimes, there would be two or three in a row, and passing them was pretty intense, especially at night. I found the best way was to just hammer it, sometimes getting my old cruiser over 160 km/hr and then once safely past dropping back to my average of 110–120. You would be flying along, and the road trains coming at you would throw the car around as well, so you had to pay attention.

The second night, I had managed to make it across the Nullarbor and had a few beers in the roadhouse pub of Penong before it closed, and I made my way into Cactus, a beach camp with really good surf. Unfortunately, when I woke up the next morning, the surf wasn't happening, so I moved on to my next garage shower and breakfast at Ceduna and made my way towards Sydney through Port Augusta. If I remember rightly, I managed to get into Sydney and park up at a friend's place the third night. Bill lived not far from Bondi Beach, so the next day, I scored my first and only surf there. What a lovely spot. Bloody hard getting a car park, though. Waves were fun, and one of Bill's mates was a lifeguard on shift that day, so I hung out with him for a bit. The next day was another long day in the seat, and I finally arrived at John and Kitty's and parked the car up, and they dropped me at the airport for my flight to Melbourne the next day. It all worked out pretty well. I had travelled over 3,900 kilometres and surprisingly entertaining.

We completed the job but a bit later than expected. Christina had flown over with the kids, and when I arrived, she had the best spot in the camping ground on the cliff face overlooking the surf break. It was all set up when I arrived, so I just cruised into it. We were there for nearly three weeks, I think, and got to have a look around up and down the coast. I surfed most days. The weather was beautiful, and the countryside was really neat. We ventured into the Glass Mountains and up and down the coast, and it is a really beautiful area with lots to do.

The last week we were there, some friends, Silvana and Marcella and their kids, joined us from Copa Cabana, a coastal town a couple of hours north of Sydney, and it was nice to hang out with them. I had decided we would use the trip to see a bit of east coast, so on the drive home, we went down and stayed with Silvana at Copa Cabana for the weekend. That is another lovely spot, with dense bush surrounding pockets of houses in amongst the hills and then you pop out on the coast. Lovely to drive and walk around. We said our goodbyes and headed south towards Ulladulla.

A friend I had just been working with, Chris, lived in a place called Batemans Bay, and we pulled up to a motel for a freshen up, and Chris and his wife had dinner for us when we finally arrived at their house in the woods. Another beautiful spot. Definitely cooler as we headed south. I discussed with Chris that night the best way over the Blue Mountains and into Melbourne, where the plan was to fly Christina and the kids back to Perth, and I would blast across the Nullarbor again by myself. Our little plan worked perfectly, and the drive through Deua and Namadgi National Parks and into Albury was just another piece of epic scenery. We copped a little rain but had clear skies where it really mattered, like the lookout on the eastern side looking back to the coast, the walk through a historic mining town, and a river valley in the middle that we stopped and I had a swim. We stopped the night in Albury and eventually pulled into Melbourne, and although we had had enough of the car, the kids most certainly had, it had still been a worthy adventure.

The family flew out, and I decided I would not miss the opportunity to surf at Bells Beach, a legendary surf break outside of Melbourne, and made my way there. After an hour stuck in a traffic jam, I gave up and turned around and headed to Adelaide and stopped in at another friend's, Brian's. He didn't believe me when I said I'd be leaving at 4 a.m. because now that I was going west, I wanted to drive the mornings and sleep from 3 p.m. through sunset. I was gone when he woke up.

My next stop was back at Cactus, and this time it was on. I surfed the main break when I arrived until sunset, three to four feet and really nice. The next morning, the wind was wrong for that, but a right hander two bays over called Caves was five feet and breaking really good, so I surfed there until the wind stuffed it around lunchtime. Then I was back across the Nullarbor for the final two days of the whole adventure. And adventure it was. I had gone coast to coast across Australia. I had seen some amazing things, from the long mundane straights of the Nullarbor with big eagles scanning the roads for fresh kills to the winding native bush roads and hidden towns in valleys along the east, central, and south coasts. This is a bloody big country.

In this industry, there are some good jobs, bad jobs, and then there are some nightmare jobs. Every now and then, you end up on a nightmare job. Now, the reason for the nightmare could be different from job to job, company to company, or personnel or environment. You dread the wake-up call for your one hour's notice to dive. It feels like you only just went to sleep. Sometimes you're in a team where one or sometimes both of the other divers you just don't get along, and the days just drag on. Or a common one is the environment and you are dreading to go out into such a hostile situation. One such job for me was on the *Rocky 2* for Subsea 7 in India in a field called Tapti. I hope I never go back there. It is shallow, around thirty metres, I think, and extremely hot in the bell to the point that even when you are the bellman, you are dreading it because it is so uncomfortable. The currents are strong, and the visibility comes and goes. We were hooking up spool pieces into T piece valve stations that were on an existing main trunk gas pipeline.

When we first arrived, there was fishing net snagged over one of the T pieces, and it took us about six days cutting it away. We had the crane hooked up to a big chunk, and we would get onto the muddy seabed, make our way along the pipe, and have to climb under this big mess of fishnet and cut away and slowly come upon the crane. With the swell and the vessel movement, sometimes it would drop on top of you, and you would spend the next half an hour cutting yourselves free. It was a bloody nightmare and a half. We would always come back to the bell with fishnet still stuck on our bailout or hat.

A couple of days after we had completed the last of that, Hector and I were landing a big spool piece in, and the visibility was that bad. We had to have the flanges of the spool tied off to running lines from the surface so we could find it once it came down. To add to our misfortune, there was a bit of swell, so the spool was heaving up and down at the same time, and to double that, the valve that I was working next to was leaking gas. We had decided we would land the spool as close as we could and disconnect the crane and use lift bags to float it in, in a more controlled and safer manner. We could see about one foot max, and when Hector was in place at the PLEM (pipeline end manifold), I instructed the supervisor to come down on the crane. The end I was working on had a two-metre-high dogleg with a standoff clamp that sat on the main pipeline, and the main pipeline was live.

We had a couple of attempts at landing it out, but it was not working, so I said to the supervisor, 'Let's just land it off to the side and play it safe.'

The current had started to pick up, and it was making things even harder. I organised with Hector that as soon as the tag line stops heaving up and down which means it's in between swells, we will land it out. He agreed, and we landed it on the seabed. When I estimated there should be enough slack in the crane, I stopped it and instructed Hector and the supervisor that we would go and locate the spool, make sure it's OK, and disconnect the crane. We both moved in. My flange had rolled over and was resting on the main trunk line, but that was OK. I went hand over hand down the pipe and came across the standoff clamp, and as I followed that around, I found out it had slid under the protection frame of the leaking valve next to the flange I had to tie in to.

I told the supervisor, 'You are not going to believe this,' and explained to him that the clamp faceplates where trapped in behind the valve body bolts, and I don't know how we were going to get it out because I don't know how it even managed to get in there.

He freaked out and got Allen, the OCM, to take over the dive panel. I asked Hector how his end was, and after he found his end, he reported that it was also wedged in under the mud mat of the protection frame. We were looking to be in a serious situation.

After going through all the options, I said to Allan, 'How about we just pick it up again and see what happens?' He agreed, so I moved to the bell side of the valve in case it blew off, asked Hector if he was clear, and said, 'Come up easy on the crane.'

Not being able to see anything, I just had all these horrible images of disaster in my head when I heard, boing, boing. Then silence. I waited another twenty seconds and stopped the crane and went back to the valve, and the clamp and spool piece were gone. I couldn't believe it. Allen was relieved to hear the news, and I asked Hector what his end looked like.

His reply was 'I don't know. I'm back on the clump weight.'

Smart man that Hector because I had been shitting myself. Eventually, we got the job done, but I have never been on another job since where I just dreaded that call for dive notice. Twenty-six days and you vow you will never go back.

Chapter 17

COFLEXIP AND GOLD MINES

With the once-a-year star job in Australia's North West on the *Venturer* for Coflexip or the *Rocky 2* for Rockwater—both the *Venturer* and the *Rocky 2* were purpose-built DSVs (dive support vessels)—Coflexip had a new product on the market that would change the concept of oilfield pipeline instillation possibly forever. Instead of hard steel pipes welded together off the back of a barge, they had invented (if that's the right word) a flexible pipeline, and the product is coiled onto these huge drums and loaded onto boats and spooled off the back over an archway and onto the seabed. It was also perfect for the new concept of floating offshore storage facilities, which was gaining popularity around the world as a cheaper alternative to expensive offshore platforms. We started installing FPSOs all over the place but more in the North West than anywhere else. It was perfect for their small pockets of oil and gas. When the field stopped producing enough to be viable, they just shut the valves and removed everything as if it had never been there. The work itself was challenging and pretty full on. A lot of the time you would get back from a bell run and just melt into your bunk. It would seem like five minutes after you fell asleep, you were getting woken up to do it all again.

In 1995, the Osprey came to the North West to install the Cossack Wanea field. This was notable for a few reasons. I think it was the first twin bell system that I worked on in Australia. Over the six months that we worked on her, a giant grouper, about the size of a VW Beetle, would hang between the bells on the bell turnarounds. You would lock out, and while waiting for diver three checks, the grouper would cruise over for a pat. He loved a scratch under the chin. The other funny thing was Jack going off at Jim because Jim decided to go fishing while being bellman. Of course, this created a shark frenzy that Jack and their other bell partner, Ray, had to deal with while diving. Jim does like his fishing.

A few months after that project, so early 1996, we were back on the Venturer and in deco after completing another project in the North West. We were tied up alongside at the Dampier Wharf while the vessel was in demobilisation. One of our LSS, Mathew, whose nickname is also Spike, went down to check on the William's and James's compressor that was transferring gas. He walked into the compressor room as it blew up. Simon, the other LST on shift, went running down and came across Mathew in a real mess. Supervisors Mick and Mitch were quickly on the scene. Without their quick actions and first aid knowledge, it is quite possible Mathew would not have survived. It is the classic example of the fact that we as divers are not the only ones in danger in this working environment. All the people, the LSTs, the techs, and the supervisors, are all working around and dealing with machinery that is under high pressure. It is easy to forget this when you see them sitting around scratching their bums and whining about winging divers. After getting out of sat, I went down to the compressor room and looked at the damage. A large piece of the compressor head had gouged a big crease through the twenty-millimetre door bulkhead. Spike, the LSS, is very lucky to be alive.

Both the *Venturer* and the *Rocky 2* were cut in half and made bigger to accommodate the large lay reels and also to put more of them on deck. As these two companies got busier, I did less and less with my mates in Divcon, a little less of the air diving jobs in Australia, but one of note was an iron ore carrier that had had a power loss while sailing out of Dampier harbour on her maiden voyage back to France. It was about to hit an island, so they dropped an anchor to stop them. The anchor stopped them, but they had dropped it too late and then floated over it, and it was too shallow, so it ripped three big tears into two different holds. It was towed back into the outer harbour, and Divcon won the contract to weld the patches on so it could make it back to its home port in France to be repaired properly. We spent close on a month wet stick welding five-metre-by-three-metre steel plates underneath, and it was good welding practice. I slowed right down on the local work, with Jim at Franmarine and Roger at Diver 1 Diver 2, after that as the Coflexip installation activity increased.

At around this time, I had been doing some local shutdown work as a mechanical fitter with Craig, a mate of ours from Napier. The company we were working for called me up and asked if I could do an emergency job for them in a gold mine in the mid-west. They knew I could weld stainless steel, and that's what they needed. So next thing, I find myself flying into a gold mine called Youanmi, not far from a township called Sandstone, which is inland from Geraldton, about an hour by ten-seater plane from Perth Airport, and we practically came in sideways because of the wind. I thought that was fun.

I got taken into a campsite and was given a donga (Australian slang for a box with a bed and a shower and toilet). I put my bag down, put on some work gear, and was taken for a drive to the mine site, into the fitters' workshop office, and was introduced to the onsite maintenance foreman, who was a fellow Kiwi. Off we went for a tour of the plant. He explained to me that the plant processed the rock from the mine by using the Batox process, the first mine in Australia to do so. Batox is bacterial oxidation and bioleaching; to put simply, these micro bugs eat everything except polished medical-grade stainless steel, rubber, and gold. He took me for a walk around the top of these tanks, telling me about the bugs in them.

He said, 'They are good for cleaning your tools,' and asked if I had any tools on me. I said no. So he pulled a hammer out of his back pocket and hung it in the top of the tank and told me we'll check it tomorrow.

At the bottom of the tank farm, he showed me the tank that was leaking and explained that tomorrow, it will have been cleaned out, and we will be in there fixing it. We went past the crusher where big dump trucks were dropping their load from the mine itself, which was at the time the steepest decline (1 in 4) in Australia. He promised he would take me down one day before I left. I was introduced to a few other guys on the maintenance team, sparkies and mechanics; one, a welder from the same company as me that I would be working with tomorrow. The camp was a good setup. It had tennis and squash courts, a big food mess with pretty good food, and of course, a separate lounge and bar with pool tables and dart boards.

I was on the 5:45 bus into the mine the next day. I was surprised how cold it was. Wish I could remember some of the names of the people I was working with. Anyway, I think it was Nigel, the foreman, who took me up to check his hammer. Blow me over, you could still tell it was a hammer, but it was riddled with holes like a termite hill.

I said, 'Jesus, glad I didn't give you my good tools,' and he laughed.

We looked down into the empty tank. There were a couple of broken paddles lying on the floor of the tank. There were a couple of cleaners still washing out the last of the mix of gold dirt and bio bacteria. It'll be a couple of hours yet. He explained the process.

In the earth, the gold forms in veins vertically but can be wide horizontally. The decline, which is the road that circles down following the gold sheet, runs down along the course but shoots off in what they call stopes. These are situated where the gold deposits are strong. The drillers, who are called airleg operators, operate these large air-operated drills called widow makers because they have a habit of killing people. They drill up from the stopes, which I think they call drives. Then when they have drilled all their holes, they pack them with dynamite, and at 3 p.m. every day, all the dynamites are let off. Boom. The dirt and rocks fall into the stope.

A bogger comes along, which is a flat version of a front-end loader and loads the trucks that have wheels the size of houses and take something like twenty tonnes a load. They go up the decline to the top of the cut (mine) and dump it over the dump site, where it is loaded by a normal-looking but extremely large front-end loader and bulldozer, and it's pushed onto a conveyer belt that takes it to a series of four crushers that get the boulders down to pebbles, and the last conveyor takes it to the tank area, and it gets loaded into the tanks. By then, the rocks are like pebbles. Big electric motors run these big paddles that churn the dirty bio mix around and around. The bugs eat the rocks, and the gold drops to the bottom of the tank and is sucked out and sent to the cyanide tanks. In the cyanide tanks, there is a big cathode in the centre. After x amount of time, they turn on a power source to the cathode. It grabs all the gold dust in the muddy water mix, and when they turn it off, the gold drops into the gold room. That is a rough version of the whole setup.

Now, getting back to the tanks and the hungry bugs. The big paddles that turn it all over are steel, so to protect the steel, they wrap it in rubber. After a while, the rubber starts to deteriorate. The bugs get under the rubber, and because to them steel tastes better than rocks, they are into it. A paddle breaks off, and as it is dragged around with the dirt and rocks, it scratches the polished wall of the stainless tanks. The bugs start eating through the scratch to the other side and actually eat the tank from the outside in. I know you're thinking, *You're shitting me.* But that's how it is.

We went off and grabbed Shane and climbed into the tank with a small hammer and tape measure. The cleaners were now setting up scaffolding for us to climb around on. I was shown how to pick up a scratch, and then you just lightly tap around in a circle, and I kid you not, it was like checking the rust on your car. The real bad spots, the hammer went straight through. The tank walls were only 3 mm thick, but they would be down to 1 mm and soft. Unbe-bloody-lievable. So Shane's and my job was to measure the damage areas, plasma cut patches big enough to put over the damage, weld them on, and then polish it all up. As we were finishing the first tank, another started leaking, and so the cycle went.

One day, Nigel asked me for a hand, and off we went to pull a crusher apart to replace a couple of broken teeth. After that, he took me for a drive into what used to be the township in the mining boom in the early 1900s (it was called Youanmi by aborigines after a spring in the area). We went for a walk through the cemetery; lots of deaths between 1910 and 1920, mostly under twenty-five year olds. Lots of kids.

Another day, he told Derek, the underground fitter, to take me down the decline to show me around. I wasted my time taking a camera. We first went into the top-level stopes, but at the top, he asked if I was a schizophrenic.

'No,' I said. 'Why?'

He said, 'When we drop into the decline, we have the flashing lights on all vehicles, and the schizos trip out, so I'll find out if you're lying.' I laughed and told him to put the foot down and let's find out.

So the open cut is maybe thirty to forty metres deep. Then we hit the decline. The first stopes we walked into were circa 1925–30s small railway lines that carts were pushed along. I think we were only twenty to forty metres underground, but it was black. It actually sucked the flash of the camera away, and none of the photos came out, as Derek said would happen. Man, they were hard arses back then. We carried on down.

He said, 'We might as well service the pumps as we go.'

There were four pump stations as we headed down. At one stage, there was a dump truck on the way up, and we were caught in a narrow area. The trucks don't stop, and Derek pulled right into a water run-off, saying, 'This should be good.'

We were in a Toyota Hilux tray back, wedged up against a rock wall on the right-hand side. The white light turned into flashing orange as this huge truck came around the corner. My head was actually lower than the centre of the wheel as it knocked the rear vision mirror on my side. Then the Hilux started wobbling as the tyre rubbed past the end of the tray back.

I said, 'This is a fuckin' test, isn't it, Derek?'

He laughed and said, 'Sorry about that. Every now and then, you get caught in between safe drives. These are the proper areas you are supposed to pull off to let the trucks pass.'

The second pump station was just a grotty mess, and I helped scoop out the unburnt cordite and other shit that get washed down the waterways and into the catching ponds and then into the filter boxes. We cleaned the filter boxes. The water underground in this mine was seven times saltier than seawater.

The third station was quite picturesque when you hit the lights on. I couldn't believe how clear the water was. This pump station was situated next to a natural underground stream and lake and was about 250 metres from the top of the decline. We went all the way down to the bottom, and just before that, he pulled up at another underground lake. It was dry because they had opened it up so they could build another pump station there. It was the nine-hundred-metre level. And they called it the Golden Gate because of the design they had for it. So what I found out was we were nine hundred metres above sea level. The top of the decline was 1,300 metres above sea level. So that made it four hundred metres from the top of the decline vertically. The decline is a circle road like a stairwell.

At the end of my first week, Nigel rotated out with his boss, who was actually the head of maintenance. And over the next few days, I worked with him a bit. He introduced me to the big boss of the whole mine. He just happened to be a South African, which coincidentally is where the Batox system comes from. I told him of our six months in South Africa, and he loved hearing about it. I did one more tank with Shane. Then he left, and I ended up helping Derek with a pump overhaul at the second pump station. They decided I needed to get my decline drivers licence, so I sat that the day before I left and was organised to rotate back after a week off. *Bloody awesome*, I thought. It was pretty good money, call home free every night, only one-hour flight to work, and two weeks on, one week off. No more having to do shit overseas low-paying jobs. Yahoo. This also came in handy when Christina, while cutting out one of her frames for her artwork, had slashed her wrist open and ended up in the hospital. I was able to be on a flight the next morning and home by lunchtime. She ended up winning a couple of awards for her mirrors, but I made a rule—no more using a scalpel.

On my second trip, I ended up taking over Derek's decline job for him while he had his week off. So I was on five bucks an hour more, plus double time on call-outs. And my main project was getting the Golden Gate pump station ready. I built this bridge walkway over what was now a six-metre-deep lake again. We had to get over to the other side to clear out the water traps. When Derek returned, I just went back to general maintenance and tank repairs whenever they started leaking.

The *Venturer* was heading down to the North West for a project, so I told Nigel I would be away for a while and asked if they want me to organise my company to send someone else. He said, 'No, no need. Just ring us when you're ready to come back and we'll rotate you back in.'

The second time I took off for a dive project, I called a couple of weeks after I had gotten home and was told the mine has shut down because of the drop in gold prices. I was sent my tools and a Gold Mines of Australia sports jacket as a thanks for the work I had done for them. That was in 1997. I had had a really good time working there. But, man, it gets cold when the sun goes down out in the desert.

Towards the end of the 1990s, we did a trip to China. Flying into Hong Kong and landing on the old runway was an epic way to land, and I am relieved I got to witness it a couple of times before they opened a new one on a man-made island. My first run into Hong Kong, it seemed like we were heading into a mountain when the plane banked to the right and then, all of a sudden, there were skyscrapers everywhere, lights all over the place, and as we dropped slowly down, you could see into the units of these large housing complexes—it was bazaar, with people clearly visible in their kitchens or on the balconies tending their clothes that are hanging on poles sticking out from the side of the buildings. I was totally blown away. When we landed, I just wanted to go and do it again like a joy ride. The next time I flew into that airport was at night, and it was even more spectacular. Unfortunately, that was my last time as they opened the new airport before my next visit.

From Hong Kong, we went by ferry to a place in Southern China called Shekou. On that first trip, we didn't get a lot of time to look around, but we did do a bit of bar-hopping in both places. I made the mistake of being talked into trying fried duck's feet in the bars of Shekou, and never again. Man, that was disgusting. I was nearly dry reaching and had the taste in my mouth for the rest of the night.

One year just before Christmas, we got a call to get to Vietnam ASAP. On the twenty-third, we flew to Singapore and met up with the rest of the crew, and the next day, we flew into Ho Chi Minh City. From the airport, we were put in a bus to travel to a harbour village called Vung Tau. The Americans, Kiwis, and Aussies went there for their R & R during the war.

I was sitting close to the front of the bus and could not believe the mayhem on the roads. At one stage, we were on this major road, four lanes in both directions and chock-a-block with pushbikes, motorbike, cars, buses, and trucks, horns blaring, goats on the back of trucks—total organised chaos. We slowly got closer to a major intersection of four lanes, both into four lanes, and we were about three cars and a hundred bikes from the lights. The lights went green, and I was not really sure of their interpretation of what green means because everyone just seemed to take off. I spotted this old man with a pushbike loaded with a ton of shit on. He's actually on the other side of the road supposedly with a red light, but he just headed out amongst all the other traffic, weaved and wobbled his way through trucks and cars and bikes, and went across the front of our bus like he was a cat with nine lives. It was bloody unbelievable and very comical. You just have to shake your head at the madness.

We arrived I think two to three hours later and were put into a hotel/motel because they had made a stuff up with our offshore visas and didn't know when we could join the vessel. It was Christmas Eve, so we were not going to argue and dropped our bags off in the rooms and headed out along the beachfront bars, had a couple of beers and then walked around and then settled into a bar called the White Elephant, which had a pool table and a dart board.

There wasn't much going on. The bay was very pretty and very flat being protected from the South China Sea by a peninsula and making it a good area for the local fishing fleet. Not long after dark, I was playing darts with a couple of others, and a firecracker came flying through the window and landed on Seagull's (Mark's) feet and went 'whiiirrr' and seemed to go out. Seagull jumped, and then as he was about to tell Ned, the cracker thrower, that the cracker had fizzled, it went *bam*. Holy shit, we all jumped out of our skin; it was like a hand grenade. Ned was pissing himself, but Seagull was pissed. Our ears were ringing.

We said, 'Where the hell did you get that?'

He said, 'They are all up and down the street in the vendors' little shops.'

We said, 'No way.'

He said, 'Way. Check this out.' And out of a bag, he pulled out this big roll of firecrackers that looked like a rack for an M16.

We followed him out the front of the bar, and a local man told him, 'You have to tie it to a tree branch, hang it down, and light it on the bottom.' All sign language and pidgin English, of course. So he hung it down, lit the bottom, and casually started to walk when, all of a sudden, this bloody thing just started exploding like an M16. He dove out of the way but not before his shirt caught on fire, and we had to smother it out. That was it. We were all off down the street buying anything we could. No one was safe for the next four to five hours; it was mayhem. Everything they had imitated, the noises of gunfire or rockets or bombs from the war. It was bloody unreal. By the end of the night, there was a motorbike and two rickshaws on fire. If it weren't for the amount of money we spent drinking and blowing things up, I'm pretty sure we would have been locked up.

Breakfast the next morning was full of funny stories from people looking very under the weather. We found out at lunchtime on Christmas Day that we were stuck there for at least another two or three days. What a bummer, ha ha. Some of us hired motorbikes and rode around touring. I took off around the peninsula to look for surf. Once I got around the other side, I couldn't believe the nice three-to-four-foot swell washed with a gentle offshore. As I rode from bay to bay seeing waves peeling here and there, I was wondering where I was going to find I surfboard. As I had come near full circle, I could see a long white beach with waves breaking everywhere.

There was another village along the beach with restaurants and bars, and a bit further on, I came across a big hotel complex. I parked the bike, walked down to the beach in front, and there was a windsurfing hire stand. I asked a guy working there if they had any surfboards, and fifteen minutes later, I was paddling around catching fun little beach break waves. I had a few beers after that and went to get my bike, and, oh shit, could I remember what it looked like. No way. There were about fifty bikes parked where I put mine. I ended up having to put my key in and take the one that started, ha ha. The party that night was a lot quieter as they only had fireworks for sale on Christmas Eve. I got another day to surf as the swell backed off and disappeared, and the day after that, we joined a vessel called the *Wellchief* and went to work.

When I returned home and told Christina about our little mad Christmas, she was really pissed off, so I said, 'I'll make it up to you and take you to Bali.'

That gave me some good brownie points, and around February/ March, we hit Bali, with Jay joining with his first trip overseas. Riding around with four on the bike was not as easy as the Balos make it look, so I ended up getting a car for the first and maybe the last time. At least on a bike, you could get around the traffic jams that had started to increase since our last trips over to what we loved as our little surf and shopping paradise.

We had a good hotel that had the original losmen-style rooms with lovely gardens, not far from the beach and still in Legian. But every now and then, you would come back to the hotel, and there was the trailer trash sitting in the pool, pissed, loud, and swearing, or even without kids, it was making it hard to hang around. We started looking for places to stay a bit more out of the way. Seminyak was opening up a bit by then. Where there used to be rice paddies and grazing cows were now an occasional restaurant, and closer to the beach, big hotel complexes were being built. It wasn't our style, but Christina managed to find a little spot back in the Kuta end down Poppies Lane 1 that had a similar feel with separate losmen spread through the gardens, so we moved there. We couldn't believe we hadn't come across it earlier. While Christina was walking around one day, she walked straight into a friend of ours from Napier who was passing through. We have a lovely photo of the two of them on the porch surrounded by flowers and very tanned.

My next trip to Africa was to join the *Wellchief* off the Congo in a French-colonised town called Pointe-Noire. This involved flying direct from Perth to Johannesburg and then bouncing through the Congo and finally landing in Pointe-Noire. At the airport, we boarded with a few of our friends coming through from New Zealand. We arrived in Johannesburg about mid-afternoon and had a couple of nights in a hotel, so the bar was pretty full, and we were up to heaps of mischief as usual. At about midnight, I had decided to call it quits. Stew, who was sharing my room, was still gas bagging to someone, so I told him I'd leave the door unlatched so he could get in without waking me, and off I went.

An hour or so later, there was a banging on the door. I got up wondering why the door was locked and let Stew in and fell on my bed. He blabbered on about something and went to go into the bathroom. The door was locked, and he was farting around.

Eventually, he said, 'Spike, are we sharing the bathroom with the room next door?'

I said, 'I doubt it. This is a Hyatt or something, isn't it?'

'Well, it's locked.'

I said, 'It can't be.'

He turned the light off, and we heard this African accent yell out, 'Turn the light on. We can't see.'

Blow me down, there was someone in our bathroom. It turned out a honeymoon couple we had talked to earlier that night had come up the stairs instead of the lift and thought they were in 504, but they were in 404. Because I had left the door lightly unlatched with the lights off, they had staggered up with the pass card, opened the door, and gone straight in for a hot sexy shower. Ha ha, bloody funny. Poor lady was so embarrassed. What a crack up.

The next day, I had organised with Mark, my friend who used to live in Port Shepstone, to catch up with his wife who had returned to South Africa from Perth. Michele picked me up and took me to a spot out of town called Ranford, a man-made shopping and dining district around a large lake with lots of bars and stuff. It was nice to see her, and there were some tears on the farewell.

Next day, we took off and landed in Congo, took off again, and while we were still heading up, all of a sudden, we lost cabin pressure. The O2 masks dropped down. The plane did a big bank, and the captain came on to say we had lost cabin pressure because none of us knew that and that we were turning back to Congo. It wasn't very reassuring when we flew over a plane similar to ours that was strategically parked in a swamp at the end of the runway. We got off the flight.

An hour later, we were told that the plane will fly tomorrow so they can fix the problem. There will be no hotel, so we were stuck in the airport. We got on the piss in the lounge, and after realising the toilets were pig troughs, we barged our way past the AK47s and parked up in the business lounge. What a long night that was. In the morning, no one had touched the plane. There were three or four guys that refused to get back on and stayed behind. I guess we played Russian roulette and walked out onto the tarmac.

Phil, an LSS (life support supervisor), spotted someone going through some bags in the hold, called over a lady that looked like she had some authority, and told her he saw that guy putting a camera out of a bag and into his overalls. She called over said workman and asked him if he had taken anything out of a bag. He said no. She turned to Phil and said he must be mistaken. We flew out and managed to land alive in Pointe-Noire.

It was midday when Stew, a dive tech, Mike, and I went for a walk. We heading down towards the coast. The place was a bit of a mess. Potholes were all over the roads. The train station had an amazing building obviously built in early colonial days but was falling apart from lack, if not no, maintenance. After that, we arrived on a beach with this really nice three-to-four-foot swell. I started freaking out. 'Let's head this way.'

As we walked, I could make out a few kids way down the beach on boogie boards, so I made a beeline for them. The closer we got, the more it looked like a surf break. There was a beach cafe/restaurant with a few expats sunbathing. I walked up to the bar and asked the lady behind if they hire out any surfboards by any chance. Next thing, I was out surfing while the boys sat back with some cold beers. When I came in, they were gone. I talked to the owner, who was happy I had a good surf, and I went off to join the crew.

The next day, we joined the *Wellchief.* The boys we left behind in the Congo turned up a day later, and we sailed for a two-to-three-week job. When we arrived back, we had two nights before the return flight to Johannesburg, and the day in between, the swell was about six feet and pumping. I had a pumping headache from the nasty beer we had the night before, but it didn't stop me. The Pyramid Bar and Restaurant owner was happy to see me and lent me his board instead of hiring it out. I was out there. When I got back to the hotel, I talked the crew into having dinner on the beach at the Pyramid, so the guy and his wife were very pleased to see about thirteen of us turned up and raced around sorting a table out for us. It was a lovely sunset and pretty good food.

We also had two nights in Johannesburg waiting for the flight to Perth, and I had talked everyone into trying to organise a safari because I had been the only one on one and told them they were mad to come through Africa on free tickets and not give it a shot. Don, our boss, was in agreement, and when we landed and were taken to the hotel, he got with our beach coordinator to get something going. I had also suggested that instead of eating at the hotel, we go to where Michele had taken me. So he organised both trips, and we had a blast. Only trouble was the drive the next day was early start because the safari park was miles away. We finished the safari with a visit to Sin City and a few beers. Then the long drive back. We were unlucky not to catch any elephants, but we got on to some rhino, had a nice picnic lunch overlooking the veld with giraffes, zebras, and kudus all around us. A long day, but I think everyone was happy they put themselves through it. We flew home late that night.

Chapter 18

SARDINIA, LIBYA, ROME AND LONDON

When we decommissioned the Skua field, I think it was the first time that Coflexip had completed one in the world. The field was stripped down, and what was to be reused was sent off to Singapore for refurbishment and then brought back and reinstalled as Elang, all for Woodside. We arrived on the *Venturer* after the FPSO was reinstalled to tie in all the field and risers. The first job was up at the chain lockers to cut the access anchor chain after they had pulled the anchors to the correct tension. The chain came up through the lockers through a pull-through shoot and was tied off on the railing above water, waiting to be picked up by the crane after we had cut the chain off.

I did the first lockout, and Nathan was bellman. Because it was only a one-man job, we had left our other bell partner, Gilly, back in the chamber. I got on the job, got the Broco burning gear down, and started cutting the first chain. The chain links are about 90 mm think, and once I had made the two cuts, I kicked the chain. It swung off, and I moved to the next one. As usual, I cut the underneath first on both links and then got up top and cut down from a safe position. Then I kicked it the same as the previous one, but there was no movement.

I kicked it again, and it was solid, so I said, 'Make it hot again, John.' I cut through from the top again and kicked it a couple of more times, but it still wouldn't budge. I went back down underneath and said to John, 'Not sure what's stopping it. There must be a bridge down here, so make it hot again,' and I did another cut.

I had barely struck the arc when I was smashed into the locker swing arm and jammed under a lot of chain. My breathing gas line to my hat was smashed off, and I had nothing to breathe. I was jammed under the chain, but with nothing to breathe, I knew I had to get out of there. The alarms were going off. John was yelling over the raw of gas around me. 'Spike, Spike, are you all right, Spike!'

I managed to wiggle and twist my head out from all this chain. I couldn't breathe, so I couldn't talk. I was looking back at the bell as I went to find my pneumo and jam it into my hat in the hope that John had automatically turned it on. As soon as it was jammed through my neck dam, I went for my bailout. I remember looking at the bell and thinking, *Is that starting to sparkle?* I found the bailout valve was still on my hat but jammed against it, and it wouldn't turn. By now, I really needed to breathe. I got both hands around the valve while all these alarms and roaring gas and the supervisor were all ringing in my head. I got to pull the valve off the hat enough to turn it on, took a big tug of gas, and said, 'On bailout heading back to the bell.'

I flew back the twenty-five metres to the bell in an instant and rammed my head up in the trunking. Bloody hell, that was a close call.

We shut everything down, and after a fifteen-minute chill-out period, I said to John I wanted to lockout on the Diver 2 rig and go over to find out what had happened and maybe finish the job. I got over there and looked at the big pile of chain that had dropped on me. It was still going up through the shoot, so it wasn't until I went and looked at the other six that I worked out the cause. Two of the remaining six chains went from the locker straight through the shoot and up to the surface like they were supposed to. The other four had various lengths of chain jammed inside the shoot and sitting on top of itself. The pile that had dropped on me was about one and a half metres long if you pulled it out straight. If I had cut any of the other ones second, it would have dropped but not enough to smash me up like that one. I finished cutting the last six without any problems, but that just goes to show you, sometimes, it's the simple operation that can catch you out. By going back over, I found out what caused my accident, but in doing so, I also dispelled any apprehension I had for wearing an enclosed breathing apparatus. The first decommission and reinstallation of an offshore FPSO was completed successfully and without any more mishaps.

Not long after that, I was off to Libya. To do this job, we went to Sardinia, an island off Italy. This was my first travel into Europe. Unfortunately, we flew straight in and out of Rome and landed at the international airport on the southern end of the island called Cagliari, and lucky for me, the vessel we were mobing for the job was a couple of hours' drive on the south end of the island, so a driver was there to pick me up and two others that I didn't know and transport us there. What a bonus. We travelled through the mountainous countryside, pretty dry as I recall. Not sure if I would like to be a farmer there; very steep and rocky, extremely picturesque. We went through quite a few neat little villages, and because the driver had the smallest car in the world and he had picked up three of us, we didn't have a lot of room, so we managed to get him to pull over in one village, and we went into a bar and had a couple of pints while he went off to re-gas the car. Wish I had taken a photo of the local elders sitting outside the pub under a big, possibly oak, tree talking and watching. Not sure what it was that drew my attention, but the picture in my head is always there when I think of that job. The roads through that town were cobbled and very narrow; I would assume the village to be very old.

We eventually made it to the vessel, and I think to this day, it could be one of the most picturesque harbours that I have had the privilege to work in. The water was a very clear emerald blue, and the bay was surrounded by steep mountains, and amazingly enough on the other side from us, there were these small villages that looked like they were carved into the countryside. I would actually like to go back there and see if what I saw was actually what I saw.

We spent a week or so getting the diving gear and sat system up and running. Then off we went into Libyan waters to install a riser and hook it up to a new manifold. We were doing the shallow clamps in the air range first when the vessel we were on did a run-off and smashed into the platform. It was pretty scary. The boom of the crane was hitting the walkway on the platform two levels above our head. We had a diver in the water that we had to get out, so we couldn't take shelter. We just hoped nothing fell on us. Luckily, we got Gery up without getting him caught up underwater and us with no walkways on the head. The vessel got its power sorted and was able to pull off without major damage.

We were out of the field doing sea trials for a few days before they would let us back in. This was the first time that I had dived in the Mediterranean, and the water was crystal clear, and there was no current for most of the time. As we moved down from the surface installing clamps on the platform to hold the riser, we seemed to have a pet cod that was there every day watching us. When we were cleaning the bracing to install the clamp, it would be very happy and hang around like a puppy dog. The ROV took a really good photo of me with my fishy mate one day when we were at the 110-metre level, and it was on the fridge in our kitchen for years until it mysteriously went missing. When we finally completed the riser and moved to the seabed at, I think, 167 metres, it was the deepest I had ever dived at the time and also the first time I had ever seen schools of John Dory, the very ugly fish that one of the surf companies, Hot Tuna, use in their company logo. I missed my little mate; it stayed on the platform.

The deco out of that job is quite possibly one of the worst I have ever done. Hector and I were in a chamber two metres around and one and a half high. We couldn't stand up. There was a sink to wash our hands and face, and a toilet. We basically lay side by side for five or six days, I can't remember exactly. I do remember my legs hurt when I got out. I crew changed off with five or six others, and we went by crew boat for thirteen hours to Malta. Man, that was really cool coming around the headland at sunrise heading into the harbour. The place just oozes history. When you have lived in such young countries as Australia and New Zealand, places like this just explode of stories of Knights Templar and stuff.

We were hoping to be taken to a hotel for a couple of hours to wash and prepare for the long flights home. Wrong. We were met at the harbour by a lovely-looking young lady who said she was sorry but she was dropping us at the airport where we had to wait for six hours for our flight out. Big bummer. No looking around, I was devastated. After finally arriving in Rome and heading towards the check-in desk, I saw the airline's info counter and decided to try my luck. We had been told by our company we were not allowed to change our tickets. No one else was interested, so off I went. To my amazement, the guy asked me what I would like to do, which was stay twenty-four hours in Rome and twenty-four hours in London. He punched away on his computer and, smiling, handed me back my tickets for as-said travel. I was wrapped. I looked over to the check-in. The guys had gone. So I turned back to the man and asked for the best place to stay overnight to get around the next day to see as much as I could. With his info, I was on a train into the city centre, booked into a bed and breakfast, and went out walking around Rome city and knocking a couple of beers down.

In the morning, I managed to jump on a six-hour tourist bus that took us around some central spots, like the Fountain of Youth and the market area that has been a market area for a couple of thousand years. We walked over a little bridge not far from that that when you look down, you see three different levels of Rome, as over the centuries, they have built on top of themselves. Then we hit the Pantheon. Well, that blew me away. It didn't just look cool; the doors were huge; they swung better than the doors in my house. Walking around inside was just mind blowing. I probably only took in half of what the guide told us. Then we headed off to the Vatican. Once again, I was blown away by the history oozing out of these places. I could be there for hours reading all the stuff on the walls, and the grandeur of the buildings is breathless. The crowds disappeared as I walked from one place to another trying to take in as much as I could.

As we were heading back to the drop off early afternoon, I asked if the bus driver could drop me off close so I could have another look at the Pantheon, mainly because I wanted to go back and also because there was a street we passed that had what looked like some nice shopping. I could maybe get Christina something. I managed to find her a nice Italian leather bag that I didn't have to mortgage the house for. Message to self, though: no matter how cool and nice a bag looks, let the lady pick her own. Yes, good advice. You may think it's good and practical, but if it's not right, it doesn't matter the cost. But it's the thought that counts. I think she still has it, but I don't think she has ever used it.

Anyway, back to the Pantheon. I was hungry by then, and although there were nice restaurants around the area, I just wanted a quick feed and carry on. So before the adverts started doing it—I reckon they copied me anyway—I grabbed a chicken burger from McDonald's and walked over under the entrance to the Pantheon and sat down to eat. A local told me off, but I pretended I didn't understand English. Not sure what his problem was. Uncouth tourist, I guess.

Anyway, while sitting in the sun looking around, I spotted a tourist shop. I walked over and bought a really cool poster map. While looking at that, I realised I hadn't been to the Colosseum. I thought, *Shit*. I went back to the shop, looked at another map quickly, walked back into the Pantheon to refresh my memory, and then headed off down the road. I walked through an area called the Forum more by accident than any organised walk. I only had about an hour once I arrived at the Colosseum, but it seemed to be enough to walk through down underneath and then sit up on the stadium arena and fantasise about the events that would have been played out. And of course, they would have been very similar to those depicted in *Monty Python's Life of Brian*. So after one beer at a bar on the walk back to the hotel, I grabbed my bag and was off to London.

I had had a British passport for ten years, and the day I arrived in London was a Friday night, the day after my passport expired. Never mind I was stuck in the expat queue; it only took a half hour longer. I was told by someone to go to Earl's Court; not sure why, but by the time I found a bed and breakfast, I went out for maybe two pints and then started doing head dips. Once again, in the morning, I just organised to jump on a tour bus. We did the rocket ship in and out all these amazing spots: the Tower, of course, and St Peter's Cathedral. We watched the Changing of the Guard and had lunch at a really nice restaurant with a group of South Africans on the same tour. And the day was finished with a nice cruise up the Thames, taking in the sites on sunset. I mean, the Tower/Castle and St Peter's are amazing, and you can spend a lot of time there. I have been back to the Tower but yet to return to St Peter's. London is full of amazing stuff. The hardest part is finding out where it is and getting to it. But put the effort in and you will be rewarded. I finished my day with two quick pints in a pub somewhere and then back on the plane to the relatively young country called Australia.

Over the next year or so, most of my work were based around North West Australia. We were lucky if we were doing a sat job. The deco would take us long enough that the vessel would sail to Singapore while we were decoing. We would usually arrive on surface a day or more before we went past Bali, so they started dropping us off there. Because of that, I had left one of my good boards in Bali after a family trip and stay for a couple of days' surf afterwards, and sometimes I would fly the family up for a week, so they got a bonus as well.

It was possibly the early to mid-1990s that I was first told about Gnaraloo Station. This is a huge sheep station about a thirteen-hour drive north of Perth. It has one of the top three waves in Australia plus a few other extremely good waves in the area; the Bluff being another in the top twenty. So on our first trip, I hired a Jayco camper van; the kids love that shit. And off we went. We pulled into Kalbarri for a couple of days to break the trip up. We arrived in Carnarvon late afternoon after a longer drive than I expected and stocked up with food, water, beer, wine, and petrol because the camp we were going to had nothing except a shop with lollies, ice creams, and not a lot else. Anyway, on our way to the station, we stopped at the blowholes. There was a bit of swell, so we watched that for a break out of the car. Thinking not far now, off we went.

The road went from tar-seal to shingle, and we rattled on. It went dark. Even Christina was saying, 'Shouldn't we be there by now?'

We finally went through the Gnaraloo farm entrance and finally pulled up at three-mile camp. The shop was shut. Luckily, someone was there. It was 9 p.m., and she couldn't believe me when I said, 'I didn't realise you had to book.'

Anyway, she shuffled around and said, 'I can put you on this site, but you will have to move when they arrive in a couple of days.' I thanked her and apologised for not booking, and again for arriving late. And off we went to set up the caravan once again in the dark.

We awoke to a very cold but clear morning with blue sky and offshore winds. We were overlooking a sea lagoon of crystal-clear water with waves breaking on an outside reef about three hundred metres away, very picturesque. After breakfast, a friend from Perth, Brad, that had told me about the place found us, and we had a catch-up with them. By ten in the morning, it is getting warm, and you are down to board shorts and T-shirts, which for July and midwinter is pretty nice. We met the campers on either side of us who were both families from the Margaret River area. At around three in the afternoon, you start putting your clothes back on, and you don't stop until you light the fire or go to bed. Man, it gets cold.

The camping here is unreal. We had been taken out that day by friends to collect firewood on the farm, very hard because there were not a lot of trees. The land is very flat and barren, as I explained a few chapters ago. But the water is teaming with life. Turtles swim past you; stingrays, dolphins, and you see whales blow off in the distance every day. But sitting around the campfire after a cook up with an explosion of stars overhead was part of the magic of the camp. There is a big sand dune to the north-west of the camp that we would take the sand board to and see who could get the best run. The main surf break called Tombstones wasn't breaking because it was too small, but we were hitting another spot called Turtles, which was about four to six feet and a really good left. In the background of Turtles is the Bluff, extremely picturesque and an amazing wave.

I was introduced to Noel, who was surfing with us and camped next to Brad and Debbie's camp. Noel is from Margaret River as well, like just about everyone else I met there. On the second night, we were invited over to their camp for dinner. Noel, when he found out we were from Napier, had said that he has been to Napier because his girlfriend lived there as well years ago. Christina, the kids, and I walked up as Noel came out of his camper. Brad was throwing some wood on the fire. Noel called out to Michelle. When she stepped out, we all nearly froze. Oh my god, there was Michelle, who had been in the hospital in Napier at the same time as Christina when Ryan was born. She was with a surf friend of mine, Bede.

Bede had left New Zealand and met her in Margaret River in the early 1980s, and they had returned to Napier, and she had given birth to their son a few days after ours. Unfortunately, a few months later, Bede had gone off on a commercial fishing trip down the east coast, and the vessel disappeared without a trace. It had been a very hard time for all of us. And I think the last time we had seen Michelle was at Bede's farewell ceremony when all hope was lost. So there was Michelle. She and Christina sat straight down and rattled away. We kept close with her and Noel over the years and often dropped in when we were down south on surf trips.

The first week went by, and still the main break slept. Then one afternoon, it started breaking, and although it was small and nothing special, I finally got to surf it. At about 4 a.m. the next day, I was awoken to a crashing of waves on the outside reefs. At 6:30, I jumped in the car and took off to the car park in front of Tombstones, and as I pulled up, I noticed one guy just paddling out when this set thundered through and totally blew my mind. It was a long way offshore and looked about five to six feet, and after offloading and spitting out the end of the barrel section, it just peeled off for ages. I watched a couple of sets and took a few photos before jumping out and getting my wetsuit on.

Just as another set was slamming down, a car pulled up with two guys in it. One wound the window down and said, 'That looks good. Are there many of those?'

I said, 'About every ten minutes, there's a set of about six.'

He said, 'Cool.'

I was grabbing my 7'4" out and said, 'Shame I've only got the 7'4 because I cracked the fin on my 6'10" at Jakes on the way up.'

He looked at the next wave and said, 'I'll think you'll be all right.'

I said, 'See ya out there.'

I managed to get out the back in between Centres and Thomby's without a big set hitting and dropped down the reef to where I had seen the only other guy out. He had just taken a wave all the way down and was paddling back.

I will never forget my first take-off. I stroked into this lump of water that as I was paddling hard was growing and draining off the reef. I finally felt a bit of push, and as I jumped to my feet, the wave just went vertical. It was between eight and ten feet, and at the bottom, I dropped over a ledge and pulled the board up through a bottom turn to line up on a wall that, as far as I could see, was pitching over. I pumped the board and bent down to grab the rail as it pitched right over me. I was going a hundred miles an hour, and as I was coming out of the barrel, out of the corner of my eye, I could see one of the guys from the car park bailing off his board. He would have been smashed as I flew out, dropped down into another bottom turn, pulled up mid face, and pumped the board as it was barrelling over me. I had to keep pumping to keep up with it, and it was pitching way over my head. I came flying out, dropped down to drain off some speed and slam another bottom turn back up into mid face, and pumped the board through another three-second cover-up barrel, and then came flying out and over the back as the wave closed out in the bottom of the bay. I was huffing and puffing. I could not believe the wave I had just ridden. It was insane.

It took ages to paddle back, and when I got there, the car park guy said, 'Far out, that was a good first wave, mate.'

Too right. I was stoked. The surf break was bloody intense. Even the pro surfers were getting smashed, but when they made them, they made it look easy. As the swell built, it probably got to solid ten feet plus. People would disappear out of the line-up. Boards were breaking. In between the sets, everyone would be chatting away about whether they got smashed or how awesome their last wave was and how they saw their mate eat it. And then the sets would come running down the point through midges, the first break, and the place would go quiet as the sets hit Centres, the second break, and everyone would be freaking out whether they are in the right place. 'Will I get one? Will I cop one? Where should I be?' Then the first line would hit, and someone would commit, and as you're paddling to get out of the way, you're hearing people down the line starting to hoot as someone is pulling in. Then you would either hear 'ooohhh' as they ate it or hoots as they made it. It was just insane.

After a few hours, I was getting tired, so I slid down the line to have a break from the intense take-offs. I had had a really good long ride and was paddling back. I was close to the second take-off spot when a guy had pulled in deep but not made it on a solid ten-footer. There was a lady in bikinis on a boogie board, and she swung around and was kicking like mad to try and get on the wave. All of a sudden, it just lurched and threw her with the lip. I couldn't believe it, when she landed on the bottom of the wave, dug the board in, her tits flew out of her bikini. She wouldn't have known as she flew past me and rocketed down the wave. I was hooting, not at her hooters but the fact that she had made the take-off. She blasted past me with the biggest grin on her face. I talked to her about it a little later, and she was stoked.

Not long after that, I couldn't handle watching the main take-off anymore and decided to go and have another shot. I paddled in deep and waited my turn. A few sets later, and I was in the perfect spot for a solid ten-foot screamer. I forced myself over the ledge, but it had drained out a bit too much, and I just dived into the bottom of the wave and popped out the back, waiting to get my leg yanked and get pulled into the impact zone. All of a sudden, my board popped up in half. That was the end of that surf.

My camping neighbour said, 'Ooh, bad luck, you nearly made that.'

Bummer, I started swimming in. When I got back to the beach, I pulled out the camera and took another couple of photos. It was absolutely pumping, and after another set, I thought I had better get Christina and bring her here to see this. This is bullshit. I found them on the beach at the lagoon and explained that she needed to come and look at this surf break. We headed back, and just as we were getting out of the car, I had the camera going and a set trucked through.

As I was taking the photo, Christina said, 'Oh my god, that looks dangerous.'

I took a few more photos. I found out from the car park gossip that so far, about 3:30 in the afternoon, four people had been taken to hospital and over twenty boards had been broken. That was why people seemed to disappear. They were either getting hurt or breaking boards or leg ropes.

My camp neighbour Brian was a board repair man, so that afternoon, I helped him fix my 6'10" so I had something to surf with the next day. The next morning was on again, about the same size but not as consistent. I was second in the car park again, and as I was running down to the spot where you hit the water, I saw the South Australian guy who was the first out again paddling for a wave, and in the face underneath was what looked like a two-metre bronze whaler midway down the face. I heard his girlfriend scream, and I stopped and reassured her he will be OK. He hadn't caught the wave, so it would still be under him.

The day was another classic of epic barrels breaking boards and bodies. I got out at about 1 p.m. and was having a beer with another bloke watching the sets when a young guy got axed. He was in trouble, but lucky for him, someone close by spotted him and managed to get him in to the beach. At first, I thought it was his hip, but it was his leg that was broken in three places, and he was nearly passing out. We used a surfboard as a stretcher to get him out of the water and up to the car park. I tried to get his pulse while we waited for the guy that had gone to get the doctor that was there on holiday. This happens so much that the camp office has a drug cabinet. If there is a doctor on holiday, he lets the office know. So the doc turned up, gave him water and a once-over, and dosed him up with morphine so he can make it along the very rough road and meet up with the ambulance coming from town. I was told by the young guy's mates that they were nearly at the tar-seal road (an hour and a half of bumping and banging) before they met the ambo.

Eighteen boards were broken the second day. Two people, including the young one we helped, went to town, and two were treated by the holiday doctor. The third day was just as good mayhem and doctor calls. Apparently, twenty boards, three doctor appointments, but no ambos from town. And that was it. The place went back to sleep, and I had one more surf around at Turtles. Then we headed home. We had had such a lovely time up there that it was our annual trip for years to come. Not every year I could get there, but for the next twelve to thirteen years until I started working in the North Sea, I did the pilgrimage to my surf mecca.

One year, our neighbours Collen and Barry brought the family up and stayed at the Gnaraloo Station holiday camp. While having dinner there one night, the ladies came back from the shower saying that there were guys filleting fish after fish. I said to Barry and Ryan that we will get the rubbish bin later and stash it overnight. The next day, I took them to Gnaraloo Bay to a spot just south of the boat ramp. The snorkelling there is amazing. The plan was to take everyone out for a snorkel. It is shallow but teaming with fish, turtles, and stingrays. After everyone had had enough snorkelling, I took the bin out with all the fish guts and bones and burlyed the place up to get the sharks in so we could watch them. Bloody typical, not a single shark showed. Then I spotted a big fish making its way along the deep section. I put my mask on and swam out to see what he was. It turned out to be a big Queensland grouper, and I yelled out to everyone to come and check it out. Well, it took me ten minutes to talk them into the water because I had spent all the night before telling them how awesome the sharks were going to be when I burlyed up. Well, they finally jumped in, and we were hand feeding this big grouper, and they said that was better than seeing heaps of sharks. I miss the place now. I hope I get back there one day before I'm too slow to take it on.

Towards the end of the 1990s, we sailed out of Singapore on the *Venturer* to do a large job off Vietnam. When I had done my days, my team and I crew changed off the vessel into Vung Tau. It had been a few years since that Christmas trip, and the place had really grown. There were different bars, but I went to the White Elephant where we had had the firecracker war. The bar owner was now an Aussie guy from Perth, and he said I could watch the Eagles play, so I did that on his TV. There were only three of us at the bar. After that, we went to a nightclub. Wow, the place had really changed from a sleepy little fishing village into a much more happening club scene. We only had the one night, and the next day, we were treated to the frightfully congested drive back into Ho Chi Minh and the airport. We were only in a small van, so it didn't seem anywhere near as hectic as the bus years earlier.

Shortly after that, I was on a job back in South Africa. This time, I was heading to Cape Town. Christina and I hadn't gotten down to Cape Town on our trip in 1985/86 as we had run out of money and time. I was picked up at the airport and taken into Octo Marine's office, met some crew, and worked in the yard for the day. The next day, we moved onto an Italian pipelay barge and started mobing the sat system.

The World Cup Rugby was on, and because I was a Kiwi, everyone thought I knew everything about rugby. We knocked off, and I got taken out for a show around. We started by just walking off the vessel into the tourist area in the harbour called the Waterfront. As you would expect, the area is full of bars and restaurants. Then we headed into the city district and later ended up in a little bar with good music. I met a sports bar manager that asked me what I thought of the All Blacks game last night, and when I said I missed it because I was in the air, he said to come to his club tomorrow night and he would put it on for me. So after a good day's work, we turned up at the club.

He introduced his girlfriend as if I was royalty and said, 'After this live game, we will put the All Blacks on.'

I said, 'Thanks, man.'

He took off and came back with two jugs of beer. He was a top bloke. At the end of the game, I bought him and his lady a nice bottle of wine, and after finishing it, we took off into the city clubs.

Towards the end of the week, the rest of the crew turned up, and we finally sailed up the coast to an oilfield off Mossel Bay. This is major white pointer territory, and I was hoping to get to see one as we worked our way down the platform installing clamps and then installing the riser. Unfortunately, that never happened, and after completing our bend watch, we were choppered off late afternoon and transported by bus back into Cape Town. I had decided to skip the first flight home and got booked on the next one four nights later. Everyone else left next morning, and I hired a car and did a drive around. One of the divers on the job had a mate with a surf shop in Muizenberg Bay, so Friday after driving right around the Cape, I went and found him. He gave me a good deal on a Mini Mal surfboard, and by the time that was all sorted, it was back down to Harbour Town.

I dropped into the sports bar and watched a World Cup game with the manager, and he told me to come in the next day for the finals, which was Australia versus France. About early afternoon, the weather cleared, and all of a sudden, it was blue skies, so I grabbed my camera and headed up to Table Mountain. On the cable car, I heard a couple of guys talking about the rugby, and when I asked the score, they said it was starting in an hour. They had picked up the accent and, one being a Kiwi and the other being the cable car driver, asked what I was up to and then told me they had the game on in the main restaurant on a big screen and invited me to join them. I trekked around, taking in the views all around the Cape for a while, and when I had seen everything, I went and joined the two from the cable car.

It turned out the Kiwi guy runs the bungee jumping off the cable car overlooking Lion's Head. And there was a large crew that worked on Table Mountain at the game, and when the game finished with Australia winning, they said I can stay back with them for an hour as they closed up the Mountain, and we returned on the workers' cable car. As they were shutting the Mountain down, I was sitting with a beer on the restaurant balcony watching the sunset. It reminded me of *The Hitchhiker's Guide to the Galaxy: Restaurant at the Edge of the Universe.* You couldn't paint a picture more perfect than that view. I was joined by a couple of the ladies as we waited, and the company topped off a lovely view as we chatted into the darkness. I ended up joining the Table Mountain crew for dinner and dancing and at the end of the night thanked them for their hospitality. I was a late riser the next day, but I still managed to get to some markets and get some African artefacts to take home.

We were coming up to the end of the millennium, so I had decided I would not be away for New Year. It wasn't that I was worried about the clocks or the world imploding; it was just that I decided I wanted to see the last sunset of the twentieth century. And what a sunset it was. We spent it on the Scarborough foreshore and without the standard howling south-west wind. There was barely a breeze, and the ocean was glassy as the sun went down on 1999. It wasn't until October 2000 that I left Australia again.

Chapter 19

GULF OF MEXICO

This time, and for the first time, I headed to the Gulf of Mexico to join a Subsea 7 vessel called the *Bar Protector*. I transited through Los Angeles to Mexico City and then into a place called Puerto del Carmen, an island in the Gulf that serves as an oilfield base. A couple of friends were at the hotel when I checked in. We ended up in a lap dancing bar later, and oh my god, some of the women there were absolutely stunning. The following afternoon, we departed on a supply boat, and I was amazed because for over eight hours steaming along, there were just platform after platform, huge barges, and drill rigs. When the sun went down, the flare stacks stood out one after the other, and it was forever.

We finally arrived on the *Bar Protector* and settled into the job. Before I went into sat, I was on night shift and used to go up on the heli deck and walk around listening to music, getting some sun, and watching the mayhem around the vessel. Usually, you would be alongside a platform, and there might be another one in the distance or on the horizon. Not there. There are platforms next to platforms, and then just over there, there's another platform next to a platform. Some had walkways connecting them to the other platforms. At shift change time, there would be crew boats all over the place going into waiting patterns for their turn to race in and pick people up and take them wherever.

Choppers were flying all over the place; it was bloody insane. We were having lunch one day, and over the Tannoy, the radio op screamed, 'Heli crew to the heli deck. Heli crew to the heli deck. Chopper in ten minutes.' People would jump up and run out, only to find out the chopper had the wrong vessel. It really is unique; there is so much going on out there.

After our sat, I headed home with Stew and Gilly, whom I had been in sat with. We got absolutely smashed when we hit the beach, and waking up the next day in Mexico City, we were pretty slow at moving. I said to Stew I was still going to force myself to head out for a look around. Gilly shook his head and went back to bed. Stew and I jumped into a taxi, and off we went. We didn't know where to go, but the taxi driver said if we wanted to shop around, there is a tourist warehouse that has everything, so we went there. Man, what a spot. He was right; it had everything from ponchos to stuffed grizzly bears and panthers. It was huge, and it was exactly what I was looking for. I got two Mexican rugs. The colours are amazing; I don't know what dye they use, but they are bright and they stayed bright, never faded, only got thinner and thinner.

But the real jewel of the spot was the jewellery. The stones and the quality of the silver and the style of the rings and earrings, bracelets, and necklaces were way above anything I had bought in Africa India or Indonesia. I ended up spending over $2,000, but I was sure I would get my money back, and I did. Stew did very well. He had done some homework on precious stones and came across some stones that are really hard to come by. The last I talked to him, he still had that stone, and it is worth over ten times what he paid for it. I'll hit him up for the name.

We arrived safely to the hotel from our shop, but there was no heading out for drinks. Because we had all arrived on different flights, we all parted company on different flights. Not sure why. I ended up in LA airport with about four hours to wait. I wasn't that impressed with the airport, but I found a bar to sit at. I was there for three hours, and everyone that walked up and ordered a drink got a shot of tequila. Bloody classic. Black, white, male, female, fat, skinny, old, or young—I mean, everyone. Bloody funny. Then I was gone.

Through the early 2000s, the *Venturer,* now owned by Technip after buying out Coflexip, and the *Rocky 2,* owned by Subsea 7, pretty much kept a nucleus of us sat divers busy enough to maintain our lifestyles. We did the occasional air job up north, which we called the holiday jobs, but mainly we did deep construction. In 2005, with our rates out of Singapore still pretty low compared to the job we were doing, a few of us told Technip and Subsea 7 to jamb it and through someone else scored a position on a vessel in the Gulf of Mexico for an American company called Global Marine.

I had come across a house in Trigg close to the beach that looked like a good investment, and after our offer was accepted, I said to Christina, 'You will have to get the real estate to put it up for rent for a year so we can get some tax back.' I didn't have time to organise it before I left, and the settlement was a week after I left anyway. I already had a couple of friends over on the vessel in the Gulf, Stew and Mike, and they warned me it was a bit dodgy, but once you commit to something, you need to see it through as far as I'm concerned. Besides, I had to go to New Zealand to get the work visa, so that meant free tickets home to see the family. I ended up with a weekend in Wellington and then headed through Mexico City to Puerto del Carmen.

The next morning, as we sailed up the Gulf to a vessel called the *Triton,* I noticed the lack of flare stacks blowing off. The stacks were still there, of course, but they weren't burning the gas as they had years earlier because the gas was now being used and piped to the mainland instead of burning off to nothing. We were definitely advancing in that respect. The *Triton* was a big steel catamaran with a big derrick crane. It had a huge old Taylor diving system on it similar to the one on my very first job. Stew and Mike had left by the time I got on board, so when I joined my shift, I just mingled in and slowly met the crew as the day went on. It didn't take me long to realise why Stew and Mike had pulled the pin; it was a little bit like the documentaries you see on TV. They definitely did things differently, and I didn't agree with some of it, but when in Rome. I tried to advise them certain things were in their own interest like doing bailout function tests and wearing the proper diving gear instead of jumping in the water looking like Jed Clampett, but got the old 'you're a dumb arse, leave us alone'. So after a while, I just had fun with them and did all my safety shit and made sure I was going to survive. The supervisors did the right thing, and that is what matters.

Katrina hit while I was there. We had done a runner into one of the shelter towns, and it was pretty hard work watching some of the guys trying to get through a day on shit worrying about family and stuff. There was no communication, and all they had for info was what was on TV. I was sitting with one guy, and he said, 'See that roof there with the chimney on the right? That's my house.'

The water was up to the gutters, and all you could see was the roof. He said he had his pride and joy in the garage and was just shaking his head. I didn't press him on it. He just wanted to listen to the TV. He had found out the next day through a cousin that lived upstate that his brother had driven down in his ute, found the keys, and got the 1969 Chevy that they had restored out of town before it was too late. But the night before, he thought it was all gone.

A couple of weeks later, I was blowing into sat and called Christina for the last family catch-up. She said she wanted to live on the beach and we were moving to Trigg. I said no. She ignored me, and she already had someone to move into our house.

I said, 'No. It'll cost me $10,000 in tax back.'

She said, 'Too late. You're over there and I'm in control. Bye. Have a nice sat.'

I started off with a Russian/Canadian, but a week or two later, he had a freak out and decided he had enough. They sent in a Mexican guy who was OK. Then cyclone Rita came through, and we started deco while heading into a safe town. There was a two-man team of Mexican divers in another chamber that had organised their mates that worked on deck to send in a few bottles of rum and vodka. We got absolutely shit-faced and had a real laugh. They were teaching me Spanish, and I picked up a bit. They also gave me the good advice on the best tequila to buy before I went home. Rita also did a lot of damage and came in at a different area, so not the same people were affected. We sailed again, and I ended up coming out and heading home. I got a taxi driver taking me to the airport to stop at a bottle shop and pick up a bottle of Corralejo Añejo and Don Julio Añejo (*añejo* means 'vintage') for $20 instead of the $65 each I would have paid at the airport.

For some weird reason, they flew me Mexico City to Vancouver to Tokyo to Perth. I had a night over in Vancouver so got a walk around the city on a sunny morning. God knows why I went that way. I flew into Perth and a new home. The next day, Christina said, 'It's too small and I want to move back to Burniston Street.' Oh, piss off.

Octo Marine got a hold of me for a job in Noverasisk, a town in the Black Sea, south of Moscow. I thought it was a sat job, but when I arrived, I found out it was a surface gas job replacing hoses on an SBM not far offshore of a marine base. The crew was all South Africans with four Russian divers to make up the numbers. Most of the team were staying in a workers' camp close to the refinery, and I was to stay on the vessel with one other diver. The food wasn't that great, but I had my own cabin. The guys had been there for three months already and had the town sorted for night activities.

They had been invited to a local wedding on the Saturday and said that I might as well take the other guy's place. So my second night in Russia, I was thrown right into Russian culture, and I love that shit. We couldn't understand anyone but managed to get by, and the mother of the bride made sure we got involved, got bloody smashed on vodka, and danced to their cultural music as well as the standard modern stuff. Pretty neat night.

After the reception, we hit a nightclub called Orange. Far out, I have never seen so many goddesses in one place. The dance floor was mostly women, and the music was that good you couldn't sit down. I was up on the dance floor, and all these girls were rubbing up against you. When you look out into the tables, you would see groups of men staring at you and making throat slashing actions when you were obviously too close to their girl. We, all of a sudden, got ushered out by all these guys in black that looked pretty intimidating.

The next day, I was working on deck when one of the main Russian divers (can't remember his name, so we'll call him Vladimir) came up to me and said, 'Morrrnning, Sspiike. You must tell Scotty and Warren they cannot go to Orange anymore. I will not be able to save them next time, OK? You tell them, please.'

I said, 'Sure.'

When Scotty and Warren turned up, I passed on the info and asked what that was all about. They said, 'Can't you remember last night getting escorted out of Orange?'

I said, 'Yeah, sort of.'

Well, when we were dancing, I noticed these heavy guys starting to group up and eyeing us up. So I called Vladimir because he is in the Mafia to come and give us back up. Vladimir brought ten of his troops, but the nightclub was run by a different gang, and he was warned next time they would disappear. Apparently, Scotty and Warren had been going there a lot and obviously playing with the wrong women.

I was there for over a month and got to check out the city. It was pretty amazing, probably more because it was such a different culture to what I was used to. There was no doubt that there were a lot of stunning women in the city. When the job was done, the boss put on a big party in town at the complex he stayed at. During the morning, Vladimir took me and Warren out to a farm in the country to buy meat for the barbecue. Now that was a different scene altogether. I mean, the countryside itself is no different to any other, but the way people were dressed and the way they looked were totally different to the city. I was really glad I went with them. Also on the way back into town, we stopped at a bottle shop to get the drinks. I was looking at all these really cool bottles of vodka to take home and decided to ask Vladimir's advice on the best stuff. He said not to bother with all the fancy-looking bottles and pulled off the shelf this cheap-looking and cheap-priced bottle called Russian Standard. He said that is government vodka and the best in the country. They actually export it now and it is as he said—very good clean vodka.

Oh, forgot to tell you about a night Scotty and I went out. The weather was up—we wouldn't be diving the next day—and I think it was Scotty's birthday. He wanted to go to this cabaret restaurant club. They do cultural shows after the restaurant shuts, and it sort of turns into a nightclub. It was cheaper to buy jugs of vodka than anything else. The show was unreal. They did about three different shows, and it was like a mini theatre. As usual, heading back to the marina, I dropped Scotty off and carried on to the front gate, left the taxi, and staggered down the hill through security. It was cold and blowing its tits off. Waves were breaking over the break wall, and the boats were getting banged around a lot.

I'm not sure what happened as I was on the gangplank, but I sobered up pretty quick when I hit the water twenty feet below. It was cold. I hit the surface and looked around, thinking what the hell just happened. There was a tyre, and I tried climbing up, but I was too heavy with wet jeans and a jacket. Next thing, the boat started moving back in. It was pitch black. I can't see anything, and the boat started pushing me against the concrete wall. Just as the pressure was hard on my chest and starting to squeeze my head, it stopped and moved off away from me. I thought, *Jesus, that was close. I need to get out of here.* I swam over to another boat that had a lower back deck and managed to climb out and get myself into my cabin for a hot shower. I was close to a statistic that morning, and it reminded me of our friend that had been found floating next to his fishing boat in Ulladulla many years earlier who had hit his head when he fell off the gangplank. I'm not sure if he got to have his twenty-first birthday. I was lucky.

We had managed to get invited to join the *Mayo* in Egypt for Subsea 7. That was really cool. We got to ride camels around the Giza pyramids and walk around the souks of Cairo. On our return, Andy, Richard, and I had a two-day wait for flights and ended up hiring a local sailing boat and doing a sunset sail with some cold beers down the river towards the pyramids. On the second trip, we went and watched the laser show from the roof of some local's house right next to the gate. They brought us cold beers and hash. We hung out up there for two shows. Then they talked us into riding horses out and around the pyramids while the last show was on. That was a lot of fun actually, and there was a moon out to add to the scene. On the way home from the second trip, I picked up a couple of belly dancing dresses for Christina, and we walked through the tourist part of the souks, the Khan el-Khalili, and down to the more local area with a guide. We were looking at gold and gemstones. It wasn't until we got right down to the produce market area that we really got a feel for the poor side of the city. It was noticeably more inhospitable but OK if you were not by yourself.

That night, at the hotel room after getting a bit smashed, I decided to put the belly dancing gear on. Luckily, Stew was pissing himself so much he didn't get a very good photo. Stew and I were worried we would miss our flight out because they had the airport shutdown because they were bringing Yasser Arafat's body in after his death. We managed to make our flight.

Chapter 20

DON'T BE SCARED OF SHARKS OR NORTH SEA TIGERS

There was a hyperbaric welding job due to start up in the North West that had everyone all excited. Then the *Venturer* headed over to do a project out of Mossel Bay in South Africa. I called up our bosses in Perth to see if we were going to crew it. They said it's being crewed out of the Aberdeen office, but they will see if we can get a slot for some of us. I was reminded about the coding up tests for the extremely high-paying welding job and said I'll have a shot for sure. As so often happens, there will be no work for ages. Then two jobs will start at the same time, and you have to pick which one and hope you make the right move. I was called and told I could get on the *Venturer,* and they were paying North Sea rates. OK, I'm in. At the time, North Sea rates were the best in the world.

I sat at home and waited. I was skipped crew change after crew change, and in the meantime, I had decided that I had better get some welding practice so hired a welding booth and started getting my eye back in. I had never done mild steel TIG, and that was the root weld, so I needed to learn that bit. The weld trials started, so I put my hand up and applied because it looked like they were going to stitch us up in Africa. Then it all fell into place. Stew, Gilly, and I were called and told we were heading over to Cape Town in two weeks. I had time to do the weld test procedures, so I went in, and we started doing practice pipes so the welding inspector could see if we were wasting his time. After four days, he said that we were all good enough to give it a shot.

The next day, we went in and set up a thirty-inch stub to weld out in pairs. I did one side, and Mike from New Zealand did the other. Mike was very keen and welding better than me, so I let him pick where he wanted to start, and I'll do the opposite. He thanked me, and as I knew he would choose to start at six o'clock, which is the hardest but the best, so I hit the ten o'clock to weld to twelve. We finished our runs at about the same time, and I moved down to six o'clock ground, his start out ready for my start. As I was coming up, I accidentally found myself walking the cone that I had been trying to do through all the practice. I still don't know how it fell in place, but once you get that rhythm, it is a lot easier. I pulled off pretty impressed with myself when I ran out of wire around the nine o'clock. I flipped up my lid and spotted the welding inspector looking down inside at the root.

Mike said, "Were you walking the cone?'

'Yeah, not sure how, but it makes it easier.'

The inspector pulled his head out and said I've failed.

I said, 'What?'

'You've failed because you have missed penetration on one side at the start at ten o'clock.'

I looked down. That was inside the grind out area, and I said so.

He said, 'No, you have failed.'

The workshop welder that was coaching us looked while I was talking to the inspector. He looked me eye to eye, said nothing, and walked away. He knew the truth, but it wasn't his job to argue. The inspector walked away and said nothing else. So I was gone. Mike and I think five others passed and went over to the UK to sit the next lot of tests under pressure. Three of them, Lee, Greg, and Gerry, passed. Good for them. There isn't a welder that I've talked to that agrees with his reason for my fail. That was in the grind out start/stop area, and that's that. I still went on the job, so don't throw the book away yet because the best shark stories are not far away.

Stew, Gilly, and I flew into Cape Town a week later. We had a day before the *Venturer* turned up for the crew change. I took them up to Table Mountain. We had a good walk around, but it went cloudy and then got cold. We met a large crew the next day as they were doing a big crew change. We sailed that night after working on deck for a few hours. Jim, the UK OCM, decided to keep us as a team, and we blew in the next day. The UK crew has a little bit of different style from us. There were a couple of supervisors we knew. The job went well. I still never saw a white pointer, and that pissed me off. We had some pretty heavy ground swells coming through, and all I could think about was how good Jeffreys Bay would have been breaking.

After the deco and while we were on bend watch, I talked everyone into doing a shark dive trip to Hass Bay. I booked it, and we were being picked up from the hotel at 0600 hrs the next morning. The project had been a success, and we were being taken out to this really nice restaurant at the base of Table Mountain to celebrate. Thirteen of us had a really good night. We all got absolutely smashed to the point where a couple were kicked out, and the rest of us had to apologise for them.

I got a call from Micky in the morning. He was the night shift superintendent and a top bloke. He said, 'The man is here to pick us up, but no one is here.'

It ended up everyone was too sick. I got down to the foyer and was told that the booking will not be reimbursed. Micky had managed to persuade a couple of Qantas flight attendants to join us. They hmmed and ahhed, so I said, 'You can come for half price.' That sealed the deal.

We jumped in the bus, and both Micky and I crashed out again. We arrived at the bay and pulled up to an old colonial house to fill out paperwork and have breakfast. This house was circa 1800s with some of the original furniture. It was pretty cool. There were some good photos on the walls of early Africa and, of course, large sharks. We boarded a forty-foot cat and headed up the coast to a rocky island outcrop in the middle of a bay. There were seals everywhere. The crew started chumming up the water, and we settled in for the waiting game after we swung the cage over the side. It was a sunny day with a little bit of wind that took some of the warmth out of the sun. A three- to four-metre shark turned up, and we started getting excited, but it stayed away from the cage so not worth jumping in the water. It was having a go at the decoy, though, so we had a bit of fun with that. The next two sharks that came by were similar, aggressive but shy of the cage, so no putting on the wetsuits. We had some whales breaching real close to entertain us for a short time. Then it went quiet.

It was nearly four o'clock and looking like a lemon day when, all of a sudden, all hell broke loose. I was sitting up in a frame over the top of the chum box, and this bloody mouthful of teeth came flying out and ripped into the decoy, splashing everyone, and even gave the deckies a jump. It was about four metres and went close to the cage, so we jumped in the wetsuits and hit the water. I was first in, just a mask and snorkel, and was trying to grab or pat it as it went past. Micky got in as it was coming straight at us. He gave me the thumbs up as it swept past and disappeared in the gloom. We could see its outline turning to come back when I saw the Qantas stewardess climb down. She hit the water and turned around right when Jaws was about five feet away and coming straight at us. She screamed and jumped back up the ladder. I called out, assuring her it's OK, She dropped back in and got her breath back.

We had about half an hour, and it started getting cold. As we were taking our wetsuits off and talking about how cool that was, the deckies were getting rid of the last of the chum and having a fight with Jaws over the last three tuna heads. He was smashing the back of the boat up, and the girls were starting to freak out. Micky and I couldn't get our gear off quick enough to join in the fun. Although a slow start, it cost me a lot more than it should have; it turned out worth it. Some of the no-show boys coughed up their money to lessen my damage. We arrived back into the hotel at about 7 p.m. We went for a quiet couple of drinks down the Waterfront and flew home the next day.

About two weeks before the welding job was about to mobilise, I was building a new boat trailer and ripped a big chunk of skin off the back of my calf muscle, causing me to miss the start of the job. If I hadn't done that, I would not have ended up bell partners with Shorty and Andy, two UK welders that I was teamed up with on the *Venturer*. I have never seen anyone drink so much tea; it was bloody amazing. So I think it may have been our first dive. We were at the bottom of *North Rankin*, about 120 metres, really good visibility, and Shorty and I were working on a thirty-six-inch valve about twenty-five metres inside the platform. This platform is huge, and everything is huge down there. Shorty's eyes were huge just watching all the fish. So I was up on top of this pipe cleaning the bolts around the flange, and Shorty had headed back out to the work basket to get some tools. Next thing, all I heard was '*Spiiikkeee, foookkaanheell, Ssppiiikee!*' I turned around I can't see him.

The supervisor was saying, 'What's up, Shorty?'

I thought there was a drama, so I was dropping off the pipe to go save him. He was still going. *'Whaaat theee fffooook, is that Spiiikeee!'*

I finally got there, and there was the local four-metre grey nurse pointing into the current. Shorty was absolutely freaking out at the size of it. Luckily for him, it was looking the other way. I said, 'Oh, fuck's sake, Shorty, it's only a shark,' and started laughing.

Shorty can't stop going on about it, and it's in his way to get to the work basket, so I jumped up to try and grab its tail so it would spin around and come at him. I was laughing but missed his tail. Shorty totally freaked out, saying I'm a mad bastard because I was running around chasing the monster. I mean, it was pretty big and scary. Shorty never shut up about it. I finally got it away far enough that Shorty could get to the basket and back without getting murdered. All I could see in his faceplate that day was these big saucer eyes. They were going everywhere to see if the monster was coming back.

The next day, it was Andy's turn to absolutely shit himself, and I was having heaps of fun with them, stirring up the sharks and freaking them out. They had both never seen so many or had so many so close. The third day, they were both in the water, and I was in the bell, so that was bloody funny listening to them freaking out to each other. As the days went by, they never got that comfortable, although Andy was getting more used to it. Shorty never settled down. We were doing some really good construction work with big pipes and equipment, so sometimes you never had time to look around, but when you did, they were always there. And when they were feeding, you knew about it. Neither Andy nor Shorty liked being in the water on those days.

One day, Shorty and I were on the clump weight under the bell. The vessel was moving along to get to a certain position so that we could go out and pick up and retrieve a cut-off section of pipe. It was dark, and the tension in the water was pretty intense. Sharks were circling the seabed just at the edge of the lights, and there were heaps of them—not nice mellow grey nurses but bronze whalers and bull sharks and black and white-tip reef sharks. There were at least three over three metres, and it was looking and more importantly feeling very hostile. The fish were moving fast, and they were worried, and the place was oozing fear.

The boat got into position, and John said, 'OK, we're on the spot. Who's going?'

Shorty said, 'I ain't going.'

He was diver 1, so he was supposed to go, but I said, 'I'll go.' John gave me a compass heading and distance to the job. I said, 'Slack the diver,' and waited to let a big bronzy disappear into the gloom, and off I went.

I was dropping down, and the bronzy I thought had gone had spotted me coming down and turned and was heading back. I said, 'All stop on the diver,' and looked up as Andy had just thrown another wrap of my umbilical out—meaning, I couldn't climb up it and carried on falling.

I turned back to the shark. I was three metres off bottom; it was five metres away and coming straight at me. As soon as I hit the seabed, I jumped up and did a kung fu kick at its head. It darted like a rocket straight around behind me, and I kicked at it again. It was my turn to shit myself this time. The place was bloody dangerous. It sneaked off into the dark to sneak up on me from a different angle, and I looked at my compass and did a runner out of the bell lights and into the safety of a bit of darkness. I found the job and crouched down, getting my breath back. John asked me if I was alright. I said I was, and we both agreed the area seemed hostile.

Anyway, the crane came down. I picked up the load. We had three more locations, but now I had to make my way back and climb fifteen metres through shark-infested waters. I got Andy up on my umbilical, and when I was straight under the bell and it looked reasonably safe, I jumped up, pulled my legs as far up my arse as I could get them, and pulled myself up as fast as I could. I got there puffing and panting, and Shorty said, 'Fook that.'

So while were moving to the next location, John said, 'Why don't you use the shark shield, Spike?'

I said, 'I thought they didn't work.'

He said, 'The other guys reckon they do.'

I said, 'What do you do with them?'

He said, 'Hook it on your harness, run the tail down, and thread it through your umbilical.'

I went to the stash area in diver 3 umbilical and grabbed this box, about one hundred millimetre square, with a tail about one and a half metres long. I hooked it up the way John told me. We got to the next spot. He gave me a bearing and distance. I waited until the least number of eyes were charging around the lights bellow me, called out slack the diver, and when enough umbilical was out, I turned on the box and jumped off the clump weight. Bang, oowwh. Bang, ooowwwwh. Bang, oooowwwwwhhhh. Holy shit, I was electrocuted three times before I hit the seabed. I nearly had a bloody heartache. I grabbed the box and turned it off. Everyone in dive control were pissing themselves. The only positive was there were no sharks attacking me.

'Jesus, John, what the hell!'

He said, 'You're not supposed to put it across your chest, for God's sake.'

'Ooh, now you tell me.'

I got to the pickup location. There were two lifts here. So while I waited for the crane to come back down, I put the shield on so it didn't electrocute me and walked over to the bell lights and waited for the biggest bronze whalers to show up. That didn't take long. I flashed my shiny tools in the light to get its attention, and it started heading my way. When it was about three metres away, I turned it on, the first pulse, and it darted off. It didn't leave town, but it lost interest in me. By the time I had picked up the second lift, the feeding frenzy had simmered right down, and things were back to normal. Shorty didn't leave the clump weight that day, though.

So over the remaining couple of weeks, we had some really good days in the water doing habitats and pipe aligning rigs. Andy and Shorty were good to be in sat with, and we had a good laugh. Our last dive was Andy and me out setting the habitat for the next weld. Andy was a lot more comfortable around the sharks and wanted to get a photo with them all around him. You wouldn't believe it, but for one of the few days of that job, there were not many around, and that was one. Bloody shame and how bloody typical.

Christina and I had lunch with them on the riverside in the city before they flew out; not sure if I would see them again. Funny enough, I ended up working with them again a few years later, and Shorty is actually a supervisor on this vessel as I write. We often have a laugh over that sat, me taking the piss out of him for being scared of goldfish, and he reckons s I'm a mad bastard, Ha ha.

I work in the North Sea now, and I miss my sharks. But a couple of years ago, I was back on the bottom of *North Rankin* with my old mate Jorma. We were doing some valve ops inside this framework just inside one of the legs. It was pretty boring until the two grey nurses that obviously lived there decided they didn't want us there anymore. They started buzzing us, and Jorma ended up getting hit in the head by one, and the other had a shot at my gum boot. Very unusual for grey nurses.

A year or so later, we had to do a forty-inch hot tap into one of the pipelines around the *Goodwin* platform, and it was a pretty big project called the Angel Hot tap. We did a week's familiarisation down in Henderson to learn how to set it all up and get the drill to drill the coupon out. Lots of fun. They brought in a backup OCM, Morris, and a supervisor, Danny, over from the UK office to back up our team. The job went really well, and when Morris was heading off, he asked for my e-mail address. He said he might have something happening in a year or so, and if so, he wants to get a hold of me. Good one, Morris. Hope to see you soon.

About a year later, I received an e-mail from Morris giving me an address to send my resume to. He was in charge of a new Technip DSV called the *Achiever* and was hoping to get me on the crew. The vessel was still in sea trials but will be starting up soon, he said. I told Stew to send his resume in as well. Six months later, we were heading over to Aberdeen, and another friend of ours, Nick, from Melbourne, joined us. We walked around there for a couple of days. Then we were on a train down to Dundee to join the *Skandia Achiever*, a joint-owned vessel with Doff and Technip. By then, Morris had been moved to a different vessel, and Jim, the OCM from the Cape Town job on the *Venturer*, was the OCM, with Mick, the other OCM. Mick is an Aussie, and he was a supervisor when I was on *Wellservicer* in 1990 in Douala, Africa.

Jim met us in the galley and welcomed us on board and told us our shifts and that we were there to get the vessel ready to do dive trials before its first job in India in a couple of months. Nick and I were put on night shift, and Stew on days. We went off to say hi to a couple of guys that were also on the Cape Town job, but one of them totally ignored us. We got a bit of that for a while, reason being we can work in the North Sea but because of our union rules and immigration rules, they can't work in Australia, and they hate us for it. I sort of think, *Fair enough, but get the fuck over it. We didn't make the rules.*

That night, Nick and I checked the sat system out. It has four three-man chambers and a six-man decompression chamber. The chambers are big and looking very comfortable. We just had to build a few bits to put in there to finish them off. We were working around, and out came an old friend, Mark, whom I've known for years and whom I was diving with on the *Wellservicer* in 1990 with Dave. He was now a supervisor, so we had a bit of a catch-up because we hadn't seen each other for ages.

About a week later, there was a shift change, and Jim went off, and Mick came on. Nick and I had been going out for a beer at six o'clock most mornings just walking up the road to a small bar overlooking the harbour. Mark and I had talked about doing an after-shift catch-up drink, and a couple of days, after Micky, the night shift superintendent, a Scotsman from Dundee, and Ned, another supervisor, arrived, we organised with a few of the other guys on the 6 p.m. to 6 a.m. shift to meet at a bar in a little village a short taxi up the road. It ended up with about ten of us in this bar. We said, 'Let's put £10 in the kitty each, and when we drink that, we'll head back to the boat.' OK, we all agreed. We drank that, and as we were loading another £10 each, another supervisor called Simon turned up. We drank that kitty and then smashed another. We were absolutely pissing ourselves over the stories that were coming out and taking the piss out of each other. We decided to end the day with a £5 each kitty, and when that was finally drunk, we staggered out. It was 10:30 a.m. Our ribs and cheeks were sore from all the laughter. To this day, it has been one of the funniest mornings I have ever spent in a pub with a group of people that I had only just met. An absolute classic.

We managed to get the vessel pretty close to operation a week or so before Christmas 2007. We had a farewell and Christmas party at the same pub that we had had the morning laugh at. The crew of us seemed to get along pretty well, and I'll never forget looking over at Ged and John, who were on my shift. Ged had bits of tissue paper sticking out of his ears, basically taking the piss out of me for talking too much. Ha ha, wankers.

Over the next couple of years, the work was a bit slow. We did a job in Holland later in the first year, and I had to go over a couple of days early to Rotterdam to get my dive tickets passed by the Dutch accreditation. It just so happened to fall on Orange Day, the Dutch Queen's birthday, so I and the other 5 divers I was with ended up jumping on a train and heading into Amsterdam. That was a bloody good idea. It was a hot sunny day. The whole dam was shut to traffic, and there were people everywhere. What an amazing place. The canals were full of boats going along like a one-way street. They all had their own music blaring out with people dancing and the occasional chick flashing her tits. Bloody awesome.

Derek, one of the Scottish divers that hadn't really talked to me much up until the day before, scored us a spot on a bridge, and we parked up for a few hours watching the boats go under and taking turns buying the rounds. I smashed down a mull cake for lunch and had a really good day. Derek kept talking to me after that, so what a bonus. Some ice had been broken through.

At the end of my sat and when I was heading home, I decided to stop in the dam for a night and fly out the next night. Bloody good idea. Billy joined me for the afternoon, and we walked around until we found a nice restaurant in the sun across from Madame Tussauds, I think, and had a few beers until Billy had to head back to the airport, and I just went walking.

The next day, I was having a coffee on the street about to go to the train and airport. I took my cup inside, and looking at the mull cakes, I said to the lady, 'Excuse me, I have about twenty-four hours of flying to get home. What would be a good cake to help me get started?'

She looked at me and said, 'You might like to try a space cake.'

I said, 'Space cake it is, then.'

On the train to the airport, I decided to smash the cake down. Thank God I had enough water in my bottle. Far out. It just sucked every bit of moisture out of my mouth. The last mouthful I had trouble swallowing. I checked in and got into a bar on the other side and washed it down with a nice cold beer. I don't remember much else. My jaw was sore from smiling. I barely slept. I didn't watch any movies because I was to out of it to concentrate. I don't remember walking through the Singapore airport at all. Bloody space cake, all right. They should make them compulsory for all flights over twenty hours instead of illegal. I'll vote for that.

Stew and I ended up on the *Wellservicer* to get our days up for the year. We arrived to a pretty cold reception because they didn't want us on there and we had taken their guys' jobs and blah blah. I was standby diver on one shift, and Stew was opposite me. The first shift change and a supervisor called John walked in.

I said, 'Hi, I'm Spike,' and went to shake his hand.

He looked at me and said, 'What are you doing here then? Isn't there any work in Australia?'

I said, 'No. I've come over here to steal all your work and root all your women,' and walked away.

Don't shoot John down yet. He's actually a funny bastard and one of my supervisors on this vessel. We got along really well and had a good laugh. In those days, core crews tended to stick together, and outsiders like we were at the time were treated like lepers. Two weeks later, there was a shift change, and a few supervisors and other crew came on that we knew. We were alongside in Aberdeen, and I was dragged out to a bar on the port called the Crown and Anchor with a couple of Irish friends, Micky and Sam.

I was introduced to Val, a heavy-accented Scottish lass. She said, 'Hi, Skippy.'

I said, 'I'm a Kiwi, not an Aussie.'

She just carried on. A little later, I was waiting to be served, and she came over and said, 'What can I do for you, Skip.'

I said, 'I'm not an Aussie. I'm a Kiwi.'

'OK, Skip,' she said.

Another few drinks and she said, 'How are you, Skip?'

I said, 'How many times do I have to tell you I'm a Kiwi, not an Aussie.'

Well, she threw the bar lid over and came racing up with her tits in my face, yelling and screaming at me in some weird language and looking all nasty.

When she finished, I turned to Mick and Sam and said, 'What the fuck did she just say?'

We all burst into laughter, and she gave me a big hug and 'No problem, Skip.' Ha ha, I gave up after that.

By the way, the abuse was in a local dialect from the old days. Doric. I still don't know what she said. What a character. A few years later, this bar was heavily included in an Aberdeen Harbour series on Sky TV called *The Harbour*. Val, of course, became a local hero, if she wasn't already. If you stopped in, which I would, drop in to say hi from time to time, get a photo, and give her £5. It would go to a breast cancer charity that she has made a lot of money for. Good on you, Val. The bar closed down a couple of years ago, and I haven't seen her for ages.

Living close to the beach in Trigg was pretty unreal, but the house was too small. Christina had come across an auction that had these circa 1830 blue crystal French chandeliers and thought they might look good in our house when we renovate. Also at this auction was a wall of leadlight five metres high and nearly three metres wide that I thought would look cool in a staircase. We went and had a look. The leadlight was made up of one main picture about one and a half metres high and a metre wide with all these other five hundred millimetre squares and a few other longer pieces that all matched up for a large wall of glass. It was designed for the house where the auction was, but they had stuffed up the size, and it didn't fit. We went to the auction, hoping to bid on the chandeliers and leadlight. Both were passed in without us even getting a chance. After a week of going back and forth, we managed to get the leadlight for $1,500, which is a steal because to get it made would have cost between $10,000 and $15,000. It had silicon all over it from when they had tried to install it.

We had a few ideas on what we wanted to do with the house, and a friend put us on to a draftsman that had done some different stuff around Scarborough. When Ed called around, I had most of the leadlight out so he could see what I was on about. We climbed up on the roof to take in the view that I wanted to capture once we had finished, and we walked around our lovely garden so he had all our energy that we could show him, and off he went to see what he could invent. In the meantime, I had seen a really nice leadlight door that was triple glassed, and I thought, that would be a lot easier to keep clean, and it looks bloody unreal. I asked around and found a place that would double glaze my leadlight and got that on the move. It ended up costing me about $3,500 but came up looking unreal. The panels were steam cleaned, blown dry, and vacuum sealed between two panes of glass. Then I designed and built a frame to install it into so that Ed could design it into our stairwell.

It was over six months before Ed came up with something he felt good about. He dropped around. We walked around again. We moved this and that and fine-tuned it. Then off he went again. By the end of the year, we had drawings in for approval. It was going to be a big mission. It took over three years to complete. It was bloody stressful and nearly broke us up a few times, but eventually, we had one of the best houses on the street. Views across the ocean to Rottnest Island and ocean sunsets every night. I will never tire of coming home walking up past the leadlight up onto the top floor and, *pow*, over the ocean. Was it worth it? Damn right it was.

By the third year, the *Achiever* started getting some good work and getting a good name. We had a pretty good team of core crew. The client companies were starting to want us on the contracts. We ended up over in America a few times working out of Mobile, where I managed to score a couple of days on the beach, thanks to a bad toothache. It was the Mardi Gras, and the place was going off at night. The vessel wasn't coming in to pick me up, so I had go to New Orleans to get a chopper out. The driver dropped me at a hotel by lunchtime on Fat Tuesday, which is the last day of the Mardi Gras. So I headed off down the French Quarter, and, wow, it was that impressive; people all dressed up, bands playing in every bar. I just street walked around and around talking to people as I went from bar to bar. I had gone into a bar to go to the toilet. The rule was to be polite. If you use the toilet, you buy a drink. A small band was setting up, and by the time my drink was finished, they were absolutely rocking the place, so I ended up staying there until they finished for the night. Then I walked off and found another place to finish the night off.

There's a bit of history in that French Quarter, and I decided when the job was finished, I would stay for a night and have a good look around, which was exactly what I did. I was lucky enough to score another nice sunny day. I walked around the antique shops and in and out of some really neat shops. I got a really neat Mardi Gras mask for the wall at home and scored Christina a nice set of earrings and a couple of cool shirts for the boys. I walked into an antique gun shop and was pretty impressed with the stock in there. I loved cowboys and Indians when I was a kid, and I couldn't believe how small the Winchester rifle was. I was looking at what was supposed to be the sixth one ever made. The gunsmith was busy with a customer, so I didn't wait around long enough to talk to him about it.

It was possibly around this time that I heard of the death in Asia of another English friend of mine from Dubai called Rob. Rob was on a construction barge in the South China Sea and about to knock off shift when he was offered to jump in for a quick dive to retrieve a sling from around the pipeline that had been left behind. He went to the location where the sling was meant to be and couldn't find it. As he was at the end of his umbilical, they decided to move the barge up and down the pipeline so he could hopefully come cross it. Unfortunately for him, the people that were supposed to tend his hose had tied it off on the handrail to go and do something else. His umbilical got snared on something on the seabed and was ripped apart as the barge moved down the pipeline, leaving him with only the contents of his bailout to find the stage that he had gone down in, and that also has spare breathing gas, which would have saved his life. His passing was another bolt of reality to the dangers of this profession. The biggest kick was the fact that the sling had been retrieved on the previous shift, but that information had not been handed over at shift change.

In 2012, after looking for a couple of years, we came across a nice boat we could afford that was penned at Hillarys. The sale was made, and our maiden voyage on our forty-two-foot Bertram was Australia Day. We had a crew of about ten to twelve on board. We went all the way around Rottnest Island, stopping at Strickland Bay, where I had a quick surf, and then Eagle Bay, but there were too many boats in there, so we ended up at Thompson Bay, where we partied out for a bit, and then went to the pub for a couple of rounds. What an excellent day, arriving back in the pen after dark.

Christina and I were able to just take off by ourselves on mini holidays when I got home, getting some sun and peace and quiet. When the surf was up and the winds stayed northerly, I would take the boat to Strickland Bay and stay overnight, get two full days of waves, and come home absolutely exhausted. After being at work and especially after being in saturation for a month, it was pretty nice having the boat to myself. I would surf till dark, watch the last boats head home while sitting on the back deck with a nice cold beer, go in, have a hot shower, throw the barby on for a feed, and then just chill out with a cocktail and couple of beers.

The very first trip I did by myself, my mates in the surf were looking at me like I was a bit nuts. But you know what, that night sitting on the back of the boat, no one else around, I had the LED lights on, and fish were charging around in the lights, and a few squid and stuff. Every now and then, a dolphin would go past. I had the music cranking, and at around eleven o'clock, I thought I'll go up the bow, check the anchor, and then crash out. I went up there, and I couldn't believe how beautiful it was. With no lights around me and no music, I could hear the sets smashing down onto the reef not far away. The stars jumped out of the sky, and the feeling took my breath away. I checked; the anchor was good. I went back down the back and turned everything off. I sat there on the Marlin board with a nightcap cocktail and every ten or fifteen minutes listened to the sets offload on the surf break about 110 metres inside of where the boat was parked. The surf had been pretty big that day and was supposed to drop. It didn't look or sound like it.

In the morning, while having a coffee and watching the sets, I realised it hadn't dropped at all, and I was in for another pumping surf. The wind turned to the south at about 1:30 p.m., and by then, I was actually a basket case, totally exhausted but floating on adrenaline. I was lucky enough to get the anchor up without any drama, and sitting up on the fly bridge with a cold beer and looking back at the peak as I cruised off was pretty special. I still do this trip whenever the weather is lined up with the swells, and sometimes, some lucky friends get to join me. Now that is living the life, surfing the dream.

The *Achiever* sailed to the southern Gulf of Mexico for some work in Trinidad, and for Stew and I, it would double our flight times. When we were called up for that our dive, medicals were due. We have to have HSE approval, and we can only get them in the UK. We flew into London, did a night over our medicals the next day, and then flew into the States and down to Trinidad. Quite a long way. Trinidad looks a real nice place. Apparently, Tobago is the holiday destination, and it has good surf there at times. We did our trip, and crew changed off and flew via Dallas and then direct into Sydney. We had flown clockwise around the world on that trip.

Another trip, I landed in LA in the afternoon and wasn't flying on until the morning, so after checking into a hotel, I took a taxi out to the coast to Santa Monica, which was where my American surfboard shaper friends were from originally. It was a medium temperature day; unfortunately, no swell. So I walked along the beach for a bit, went out on the pier, had a couple of tequilas at a tequila bar, and went along the boardwalk until I found a bar, and lucky for me, the sun came out just as I sat down. Leaving Trinidad after that trip, I had an afternoon and managed to get a walk around the area, but without any local contacts, it was hard to know where to go or what to do.

Larry, one of our Irish life support technicians and a well-known world-record Guinness-drinking holder, and his lovely wife Debbie were heading to Perth to visit his sister Lily and their family. We organised a day trip to Rottnest Island on our Bertram. It was your typical sunny Perth day, and because there was a little bit of swell running on a sandbank called transits just outside the Rottnest moorings at Thompson Bay, and the wind was still light, I decided we would drop the anchor there for a paddle around and swim. As we set up the drinks and snacks on the back deck, I couldn't believe that they had been in Australia for a while but had never had a swim because of the sharks. I promised them there were no sharks and then spotted a nice little right hander peel down the sandbank past the boat.

'Who wants a surf lesson?' The place went silent.

Then Lily piped up with 'I'll have a shot.'

So we got the big boards out and got all ready, and off we went. After half a dozen attempts at standing up, she had caught a few but gone tits up straightaway. She was huffing and puffing and wanting to go back to the boat. I wouldn't have any of that, feeling that she was close to the prize of actually standing up. She couldn't paddle anymore, so I towed her back out. After a bit of a rest, I pushed her onto another one. She nearly got up and then splat, disappearing under the water for a bit too long. I managed to get to her as the second wave pushed her under and pull her onto the board. She just lay there totally exhausted while I towed her back to the boat, where she was met with cheers and laughter.

By then, everyone was swimming in the shark-infested waters without a care in the world. We picked up the anchor and went in and picked up a mooring close to the beach. I put the tender in the water to get ready to take them to the pub for afternoon refreshments. I asked their daughter Kate if she wanted to come for a run to warm the tender up. So off we went wave jumping. She nearly flew out a couple of times, and I'm not sure if she was having as much fun as me, especially when I stuffed up a turn and a wave swamped the boat and we had to go back nearly underwater. When we got back, she jumped off as fast as she could. I think she was just thirsty. So I bailed all the water out. We went to the beach for the standard park up at the pub and enjoy the view. It is extremely relaxing, and we had the photos taken and stuff.

While we were there, their son Aidan had arrived on the afternoon ferry, and we headed back to our boat, got the bar snacks out, and got the music going. Christina was on the cocktail-making job, and all was going according to plan. I saw another couple of waves come through out at the sandbank and thought the swell might have picked up a bit so asked Aidan if he wanted to go for a blast in the tender. Off we went. We were having a grand old time jumping waves, and I was being a bit of a larrikin when we caught onto a rather good-size one. We were riding out onto the face, and I decided to do a cut back to freak him out, but I hit the wave to high, and we got thrown out and flipped the boat upside down. Not really sure if he could swim or not, but it took us three or four attempts to flip the boat back over. The motor had conked out and wouldn't start again.

A family in another boat that had been watching me came over and while he was abusing me for being an irresponsible fool towed us back to the mother ship. I said thanks, and he started going off at me again, so I told him to get over it. It's just a boat. Well, we certainly had a few laughs. There were a lot of red faces from too much sun. I had jokingly been accused of trying to murder them that day, and in a way, I had. But being murdered by fun doesn't count as far as I'm concerned. We arrived home safely. Larry assured me they still talk about the day they survived shark-infested waters with Captain Spike and his cocktail waitress Christina.

The *Skandia Achiever* had been working very well, so Technip extended the charter for two more years. We had some really good jobs in the North Sea, and I really enjoyed the short stops around Aberdeen or Edinburgh, where I would just go walking. It's like being in a museum everywhere you go. A few times, we would be mobing the vessel in Leith, the harbour of Edinburgh. Visiting the castle is pretty cool. There is an extremely old sixteenth-century bar at the top of the mile, just before the castle. Walking the mile on a sunny day is a good way to burn off some spare time.

During the Blues and Jazz Festival, instead of hanging in a bar with a whole lot of divers talking the same old shit, I jumped in a cab and headed into the city. I had been told about the piano bar and thought I'd start there for some live music. I must have walked past it by accident and ended up in a blues bar down a set of stairs. The music sounded pretty good, but the guy said I can't go in. I asked why. He said, 'Doors are closed. You will have to wait an hour for this set to finish and the next band to come on.' He told me to go back on the Main Street. There will be a queue up the road. That band will start in a half an hour.

What happens is they open the doors twenty minutes before a band starts, you pay £10 to get in, and the doors shut when the band starts, and you stay in there until they finish. I went down to where the queue was and asked a couple what the next band was going to be. They said it was four of the guys out of Earth, Wind & Fire with some others, a ten-piece band apparently. I went to the end of the queue. Doors opened. I paid my £10, found a spot to stand, and started looking around while I waited for the music. Bloody hell, we were in a sixteenth-century church. It was bloody amazing. I was looking around the church more than I was watching the band. The band was bloody good as well.

I've been back in Edinburgh a few times over the years. The walk up to Arthur's Seat is good to work the beer off and a good view from the top. I got stuck there waiting for a job to go out last year for five days, and I just walked everywhere and found heaps of interesting stuff.

The *Achiever* headed over to America again to do a deep job in the Gulf of Mexico off the coast of Pensacola. That was pretty cool because we had a couple of days of mobing the vessel, and Jim had organised with Ziggy and his wife Julie to have a barbecue dinner party at their place on the beach. That was fun, and at the end of the job, Ziggy took us out on his boat for a lolly gag around scenic tour, ha ha. Everyone was so hungover from the after-the-job party that Mick and the clients put on that we were a pretty quiet boat.

The job went well. Pretty big deal doing it because of the depth. We were stored at 240 metres and working from 240 to 265 metres. It was mid-water, which is a lot harder than when you're running around on the seabed. The visibility was bloody amazing. One day, I was hanging on the side of this huge mid-water buoy at around 250 metres, and I was waiting for the crane that was bringing a whole lot of rigging down that we needed to install. I was in with Stew and John, and we lucked in with the day shift, so I was looking up and I saw the crane and said I got a visual to Norm, the supervisor.

He said, 'No, you haven't.'

I said, 'I have.'

He said, 'You haven't because it was only at 105 metres. So that means, 145 metres, pretty clear?'

In the middle of the day, when you looked up, it was light; when you looked across, it was deep blue; and when you looked down, it was black. I think we were working in three thousand or five thousand metres of water. The chains we were working on you could just about swim through. Because our vocal cords were so stressed with the helium, it was hard to talk so that someone could understand you, and it was just as hard to listen to someone who was trying to talk so that you could understand what they were saying. I think it may have been the only time anyone's enjoyed being in sat with me because I didn't talk too much, ha ha. Having a conversation was hard work so kept to a minimum. We had to watch our breathing in the water because if you worked too hard and started breathing heavy, you would or could overbreathe the hat, and then you would struggle to get your breath back. I don't recall anyone having any issues, and I think we all enjoyed the experience.

Temperature was another thing that was really noticeable. Helium transfers heat very fast, so you would be hot one minute and then cold soon after. You could be sitting at the table with a jumper on feeling cold, having a mouthful of coffee, and a minute later, you're taking your jumper off and starting to sweat. As I said, the job went well, the client was very impressed, and the company and vessel got another big tick on the performance box.

Unfortunately, the next year was our last on the *Achiever*. The lease was up. And with a new vessel being built and a new boat called the *Skandia Arctic* already out working, the company let it go. Bit of a shame. End of a good working error, but time to move on. At the same time, there was a major downturn in work, and everyone was getting let go, or sacked, the better word, from their contracts. Jim had been moved back on to the *Wellservicer* and taken some of our good supervisors. Ned was made up to night shift superintendent, which was good for him but bad for me because we used to have a good laugh while working in the water. He kept telling me I needed to go and do my supervisor tickets before I got too old and missed the boat, so I actually did.

What was looking like our last year in the North Sea turned to turmoil when we were about to join the *Achiever* for its last job and got diverted to the *Orelia*. We were freaking out about that on the flight over because everyone used to call it the *Death Star*, and we had heard all these stories. But we got on board. Really friendly crew. As usual, we already knew a lot of guys on it. One of our old mates from Australia, Muzza, was a supervisor, and it was actually a pretty good trip. My last job on contract to Technip UK was to be in Australia on the *Wellservicer*, and it was looking like a really good job to look forward to. We left the *Orelia* and went home and waited for it.

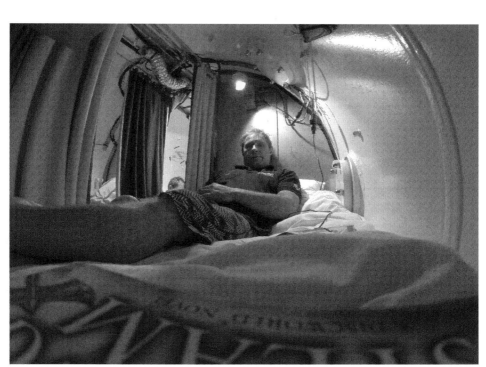

Chapter 21

BACK IN AUSTRALIA WITH THE WELLSERVICER

hile we were waiting for the *Wellservicer* work in Aussie to start up, Stew had been doing the networking on faceless and found out an old friend was running a company in Singapore that had a few months' work in India. We got all the paperwork ready, but we were not looking forward to working in India after a few years in the North Sea. But we'll worry about that when we have to. The *Wellservicer* arrived, and it was good to be back in Australia. Good visibility, lots of fish, and a really good construction job. Big diameter spool pieces, so we were using pipe handling frames as well as big lift bags. Every dive was a challenge and an adventure. A few of our North Sea mates that joined us were Jim, OCM; Tim, night shift superintendent; Jim, the supervisor; Ian and Jim, the life support techs; as well as our dive techs. It was also good to catch up with some of our Aussie mates we hadn't seen for a few years.

We had some nice grouper we were hand feeding out of the bell. My mates got a bit pissed off when they would come back for their tea break and ask for their sandwich. I'd say, 'Too late, mate, fed it to Groopy the grouper.'

There weren't as many sharks as I hoped, but we did get one feeding frenzy going off. On one dive, while standing in a huge ball of baitfish, I had a grouper about one and a half metres long right in front of my faceplate. About every minute, it would open its mouth and suck in all the fish in front of me. I just stood there without moving for maybe five minutes. It was absolutely unreal. Every now and then, a giant manta ray cruised over you. I hate it when you finish those sorts of jobs.

After the completion of the project, we were having some drinks at my place, while the UK boys waited for the flights out. Jim asked me if Stew and I were interested in joining the team on the *Wellservicer*. So, of course, that was an easy answer. She was getting old but still a good workhorse. We did a few jobs in the UK and then spent some time in Trinidad and Venezuela. Venezuela was another good big spool piece construction job but totally different from the Aussie job. The visibility was poor, and the seabed was mud instead of sand. At the completion of that project, the party at the hotel was epic. We ended up dancing in a local club until early morning. Last year, I spent most of my time with Mick, who has been the OCM on the *Deep Arctic*, and this year back with Jim, who is now the OCM on the newest vessel, the *Deep Explorer*, and the *Wellservicer* has been sold. Both the *Arctic* and the *Explorer* are state-of-the-art dive support vessels. The chambers are comfortable, the bells are good, the cranes are good, and both vessels have really good crews. Does that make my life better? You bet ya. Do I feel lucky? You bet ya. Both these vessels are diving machines. And that is really good because I'm still a diver. Why I'm still diving, I'm not really sure when I'm at work. But when I'm at home, I know exactly why—I can do what I feel like when I feel like. I only work an average of four months a year. And I can just survive our lifestyle.

Live the life

Surf the dream

Chapter 22

So Who Are We Anyway

S o who are these people who work in this industry, in this environment? That is a very tricky question. The characters are very diverse, but you would have to say they must share some form of love for the water, or maybe they just love the challenge of working in the water. From experience, the people who are not confident being under water don't last long. There is a big difference between, say, an air diver and a saturation diver. When you go on an air-diving job, the atmosphere among the team is quite jovial mostly. It's easy, like in most jobs, to get along with people you don't necessarily like. The idiosyncrasies are easily brushed aside by having a laugh with someone else. In fact, the money is not as good, but you have your life back in a way that when your shift is over, you walk away. You may go for a walk around the helideck or go to the gym, or simply go back to your cabin and watch TV or read a book. Saturation diving is quite different. When you complete your shift in the water, you return to the system you are held in with your team, one or two others in a small space usually four to six metres long and, say, two to three metres in diameter. You are under pressure and on a helium mix gas. There is no getting away, and the closest you will get is shutting your curtain and putting music on or immersing yourself into a book. And to top that off, you can be in the same chamber with another team. When no diving is happening, you are all squashed into a little table trying to eat a meal or simply having a cup of tea or coffee and a conversation. Not everyone likes everyone, and often you don't get to say who you are going to be teamed up with. In this circumstance, you just have to bite your tongue and get on with it. It is a team effort, and working together and making the best of the situation is beneficial to everyone. It doesn't always turn out that way, and there are numerous stories of people snapping and having short but fierce altercations, much to the entertainment of those who look after us. Most people think we are crazy or mad. So when crazy meets crazy, who knows what can happen? In a tribute to how professional the people I work with can be, I had been in a six-man chamber for around twenty-seven days. We had a three-day deco, but we also had a few days off during the saturation. So for argument's sake, we may have had six days when no one left the chamber. Two of the guys in the other team were from the same country and knew each other well, and I knew both of them as well. The day after we arrived on surface, I was talking to one of our bosses about people getting along because someone had had some fiery dives during that job. He said, 'You wouldn't believe so and so, and so and so don't like each other.' I said no way. I have just spent twenty-seven days with them, and I thought they were friends. I was truly gobsmacked.

Then in a separate case, we had heard of a bit of yelling and screaming with a team in a different chamber. The supervisor had to intervene to calm the people involved down. One of the divers came on the comms to say goodbye when they were due to fly off and told me he was so embarrassed because he lost his composure and snapped. He was pissed off more with himself than the other guy, even though the other guy created the tension. And in a lot of ways, we are all similar. I have snapped at people and not just my dive team members. I have snapped at supervisors and at techs who look after our system. And the worst of all, I have snapped at the LSTs or LSSs. And they are the worst to snap at because they can make your life easy or hard. As most divers will tell you, you mostly have good sats, but every now and then, you get one that will test you, push you to your edge. And every day is a chore just to get through. We cherish the good ones and fight our way through the bad. We are all very different but also very similar, from different countries and different backgrounds but all with the same goal: make as much money as possible and go home. The divers are the small part of the team, the nucleus of the operation. But for us to be able to do our job, there is a large crew of people who work in shifts to keep us working and most importantly keep us alive, from the OCMs, supervisors, LSSs, and techs to the engineers, riggers, and of course, the ship's crew. One thing I think we all have in common, we look forward to going home and dread going to work.

I guess we really are no different from anyone else who has a job.

You can go now. I have to go back to sleep. In six hours, we will be woken up to start our shift. In nine hours, I will most likely be walking on the ocean floor.

Abreviations

OCM	Offshore Construction Manager
LSS	Life Support Supervisor
LST	Life Support Technition
ALST.	Assistant Life Support Technition
TECH.	Mechanical / Electrical Technition
NIGHT SHIFT.	00:00 hrs - 12:00 hrs
DAY SHIFT.	12:00 hrs - 00:00 hrs
Days	06:00 hrs - 18:00 hrs
NIGHTS.	18:00 hrs - 06:00 hrs
Nitrox	Air and Oxygen mixed to a required percentage
O2	Medical grade Oxygen
Heliox	Helium and oxygen mixed to a required percentage
Gas	Breathing medium of the job at hand
Narced	Suffering from nitrogen narcosis
CNS	Central nervous system bend
DCS	Decompression sickness
Bib	Mask for administering O2
TUP	Transfer under pressure. The chamber the bell locks on to.
Wet pot	Chamber between living chamber and TUP. Shower and toilet.
Trunking	Pipe that the bell mates (clamps) on to on the TUP
Bell	Chamber used to lower divers to the seabed.
FPSO	Floating production storage and offloading vessel

RTM	Riser turret mooring.
Jacket.	Offshore platform
SBM	Single buoy mooring system for off loading oil.
PLEM	Pipeline end manifold
Bailout.	Reserve gas mix worn on a divers back. I case of damaged umbilical .
SLS	Secondry life support. A bailout bottle with longer breathing times.

Photo log

1. Left to Right. Steve, Steve, Martin and myself. Hanging out in the front of the Dive chamber shack.
2. Ocean Diver 2 alongside an SBM in the DPC field, Dubai.
3. Riccardo and John John with the rigging and welding crew on the Jawharah. Doha.
4. The Jawharah moving into position alongside a platform off Doha.
5. Cofferdams in place ready to pump the water out.
6. Lance and I on Jumeirah beach after a surf. Now the location of "The Palm".
7. Sonja (left) and Christina outside our traditional Balinese style losman. Legian.
8. The Masai tribe in Rift Valley. Nairobi.
9. Tshokwane, one of the four big tuskers of Kruger National Park, SA.
10. (Left) Christina just before the Ostrich bolted in panick. Oudtshoorn .
11. (Right) Oribi Gorge,Port Shepstone.
12. Hand feeding Cheaters, Oudtshoorn.
13. CSO Venturer, a real work horse.
14. Ryan's first trip to Bali.
15. My first big surf at Margaret River, Main brake.
16. A four man chamber on the Stena Wellchief.
17. The dive crew at Sun City, on our way home from a project in Point Noir.
18. One of the biggest FPSO's in the world. Located off Point Noir.
19. The Pyramid Cafe at Point Noir.

20. The dive crew in Giza, Cairo on our way to join the Mayo.
21. The family at 3 mile camp on Gnaraloo Staion.
22. After sleeping all week Tombstones awakens in impressive form.
23. Tombstones, a true surfing experience.
24. The committed, The watcher and the destroyed.
25. Heading East across the Nullabour.
26. I had to pay in the end but I finally got to dive with white pointers. Gansbaai.
27. Air Diving on the Skandi Achiever.
28. Going through pre dive checks, Skandi Achiever.
29. Day shift on the air station.
30. 3 man chambers on the Skandi Achiever.
31. Sitting in the bell on the Skandi Achiever.
32. Staying the night out the back of 6-8 foot Strickland bay. Rottnest Isl.
33. Tie'ing in spools on the Wheatstone project NW Australia.
34. Moving a spool into place with the help of a pipe handling frame.

Printed in Poland
by Amazon Fulfillment
Poland Sp. z o.o., Wrocław